"Among the vast array of comment
the theology of Joseph Ratzinger/E
its illuminating presentation of cer
vision. [*The Word Made Love*] will s
letter and the spirit of Benedict's theology."

　　　　　　　　　　—Khaled Anatolios
　　　　　　　　　　Boston College School of Theology and Ministry
　　　　　　　　　　Author of *Retrieving Nicaea*

"Fr. Christopher Collins has written a book which is both informative for
the general reader and a useful bibliographical source for the student.
There is a certain 'freshness' in the tone and a pleasing humility in the
presentation. This book is certainly a significant addition to the
commentaries on Joseph Ratzinger's work."

　　　　　　　　　　—Gill Goulding, CJ
　　　　　　　　　　University of Toronto

"I have been captured by the beauty of Fr. Collins's *The Word Made Love*.
By illuminating the dialogical theology of Pope Benedict XVI, this
masterful work brings the reader face to face with Jesus' living presence.
Thank you, Fr. Collins!"

　　　　　　　　　　—Fr. John Horn, SJ
　　　　　　　　　　President-Rector
　　　　　　　　　　Kenrick-Glennon Seminary

"Fr. Christopher Collins, with theological acumen and pastoral sensitivity,
provides a robustly Christ-centered reading of the writings of Joseph
Ratzinger/Pope Benedict XVI. This is an admirable introduction to the
universal scope of the Pope's theological vision."

　　　　　　　　　　—Robert Imbelli
　　　　　　　　　　Boston College

"Eloquently and peaceably, with a rare combination of scholarly and
spiritual discipline, Christopher Collins guides us into the very marrow of
Joseph Ratzinger's theology: God calls us to encounter Jesus Christ
through his Holy Spirit. In this simple insight, Ratzinger's whole theology
and life are enfolded. Indeed, like an icon, this book draws us into the
encounter to which Ratzinger bears witness. A stunning achievement."

　　　　　　　　　　—Matthew Levering
　　　　　　　　　　University of Dayton
　　　　　　　　　　Author of *The Theology of Augustine*

The Word Made Love

The Dialogical Theology
of Joseph Ratzinger/Benedict XVI

Christopher S. Collins, SJ

A Michael Glazier Book

LITURGICAL PRESS
Collegeville, Minnesota

www.litpress.org

A Michael Glazier Book published by Liturgical Press

Cover design by Jodi Hendrickson. Cover photo: Catholic News Service.

1   2   3   4   5   6   7   8

Library of Congress Cataloging-in-Publication Data

Collins, Christopher S., SJ.
    The word made love : the dialogical theology of Joseph Ratzinger / Benedict XVI / Christopher S. Collins.
        p.   cm.
    "A Michael Glazier book."
    Includes bibliographical references.
    ISBN 978-0-8146-8078-0 — ISBN 978-0-8146-8079-7 (e-book)
    1. Benedict XVI, Pope, 1927–   2. Spirituality—Catholic Church.   I. Title.

BX1378.6.C635   2013
230'.2—dc23   2012042302

Contents

Foreword   vii

Introduction   xi

Chapter One: The Theological Formation of Joseph Ratzinger   1

Chapter Two: "Revelation Seen Basically as Dialogue"   21

Chapter Three: Jesus the Christ: Eternal Logos-Made-Love
            in History   55

Chapter Four: Church as the Locus of Divine-Human Dialogue   93

Chapter Five: Word Spoken from Beginning to End: Creation
            and Eschatology   131

Epilogue   171

Bibliography   173

Index   179

Foreword

In his *Theologische Prinzipienlehre*, first published in 1982 and translated into English in 1987 as *Principles of Catholic Theology: Building Stones for a Fundamental Theology*, Joseph Ratzinger described the "fundamental crisis of our age" as understanding the mediation of history in the realm of ontology. He noted that the "problem of history's role in the realm of being has become a question about being as such: Is there a continuity of 'humanness'? And, if there is, at what point does the mediation of history begin?" In shorthand terms, one might call this the Heideggerian "being in time" problem. Whereas the theological establishment prior to the Second Vatican Council prided itself on being "ahistorical" or "above history," the effect of Heidegger's philosophy was to push to the front of theological speculation the issue of the significance of time and history for our understanding of the human person. Moreover, the different responses to the documents of the Second Vatican Council often revolve around different understandings of the role that history plays in theological speculation. Indeed, many of the theological conflicts of the last two centuries can be reduced to questions about the relationship between history and ontology (also described as the grace, nature, and culture relationship) and the relationship of history and revelation (which includes the territory of the relationship between faith and reason and tradition).

In this work, Christopher S. Collins, SJ, provides a most lucidly written account of Joseph Ratzinger's theology (as it developed within the historical context of the "being in time" problematic), which Collins describes by the adjective "dialogical." By this term, he means that Ratzinger's theology is driven by his interest in the relationship between God and each unique human person situated in history.

vii

Collins notes that Ratzinger learned from St. Bonaventure that "wisdom is unthinkable and unintelligible without reference to the historical situation in which it has its place." Moreover, being a Christian is about having a personal relationship with God, and relationships are by definition a two-way giving and receiving, or literally "dialogue," not a one-way missive.

One of the most revolutionary aspects of Christian revelation is the notion that Truth is a Person. As Collins observes, "In Ratzinger's thought, not only is the drama of salvation history itself unfolding, but the theological *understanding* of this history is also developing in its own kind of drama within a drama. The whole of his theology is manifested according to the pattern of narrative rather than that of proposition and argumentation." In an interview given to Peter Seewald, Ratzinger remarked that he "could not imagine a purely philosophical theology" since "the point of departure is first of all the Word."

As a consequence, for Ratzinger, humanity is rightly understood in the light of Christ and not the other way around, and for theology this means that anthropology should be seen in the light of revelation rather than the other way around. This is essentially the path taken in paragraph 22 of *Gaudium et Spes*, which appears to have been adopted almost word for word from Henri de Lubac's work *Catholicisme*. It was also the approach of Hans Urs von Balthasar, another of the outstanding sons of St. Ignatius in the twentieth century. In his book *Milestones–Memoirs 1927–1977*, Ratzinger remarked that meeting von Balthasar was for him the beginning of a lifelong friendship and that never again has he found anyone with such a comprehensive and humanistic education as von Balthasar and de Lubac. He concluded, "I cannot even begin to say how much I owe to my encounter with them."

Collins summarises the meeting of theological anthropology and ecclesiology in the works of Ratzinger in the following paragraph:

> As Ratzinger interprets Bonaventure, then, the understanding of God that comes in revelation is not what is apprehended in isolation by one thinker but rather is a discovery that is made in union with the community of the whole Church over the course of salvation history. Consequently, what comes to be known by the human person in the process of *revelatio* is not some kind of "clear and distinct" *idea* about God, but rather only the kind of knowledge that comes from personal encoun-

ter with God in history. This encounter does not take place in
private between the individual and God but in the context of
the whole complex of relations that comprise the church in
the present that is always connected to its past.

This is a beautiful exposition of Joseph Ratzinger's account of the
faith for which, in Ratzinger's own words, there is no more convincing proof than the "pure and unalloyed humanity" it fostered in his
parents.

Because Truth is a Person, truth and love are the twin pillars of
all reality and faith is dialogical. Collins, a twenty-first-century Jesuit,
gets this.

This work makes a seminal contribution to a deeper understanding
of Ratzinger's theology as *logo*-centric and sensitive to the historical
dimensional in faith and theology.

Professor Tracey Rowland

Introduction

A s a newly ordained priest, my first assignment was to be a pastor for four small parishes of the Jesuit mission on the Pine Ridge Indian Reservation. Those years of pastoral work in a sense provide the backdrop for my own interest in the present topic. The narrative of the life and struggles on the reservation, including the massive unemployment, breakdown of family structures, violence, alcoholism, etc. is a familiar one. In my experience it seemed that none of the social, political, or even religious institutions worked very well to address the needs of the people. It also seemed that in that environment nothing I tried to do programatically as a pastor *worked*. No new initiatives of mine bore any fruit. Nobody seemed much interested in new ways of being involved in the church. However, what in my opinion *did* work, on a regular basis, was the liturgy. No matter how broken down all the other institutions and activities seemed to be, for me, especially in my sensitivity as a new priest, it was palpable how "effective" the liturgy was. Even if ten or twelve people were there for a Sunday mass, or it was a funeral mass at which only a handful of people might come for communion, somehow, by paying attention in a new way to the prayers being said, knowing a bit of the personal stories of the people in the congregation including much of the sorrow and pain in their histories as well as something of the hopes for something new in the people's lives—all of this made for a profound encounter I had the privilege of entering into every day. I listened, in a sense, with new ears to what Christ was speaking to his people gathered around him in the Eucharist and I heard with new ears the responses and pleas of these same people. There was speaking and listening . . . and silence. There was dialogue that was very fragile and on the surface did not achieve much. But I had a profound sense that this encounter—this dialogue—was the only thing that *worked* during my time on "the Rez."

With that pastoral and spiritual experience as a kind of catalyst for the research and writing I have taken up in the last few years I came to discover the figure of Joseph Ratzinger, now Pope Benedict XVI, as a guide and an exemplar of a contemporary theologian who does theology, it seems to me, with a profound pastoral and spiritual sensibility. I had never read his works before he was elected pope. After that I would occasionally see one of his homilies or Angelus addresses given in ordinary pastoral settings. I was struck by the simultaneous simplicity and profundity of his words. It was captivating how he could so succinctly encapsulate the mystery of the encounter with Christ in such a concrete and simple narrative manner. Again and again he would reiterate that Christianity is not a set of ideas to believe, much less moral principles or laws to follow. Rather, Christianity is about a person and, specifically, our own encounter with that person. He stresses repeatedly that God has spoken to humanity, ultimately and most perfectly, in the person of Jesus Christ.

The more I read of Ratzinger, both in his academic theology and in his preaching, the more I gradually came to detect a very basic structure in his work. Whether he was speaking of the liturgical season of Advent, the mystery of Christ's suffering on the cross, the life of any given saint or the need for justice and solidarity in a broken political and social structure, one way or another I would always glimpse his method of describing the transformation that happens when one enters into a personal encounter, into dialogue. This is the way he articulates the whole of the Christian vision, it seems to me, and here, in the pages that follow, I have attempted to trace this pattern, to describe this dialogical principle of coherence in various and diverging aspects of his thought.

Ratzinger sees God as the one who *speaks*. Humanity is best understood as those who listen to God's Word and then are able to respond. God and humanity are dialogue partners. But this is not a dialogue of equals; it is necessarily *asymmetrical*. It matters who speaks the first word. For Ratzinger, God is always the one taking the initiative, and humanity is always in the posture of responsiveness. So for Ratzinger all of reality is dialogical, but dialogical in an asymmetrical manner. Indeed, even in the very essence of God there is dialogical communication and communion in the eternal trinitarian relations.

But here too there is an asymmetry to the communication. The priority of speech always lies with the Father. Furthermore, not only is the *inner life* of the Trinity asymmetrically dialogical but this same God also communicates himself in creation and in human history. This communication that unfolds throughout human history culminates in *speaking himself* in the person of Jesus Christ. The basic structure of all reality, then, is dialogue. My aim here is to show how this dialogical, communicative structure that is always unfolding is the unique way Joseph Ratzinger constructs his theology. I argue that he represents a unique contribution to the renewal of theology that is more personalistic and therefore more communicable in contemporary culture.

This study begins with a brief exposition of what I think are the most significant dimensions of Ratzinger's own theological formation that produced such a communicative, dialogical approach to theology. The subsequent chapters will attempt an exposition of how the dialogical structure of his thought, based on the eternal Logos of God communicated both in eternity and in human history, provides a framework for the whole of his theology. In chapter 2, I focus on how this communication of the eternal Logos pertains to his theology of revelation, which he sees as necessarily involving the active *reception* of God's Word by God's people in history. Chapter 3 examines Ratzinger's Christology, which follows this same dialogical framework in which God's speaking of the Word is not only the source of an intelligible creation but also becomes the center of human history when that Word becomes human. Chapter 4 gives an exposition of Ratzinger's ecclesiology, which flows directly from his Christology, so that the church becomes the privileged place to encounter the fullness of the Word in Jesus Christ. Special attention will be given to the role of the liturgy in this expression of ecclesiology. Finally, chapter 5 describes the implications of this dialogical framework for a renewed eschatology and theology of creation that especially provides a basis for the theological virtue of hope that is of such concern to Benedict in the current cultural and religious context. Throughout all these aspects of his theology it will, I hope, become evident how this dynamic of the Word of God being spoken, heard, and responded to provides a basis for a contemporary kind of "personalistic" theology that is narrative in its texture and provides an alternative to the abstraction characteristic of much of modern theology. In this, an exemplar of a theologian who is able to communicate the content of the Catholic faith in a manner accessible not only to the minds but also the hearts of a contemporary audience can be found in Joseph Ratzinger.

Chapter One

The Theological Formation
of Joseph Ratzinger

*"Yet it was I who taught Ephraim to walk, who took
them in my arms; I drew them with human cords, with
bands of love." (Hos 11:3-4)*

A
s he began his opening lecture of the last course he would ever
teach, a class on the theology of Pope Benedict XVI, Avery
Cardinal Dulles remarked, "The real leader of the seminar,
under the Holy Spirit, will be Pope Benedict himself. By virtue of his
intelligence, his learning, and the positions he has held, he is in my
judgment the most important Catholic theologian of the day."[1] Benedict can perhaps be considered as such not only because of his role
as prefect of the Congregation for the Doctrine of the Faith for nearly
a quarter century and then as the elected successor of Peter, but because he has so clearly cultivated his theological project in the pattern
called for in the Second Vatican Council: to return to the sources of
Scripture and the patristic tradition while being consciously open to

---

1. Class lecture notes, January 16, 2008. Thanks to Sister Ann Marie Kirmsie,
OP, the long-time secretary of Cardinal Dulles at Fordham University in the Bronx,
NY, for this reference.

1

translating the Gospel in a mode intelligible to the modern world, according to the signs of the times.[2] Whether or not one might agree with Dulles's assessment, it is clear that in the landscape of Catholic theology at the beginning of the twenty-first century Pope Benedict XVI stands out as a major figure who has served as a catalyst toward encouraging an approach to theology that simultaneously involves a return *ad fontes*, to biblical and patristic sources, and at the same time one that is able to speak the new language of personalism hungered for in contemporary culture.[3] Before elaborating on those early intellectual influences that produced such a theological sensibility, however, we take a brief look at the context of this formation.

Brief Biography

Joseph Ratzinger was born and baptized on the same day, April 16, 1927—Holy Saturday—at Marktl am Inn in Germany. He studied philosophy and theology from 1946 to 1951 at the Higher School of Philosophy and Theology of Freising and at the University of Munich. He was ordained a priest on June 29, 1951 and taught briefly at the Higher School of Freising. In 1953 he obtained his doctorate in theology with a thesis entitled *Volk und Haus Gottes in Augustins Lehre von der Kirche* (*The People and House of God in Augustine's Doctrine of the Church*).[4] Four years later, under the direction of Gottlieb Söhngen, professor of fundamental theology, he wrote a second thesis, the *Habilitationsschrift* that made him eligible to teach in a German university. *Die Geschichtstheologie des heilegen Bonaventura*,[5] published in 1959, was translated into English in 1989 under the title, *The Theology of History in St. Bonaventure*.

2. Austin Flannery, ed., *Vatican Council II: The Basic Sixteen Documents: Constitutions, Decrees, Declarations* (Northport, NY: Costello Publishing Co., 1996), *Dei Verbum* 24.

3. John W. O'Malley, *What Happened at Vatican II* (Cambridge, MA: Belknap Press of Harvard University Press, 2008). A consistent theme for O'Malley is the new "style" indicative of Vatican II that speaks to the hearts and minds of more contemporary people. This style includes a responsiveness to the reality of the "turn to the subject" in modern philosophy and theology.

4. Joseph Ratzinger, *Volk und Haus Gottes in Augustins Lehre von der Kirche* (Munich: Zink, 1954).

5. Joseph Ratzinger, *Die Geschichtstheologie des heilegen Bonaventura* (Munich: Schnell and Steiner, 1959).

After lecturing at Freising, Ratzinger went on to teach at universities in Bonn from 1959 to1963, Münster from 1963 to 1966, and Tübingen from 1966 to 1969. In 1969 he assumed the chair of dogmatics and history of dogma at the University of Regensburg. For the duration of the Second Vatican Council, from 1962 to 1965, he served as a *peritus*, a theological "expert," for Cardinal Joseph Frings, Archbishop of Cologne. In 1977 he was named Archbishop of München-Freising by Pope Paul VI and served there until 1981 when he became the Prefect for the Congregation for the Doctrine of the Faith. He was named a cardinal that same year. Ratzinger served Pope John Paul II in this capacity for the remainder of his pontificate and ultimately succeeded him to the Chair of Peter on April 19, 2005.

I. Formed by a Living Tradition

The Word Spoken at Home

Ratzinger's theology of the Word stems from a rigorous philosophical and theological formation. But it also carries weight precisely because it derives from both the ordinary and the extraordinary moments of his personal life. In the course of his father's dying, he recalls, "We were grateful that we were able to stand around his bed and again, show him our love, which he accepted with gratitude even though he could no longer speak."[6] And again, at the time of his mother's death he would speak about this mystery of the truth of love being communicated in life and perhaps most poignantly in death in terms of the theological framework he had been building: "On the day after Gaudete Sunday, December 16, 1963, she closed her eyes forever, but the radiance of her goodness has remained. . . . I know of no more convincing proof for the faith than precisely the pure and unalloyed humanity that the faith allowed to mature in my parents."[7] This sensibility of recognizing the resonance of the faith within very human events has continued to echo in his life where his great love for music is concerned. He famously recalls:

> For me an unforgettable experience was the Bach concert that
> Leonard Bernstein conducted in Munich after the sudden

6. Joseph Ratzinger, *Milestones: Memoirs, 1927–1977* (San Francisco: Ignatius Press, 1998), 119.
   7. Ibid., 131.

death of Karl Richter. I was sitting next to the Lutheran Bishop Hanselmann. When the last note of one of the great Thomas-Kantor-Cantatas triumphantly faded away, we looked at each other spontaneously and right then we said: "Anyone who has heard this, knows that the faith is true."[8]

The tangible, intimate, and expressive nature of this faith in the course of ordinary (and perhaps extraordinary) human experience sheds light on his later theological formulations of that faith. Though he would soon enter into an academic environment, his theological project would never become so abstract as to be removed from the simple and profound experience of his Catholic faith and the bonds of familial love that mediated this experience of God early in his life.

Seminary Formation

Such was the affective sensibility he brought with him into the experience of seminary studies. In his memoirs, however, then-Cardinal Ratzinger recalls plainly his dissatisfaction with the arid neoscholasticism in some aspects of this early theological training. The modern person, the young seminarian could see, longed for authentic encounter with the living God—an encounter that could lay a claim on the whole person and not merely on the mental faculties. He recalls the version of Thomism being presented in those years in the seminary: "the crystal clear logic seemed to me to be too closed in on itself, too impersonal and ready-made."[9] Consequently, he sought out—and discovered—a way of doing theology that would speak to the contemporary cultural needs, that would draw modern men and women out of their anxiety and isolation into communion with other believers and with the living, Triune God who is, above all, relational and personal. To enter into that vision, he came to see, the starting point must be an engagement with the biblical narrative.

A New Biblical Point of Departure

One of the most significant influences on the mind and heart of the young seminarian Ratzinger at this time was the set of exciting new developments in biblical exegesis and its import for all the other

---

8. Joseph Ratzinger, *On the Way to Jesus Christ* (San Francisco: Ignatius Press, 2004), 37.

9. Ibid., 44.

branches of theology. Friedrich Maier was the "star" biblical scholar at the Munich University faculty of theology while Ratzinger was a student there from 1947 to 1951. Maier was a significant proponent of the "two-source theory" of the Synoptic Gospels, which proposed the existence of another *Quelle* (source) from which Matthew and Luke must have drawn, in addition to Mark, to write their own gospels. This hypothesized alternative source for the gospels came to be known as "Q." Ratzinger recalls coming to a greater appreciation of the need to pay attention to the concrete setting of the gospels and the historical settings and particularities within which they were written, the great excitement surrounding Maier's lectures, and how he took to these new studies with great hunger for learning the newly emerging methods for doing biblical exegesis.

Ratzinger would later come to a more critical reception of a certain mode of historical exegesis because he could see how, in its attempt to be highly objective and analytical in its practice of situating the gospels in their historical contexts, "it is not in a position to see the full depth of the figure of Christ."[10] He soon had a sense of the tension between appropriating the Gospel as historically embedded and yet only accessible by way of an ecclesial hermeneutic that allows the reader to understand Scripture for what it is: texts written *from* the experience of faith and *for* the experience of faith. Nonetheless, from this point on in his early seminary study he would say that biblical exegesis would always remain "the center of my theological work."[11] It is worth mentioning how, in hindsight, he has conceived of his own theological method throughout his whole career. In the course of an extended interview, he explains:

> I have never tried to create a system of my own, an individual theology. . . . I simply want to think in communion with the faith of the Church and that means above all, to think with the great thinkers of the faith. For this reason, exegesis was always very important. I couldn't imagine a purely philosophical theology. The point of departure is first of all the Word.[12]

10. Ibid., 53.

11. Ibid., 52–53.

12. Joseph Ratzinger and Peter Seewald, *Salt of the Earth: Christianity and the Catholic Church at the End of the Millennium* (San Francisco: Ignatius Press, 1997), 283.

This brief sentiment gives a clear sense of the contours of his theo-logical vision, his desire to operate within the *communio* of the whole Christian tradition and to do so always based first and foremost on the Word of God, particularly as encountered in Sacred Scripture.

Ratzinger attributes great importance to the teaching and schol-arship of Friedrich Stummer, an Old Testament scholar, for the de-velopment of another important aspect of his thought. Stummer demonstrated the importance of the perspective of the *inner unity* of the two biblical testaments. Based on this perspective, Ratzinger recounts, "more and more I came to understand that the New Testa-ment is not a different book of a different religion that, for some reason or other, had appropriated the Holy Scriptures of the Jews as a kind of preliminary structure. The New Testament is nothing other than the interpretation of the Law, the Prophets and the Writings found and contained in the story of Jesus."[13] The two testaments, he could see, are really one expression, unfolding in a coherent way, of the one Word from God spoken in salvation history, culminating in the person of Christ. He came to see that attempting to analyze and interpret each book of the Bible and each part of each book as iso-lated, historically conditioned artifacts of a given historical and cul-tural setting results in losing sight of the forest for the trees. The insight offered by Stummer regarding the inner unity of the biblical testaments would have significant impact later in Ratzinger's under-standing of the deep structure of revelation itself and how it is con-veyed in the course of salvation history. He was beginning to formulate not only a *historical* sensitivity to the nature of biblical exegesis but also the need for a *literary* approach that can appropriate in a unified way the integration of many texts that offer a multifaceted but never-theless coherent vision and basis for a whole people's experience of God.[14] Throughout all of Scripture, he realized, the interpretive ten-sion that simultaneously appreciates the particularities of any given aspect of the scriptural narrative and keeps a sense of the unity of the *one narrative* that is expressive of one ongoing dialogue between the eternal *Logos* and historical humanity must be kept alive. Ratz-inger would later describe this historical and literary approach to biblical interpretation as the *analogia scripturae* that is suggested by

13. Ibid., 53
14. Ibid., 53–54.

the biblical texts themselves: "texts have to be referred back to their historical setting and interpreted in their historical context. Then, in a second process of interpretation, they must also be seen from the perspective of the movement of history as a whole and of Christ as the central event."[15] The impact of this recognition of the inner unity of the testaments and the christocentrism of all of history on Ratzinger's thought will be explored in further depth in the next chapter on revelation.

A Liturgical Horizon

Next to the exegetes, Ratzinger recalls that his greatest influences at the time were the dogma specialist Michael Schmaus, the fundamental theologian Gottlieb Söhngen, a pastoral theologian named Josef Pascher, and a canonist, Klaus Mörsdorf.[16] Each in his own way pointed toward deeper sources for the various branches of the theological disciplines he taught. If he saw that the biblical narrative is the "soul" of fundamental and dogmatic theology, so too in moral theology, for example, he gained the perspective that sought to "end the dominance of casuistry and the natural law and to rethink morality on the basis of the following of Christ."[17] If Scripture served as the primary basis for the various aspects of theology, liturgy too became primary as a source for theological reflection. Michael Schmaus, seeing the limitations of the neoscholasticism of the day, offered an innovative, systematic portrayal of doctrine "in the spirit of the liturgical movement and the recent return to Scripture and the Fathers, which had developed in the years after the First World War."[18] Ratzinger could begin to see more and more clearly the inner relationship of all the branches of theology, reflecting in various ways one coherent vision of the dialogical encounter of God and humanity in the living tradition of the church.

Being introduced to the work of Odo Casel and Romano Guardini was also significant for Ratzinger in the focus they provided on the liturgical "shape" of the Christian faith. Casel's contribution, highlighting

---

15. Joseph Ratzinger, *God's Word: Scripture, Tradition, Office*, ed. Peter Hünermann and Thomas Söding (San Francisco: Ignatius Press, 2008), 121.

16. Ratzinger, *Milestones*, 55.

17. Ibid.

18. Ibid., 49.

the fact that early Christian liturgical life drew especially on the reality of *mystery*, helped contemporary theologians to reexamine sacramental theology not so much through the scientific/analytical approach characterized by reliance on the ontology of Aristotelianism and neoscholasticism, but rather through the lens of personal engagement in worship that could not be tamed and defined easily by the mode of propositional logic.[19] Ratzinger notes that Casel's emphasis on *mystery* had emerged from the renewed interest in the liturgy as a source for Christian theology. The very existence of this "mystery theology," he said, "posed with new acuteness the basic question concerning the relationship between rationality and mystery, the question concerning the place of the Platonic and the philosophical in Christianity, and indeed about the essence of Christianity."[20] This "mystery" can only be experienced when the individual, isolated person lets go of the prospect of self-security and opens up to the dynamic of conversation with the sovereign God who has "spoken" Himself and called for a response from all humanity. Casel explained that "modern man thinks he has finally driven out the darkness of the Mystery" thanks to the efforts of technical rationality, and yet the human "remains wholly circumscribed in the bounds of the material world. By imagining he is the ruler of this world, he is forced more and more to do its will."[21]

See Spaemann

This notion that a human being finds authentic freedom only in entering into and surrendering to the dynamic of relationship with God in the context of worship would become the chord struck again and again in the thought of Joseph Ratzinger. He notes, for example, in his *Der Geist der Liturgie: Eine Einführung*[22] that the real purpose for God's call through Moses to the people of Israel to go out into the desert is not just so that they can pass through it on the way to the promised land. Rather, they are to go where there is no other source of security, *in order* to freely worship the living God. When God says, "Let my people go to worship me in the desert" (Exod 7:16), Ratzinger

---

19. Most prominently in Odo Casel and Burkhard Neunheuser, *The Mystery of Christian Worship, and Other Writings* (Westminster, MD: Newman Press, 1962).

20. Ratzinger, *Milestones*, 55–56.

21. Casel, *Mystery of Christian Worship*, 3.

22. Joseph Ratzinger, *Der Geist der Liturgie: Eine Einführung* (Freiburg: Herder, 2000); ET: *The Spirit of the Liturgy*, trans. John Saward (San Francisco: Ignatius Press, 2000).

lets this command speak for itself: that the essence of God's call to his people, and therefore the fullness of the freedom God has in mind for them, is ultimately rooted in their capacity to enter into this worship, into this dialogue with the living God.[23]

Romano Guardini, too, did much to open up new horizons for Ratzinger through his theology that reminded people of the core of the Christian experience as liturgical worship.[24] For Guardini the church realizes the deepest expression of its identity only in the context of corporate worship. For "in the liturgy," he explains, "God is to be honored by the body of the faithful, and the latter is in its turn to derive sanctification from this act of worship."[25] Consequently, it is essential to be reminded that there is a primacy of *logos* over *ethos* in the Christian life. That is to say, contemplation of divine truth in the liturgy must always precede any authentic efforts to *work* for the kingdom of God. Guardini writes that the liturgy is "primarily occupied in forming the fundamental Christian temper. By it man is induced to determine correctly his essential relation to God. . . . As a result of this spiritual disposition, it follows that when action is required of him he will do what is right."[26] Entering into the dynamics of the liturgy wherein the human person discovers who he or she truly is in relation to God is essential for shedding light on the rest of the Christian life. These insights that became so central to the liturgical renewal of the early twentieth century were, of course, based on the historical retrieval of more ancient Christian sensibilities, and it is to these (and their influence on Ratzinger) that we now turn.

The Influence of the Fathers

Ratzinger embraced the insights of Casel and Guardini regarding the centrality of the liturgy all the more, given his simultaneous realization of the fruitfulness of patristic biblical exegesis and theological conclusions drawn from this approach. He was shaped by the fathers in the conviction of the normativity and unity of Scripture. All theological reflection must therefore begin with a posture of faith that

23. Ratzinger, *Spirit of the Liturgy*, 15.

24. Ratzinger, *Milestones*, 43.

25. Romano Guardini, *The Spirit of the Liturgy* (New York: Crossroad, 1998), 19.

26. Ibid., 86.

God has taken the initiative and has indeed spoken in history. Origen, for instance, is a great model for Ratzinger in this regard. Reflecting later in life in a "Wednesday audience" on the fathers, Benedict recalls Origen's influence on the history of theology. He reflects: "Theology to him [Origen] was essentially explaining, understanding Scripture; or we might say also that his theology was a perfect symbiosis between theology and exegesis."[27] Origen himself notes in the first lines of *On First Principles* that those who find confidence in a way of life that will be "good and blessed" do so because of the "words of Christ." But "by the words of Christ, we do not mean only those which formed his teaching when he was made man and dwelt in the flesh, since even before that Christ the Word of God was in Moses and the Prophets."[28] As Sacred Scripture is a conveying of these moments of God's speech, Ratzinger, along with his patristic teachers, recognizes it must be the starting point for further theological reflection and, as such, provides the normative framework for all that follows. The scriptural witness, though it is expressed in a variety of different genres and comes from various historical and cultural settings, nevertheless is a coherent and unified "word." It must be taken, in this patristic vision, as a whole and not as a collection of isolated historical documents. Furthermore, from the fathers Ratzinger learned that the living tradition since the age of the scriptural witness is always essential to the present understanding of the faith. How the ecclesial community has appropriated the Word of God spoken in the past serves always as a clue as to how to remain in the dialogical exchange with God in the present. This is especially true when one considers the nature of Christian worship that has been inherited from previous generations. The *lex orandi* of the living tradition becomes essential for the current ecclesial community's grappling with questions of the *lex credendi*.

Underlying the reliance on biblical and liturgical sources for theology is a presumption of the importance of historical experience of God's salvation among the people of God. Ratzinger's professor for fundamental theology, Gottlieb Söhngen, was especially influential in helping to form this vision. In his own scholarship he argued: "the

27. Benedict XVI, *The Fathers* (Huntington, IN: Our Sunday Visitor, 2008), 36–37.

28. Origen, *On First Principles*, ed. George W. Butterworth (Gloucester, MA: Peter Smith, 1973), 1.

Christ mystery is no kingdom of 'pure' values like the kingdom of 'eternal truths.' "[29] Rather, at every turn in the Christian tradition, it is clear for Söhngen that truth is necessarily communicated by God to humanity in a manner that is *historical*, and not as ideas somehow disengaged from historical reality.[30] The development of Christian dogma, by way of the age of the fathers, comes to be an essential aspect of how God's word continues to be communicated to the church in every age.

Another major influence, Alfred Läpple, also directed Ratzinger toward Hans Urs von Balthasar's translation of Henri de Lubac's *Catholicisme*.[31] De Lubac became for Ratzinger a guide to the fathers, especially Augustine. He describes how de Lubac helped him to discover the "essentially social" nature of the Christian faith.[32] He found there an alternative to the presentation of the faith sometimes narrowly conceived as an individualistic following of moralistic codes or private assent to particular propositional truths. This opening up of the horizon of the essentially communal and ecclesial nature of the Christian faith made it clear to him how the celebration of the sacraments by the whole church really expresses the fullness of the Christian life. In particular he realized in a deeper way the essential link between the Eucharist and the church, namely, how each one "makes" the other.[33] By placing the Eucharist at the center of ecclesiology he simultaneously insists, with Augustine, that the substance of ecclesiology is essentially Christology. This is so since the unfolding of the life of the church whose members are in communion with one another and with the tradition that has preceded them is always

---

29. Gottlieb Söhngen, "Das Mysterium des lebendigen Christus und der lebendige Glaube . . ." in *Die Einheit in der Theologie: Gesammelte Abhandlungen* (Munich: Zink, 1952), 344–48. Cf. Patrick W. Carey, *Avery Cardinal Dulles, SJ: A Model Theologian, 1918–2008* (New York: Paulist Press, 2010), 168.

30. Ratzinger, *Milestones*, 55.

31. Henri de Lubac, *Glauben aus der Liebe: Catholicisme*, trans. Hans Urs von Balthasar (Einsiedeln: Johannes Verlag, 1970). See also Ratzinger's own introduction to a later edition of the same work by de Lubac *in Henri de Lubac, Catholicism. Christ and the Common Destiny of Man*, trans. Lancelot C. Sheppard and Elizabeth Englund (San Francisco: Ignatius Press, 1988).

32. Ratzinger, *Milestones*, 98.

33. Ibid. More will be said on this in the later chapter on church and liturgy.

centered on, in imitation of, and participating in the mystical body of Christ himself.[34]

The encounter with Augustine would ultimately lead to the focus of Ratzinger's later doctoral work on the great Latin father's theology of the church as communicated in the images of "people" and "house" of God. Here a familiar theme in Ratzinger's theology would be developed: his sense of the "collective I" of the church. Ratzinger notes that Augustine's use of the term "people of God" often recalled Old Testament foundations wherein God gathered his people together for them to listen to the word spoken through Abraham, Moses and the prophets. This notion of the people of God is recapitulated and fulfilled in the New Testament when the apostles gather together as an *ekklēsia* around the person of Christ.[35] In the process of hearing the Word of God the church becomes a true subject, able to speak back, to enter into dialogue with God who has spoken first. In the course of this exchange of listening and speaking, the church becomes its "true self." Though Ratzinger drew on an ancient source in Augustine for such a vision, the theme would resonate in at least some strands of contemporary hermeneutics as well. The proposal in "reader response theory" that meaning in a text is not fully realized until the reader appropriates that meaning, and further, that this appropriation is a matter not simply for the individual reader but for the whole "interpretive community," would find a certain resonance in Ratzinger's recognition that "by definition, [divine] revelation requires someone who apprehends it."[36] More on this aspect of Ratzinger's thought will be taken up in chapter 4, on the relationship of the Word to the church. But suffice it to say for now that Ratzinger found in the insight of the "essentially social" nature of the church gathered from Augustine yet another place of contact with contemporary thought that was rediscovering some of these ancient anthropological and epistemological insights. We turn now to an elaboration of Ratzinger's contact with some other strands of contemporary philosophi-

---

34. Emery de Gaál Gyulai, *The Theology of Pope Benedict XVI: The Christocentric Shift* (New York: Palgrave Macmillan, 2010), 65.

35. Maximilian Heinrich Heim, *Joseph Ratzinger: Life in the Church and Living Theology. Fundamentals of Ecclesiology with Reference to* Lumen Gentium (San Francisco: Ignatius Press, 2007), 159.

36. Ratzinger, *Milestones*, 108.

cal movements that would find resonance in the Christian theological tradition.

Philosophical Personalism

Ratzinger says that in first being introduced to the "philosophy of dialogue" of Martin Buber he was given "a spiritual experience that left an essential mark" not unlike his first encounter with Augustine's *Confessions*.[37] Though he does not go on to elaborate much about what this experience was like, it is evident in his later writings how much Buber has been an influence.[38] This new horizon of a "metaphysics of dialogue"[39] suggested by Buber would give a contemporary philosophical grounding that would allow Ratzinger to appropriate the Christian vision from the ancient biblical and patristic sources while enabling him to simultaneously engage contemporary culture in the sphere of its own concerns.

Buber first published his landmark essay, "Ich und Du" (*I and Thou*) in 1923. His "dialogical philosophy" offered a basis not only for a renewal of ethics, politics, and hermeneutics, but also for an understanding of authentic religious experience. Conscious of the needs and concerns of modern culture, Buber's "Ich und Du" spoke to the "sickness of the age" and offered an antidote to it. In this age between the wars Buber sensed, like many of his contemporaries, an alarming isolation, anxiety, and alienation in his contemporaries. The way to healing this sickness of alienation, for Buber, lay in humanity's return to the dialogue with "the Eternal Thou."[40]

In this foundational work Buber points to the possibility of a real encounter of the human person with God, a proposal called into question in the modern philosophical and theological landscape. Only in this encounter, however, would the human person find a way out of the oppressiveness of the modern mentality that had come to objectify all around him. This way of objectification Buber deemed the

---

37. Ibid., 44.

38. Markus Rutsche, *Die Relationalität Gottes bei Martin Buber und Joseph Ratzinger* (Norderstedt: GRIN Verlag, 2007).

39. Paul Arthur Schilpp and Maurice S. Friedman, *The Philosophy of Martin Buber* (La Salle, IL: Open Court, 1967), 49–68.

40. Tamra Wright, "Self, Other, Text, God," in Michael L. Morgan and Peter Eli Gordon, *The Cambridge Companion to Modern Jewish Philosophy* (New York: Cambridge University Press, 2007), 102–21.

"I and It" relationality. He admits that relating to objects—"Its"—is the way in which we must live much of our practical lives, but when it comes to interacting with the world around us, with other people, and even in attempting to relate to God it is impossible for us to remain constantly standing in this objectivist posture, relating only to "It." For Buber, this objective relationality is precisely what creates a sense of isolation and "sickness" in the human subject. Offering a critique similar to that of Odo Casel, Buber explains that to have our way of interacting beyond ourselves limited only to this "objectifying" mode is to have the essence of our true human nature stifled. Rather, what is necessary is an entering into the "mystery" of the encounter that is established in an opening up to "the Thou."[41] The most authentic human experience, for Buber, is an "I-Thou" encounter. This is indeed what makes us human. Too often, however, we become content to remain in the realm of talking about these encounters from the safe distance that "various conceptual, aesthetic, instrumental or mathematical" mediations afford us.[42] Insofar as we do not allow ourselves to be drawn into and changed by these encounters we become closed off from authentic human existence. Rejecting the objectification of God, then, Buber reintroduces his reader to God as divine *subject* with whom the human person is able to enter into real relationship and thereby actualize authentic human identity.

Joseph Ratzinger found in this "I-Thou" paradigm a way of talking about relating to God that opened up new horizons that could speak to the longing for relationship and overcoming the isolation so characteristic of the modern person. Ratzinger would concur with Buber in his belief that the crucial turning point in this authentic coming to be of one's true self is the conviction that God must be "addressed" and not simply "asserted" or "expressed."[43] Tamra Wright describes Buber's strong critique at the end of *I and Thou* both of modern theology and of many traditional religions that are often drawn into an objectification of all that pertains to the encounter with God.[44] While God can be spoken of in certain circumstances as an "It," it is not true that God *is* an "It." Making a kind of liturgical argument that reso-

---

41. Martin Buber and Ronald Gregor Smith, *Between Man and Man* (New York: Macmillan, 1965), 229.

42. Wright, "Self, Other," *Cambridge Companion*, 108.

43. Ibid., 110.

44. Ibid. See the whole section on "The Eternal Thou," 109–11.

nates with the biblical admonition against idolatry, Buber reminds his reader: "God, the eternal Presence, does not permit himself to be held. Woe to the man so possessed that he thinks he possesses God!"[45] Worship, then, that activity in which the human person *addresses* the personal God and allows the God who is not object but subject to *speak*, is essential for healing the modern sickness of humanity.

For Ratzinger's part, it seems that he has drawn especially upon the Jewish philosopher Buber to suggest the very shape of the Christian faith itself. Emery de Gaál Gyulai argues that for Ratzinger, by following the "grammar" of Buber's description of the God-human relationship, both Christian theology and anthropology may be redefined precisely because "through a human being God has entered history as a speaking subject."[46] Buber's dialogical philosophy was certainly an impetus in Ratzinger's development of this "grammar" of the Christian mystery. Later, in reflecting back on the development of the church's teaching on divine revelation in *Dei Verbum* at Vatican II, Ratzinger would note that there emerged "an understanding of revelation that is seen basically as dialogue."[47] The dialogical understanding of revelation taken up in *Dei Verbum* was influenced in no small part, according to Ratzinger, by the "personalistic thinking" of Buber that had helped to shape so much of philosophy and theology on the eve of the council.[48] It is to this dialogical conception of Christianity embraced by Ratzinger that we now turn.

II. A Post-Conciliar Theological Alternative

The ecclesial divide that has emerged in the wake of the Second Vatican Council has been frequently described, typically framed in the sociological and political terms of "conservatism" and "progressivism." This paradigm, however, does not easily offer a way of understanding the likes of Joseph Ratzinger. In the years around the council he is easily placed in the "progressive" category, and yet in more recent decades his identity has been more often associated with

---

45. Martin Buber, *I and Thou* (New York: Scribner, 1958), 106.

46. De Gaál Gyulai, *The Theology of Pope Benedict XVI: The Christocentric Shift*, 61.

47. Herbert Vorgrimler, ed., *Commentary on the Documents of Vatican II* (New York: Herder and Herder, 1967), 3: 171.

48. Ibid.

conservatism. People search for political and sociological reasons for such a "change" in him: he was unsettled by the social upheavals of 1968; he became motivated by ecclesial ambitions, etc.[49] These must be the reasons, so the conventional wisdom goes, for his "reversal" of thinking. However, if the social and political hermeneutic can be suspended for a moment and the theological perspective allowed to come to the fore, the development of Ratzinger's thought becomes more intelligible.

Ratzinger, following Hans Urs von Balthasar, places the mystery of the drama of salvation at the center of the theological project. In fact, he describes von Balthasar's use of the drama of the Christian narrative as the proper hermeneutic lens for understanding the Second Vatican Council's understanding of the task of theology.[50] The Christian is the one called into the tension of *living within* this dramatic narrative of the salvific dialogue of God and humanity. To use Buber's category, it is a way of "in-betweenness" that indicates the tension between God, who speaks to the world, and the world that is able to listen, but perhaps afraid to do so.[51] The "deep structure" of reality is based not primarily on the individual's knowing and understanding reality according to this mode of knowing. Rather entering into relationship with both God and others sets the conditions for the emergence of the possibility of *knowing* at the deepest level. Indeed, this knowing that is consistent with faith takes place most perfectly in the life of the church and occurs only by letting perception of the whole of reality be shaped by the vision from within these sets of relationships. Tracey Rowland cites in Charles Taylor a similar understanding of the encounter of the church and modernity: "It is not that we have sloughed off a whole lot of unjustified beliefs leaving an implicit self-understanding that had always been there, to operate at last untrammeled. Rather, one constellation of implicit understandings of our relation to God, the cosmos, other humans, and time, was

49. Clifford W. Mills, *Pope Benedict XVI* (New York: Chelsea House, 2007); John L. Allen, *Cardinal Ratzinger: The Vatican's Enforcer of the Faith* (New York: Continuum, 2000), 98; Michael Collins, *Pope Benedict XVI: Successor to Peter* (Blackrock: Columba Press, 2005), 98.

50. Joseph Ratzinger, "Communio: A Program," in *Communio: International Catholic Review* 19, no. 3 (1992): 436–49.

51. Maurice S. Friedman, *Martin Buber: The Life of Dialogue* (Chicago: University of Chicago Press, 1976), 3–10.

replaced by another in a multifaceted mutation" in the course of the emergence of secularized modern culture.[52] For Ratzinger, in order to address this challenge of the culture of modernity what is required above all is "receiving" the truth of the reality of the revelation from God, thereby giving impetus for a Christian culture to be revivified according to what has been received in the community of the church.

As Ratzinger would put it in a 1992 essay, "Christianity is not speculation; it is not a construction of the intellect. Christianity is not 'our' work, it is a Revelation, a message that has been given us, and we have no right to reconstruct it as we wish."[53] This revelation that is given constructs the whole of reality for the Christian. Reliance on revelation and its historical-symbolic nature, as opposed to the abstract character of other modes of contemporary theology, has been an essential characteristic of Ratzinger's manner of doing theology. This approach, I suggest, might be considered uniquely "dialogical." It also allows for the possibility of coming to new judgments about current social, political, or ecclesiastical issues, depending upon how historical circumstances are evolving. So rather than trying to lock Ratzinger in as either conservative or progressive, it is more accurate to see him as one attempting to discern responses to current matters of the day in light primarily of the revelation of God in Scripture and tradition and how this revelation has recently been appropriated in various historical contexts. He has proceeded in this "historical-symbolic" manner of doing theology that is most given to a *narrative* theology whose central motif is the dialogue between God and humanity. I would argue that he chooses this mode of doing theology not only because he sees it as being true to the core of the faith that has been given, but also because he believes that this is pastorally the most effective way of communicating the saving power of the Word in history.

But Ratzinger's theology of the Word does not limit itself to an *ad intra* discussion among Christians alone. By appealing, not unlike the early church father Justin Martyr,[54] to the ancient category of *logos*,

---

52. Tracey Rowland, *Ratzinger's Faith: The Theory of Pope Benedict XVI* (New York: Oxford University Press, 2008), 145–46. Cf. Charles Taylor, "Two Theories of Modernity," *Hastings Center Report* (March–April 1995): 24–27.

53. Joseph Ratzinger, *Co-Workers of the Truth: Meditations for Every Day of the Year*, ed. Irene Grassl (San Francisco: Ignatius Press, 1992), 265.

54. Justin Martyr, *The First and Second Apologies*, ACW, trans. Leslie W. Barnard (Mahwah, NJ: Paulist Press, 1997).

Ratzinger makes a case to the world beyond the church for the intelligibility of all of creation—human existence in particular—in light of the Word being spoken by God that is the basis for all reality. In so doing he provides a challenge to a postmodern tendency toward relativism that has called into question the human capacity to discover and know truth.[55] The case he makes is based not on abstraction and rationalistic argumentation but rather on the narrative of salvation history. As this historical narrative unfolds, the *Logos* comes to be known as a person, as love itself. The *Logos*, then, becomes the basis for a more personal sense of the Christian mystery for believers themselves and also provides a criterion for dialogue with secular culture.

III. Conclusion: A Dialogical Vision Formed

The process of the formation of the "dialogical structure" of the young Joseph Ratzinger's thought was multifaceted. That formation was in itself, of course, the fruit of ongoing dialogue with sources both ancient and new. As he matured, he cultivated what might be termed a "personalist theology," or perhaps better a "dialogical theology" shaped ultimately by biblical and patristic sources but also reaffirmed by contemporary philosophical lines of inquiry. The basis of this personalist theology is the eternal *Logos* who is speaking, is being spoken and being heard. In Ratzinger's theology, whether it pertains to the inner life of the Trinity, Christology, or theological anthropology, there is always present what might be called a dialogical principle in which the Eternal Word is continually being spoken in history, in human words. This reliance on the Word, which is by definition both intelligible and communicable, lays the groundwork for a theology that is inherently relational. Ratzinger's dialogical mode of doing theology, then, serves his preference for the "communio" shape of theology.[56] For example, when he reflects on the intrinsic link between Christology and the eucharistic liturgy and its significance for ecclesiology, he notes:

> The Eucharist is never an event involving just two, a dialogue between Christ and me. Eucharistic Communion is aimed at

---

55. James V. Schall and Benedict XVI, *The Regensburg Lecture* (South Bend, IN: St. Augustine's Press, 2007).

56. Ratzinger, "Communio: A Program," 436–49.

a complete reshaping of my own life. It breaks up man's entire self and creates a new "we." Communication with Christ is necessarily also a communication with all who belong to him: therein, I myself become part of the new bread that he is creating by the resubstantiation of the whole of earthly reality.[57]

Thus at the heart of how he understands all these aspects of theology—Christology, liturgy, ecclesiology, creation and eschatology—lies the communicative structure of dialogue.

Ratzinger's dialogical structure of theological reflection follows a consistent pattern: Scripture, the "soul of theology," must be its methodological starting point. Scripture as a whole is the narrative of the unfolding relationship between God and humanity. A narrative is always set in history; it is never merely abstract reflection. It is in history, then, that God speaks to humanity and reveals himself ultimately as Word-made-flesh in the protagonist of the entire narrative: Jesus of Nazareth. This is the culmination of the narrative in which God and humanity are rediscovered in a new way. Indeed, in the person of Jesus himself appears the perfect dialogue between God and humanity.

A More Historical, Spiritual, and Pastoral Systematic Theology: *Logos* Manifested as Love

Characteristic of Ratzinger's thought is a re-conception of the basis of Catholic theology by way of renewed attention to the historicity of the Christian mystery. His formation was influenced very much by the emergence of historical consciousness in biblical exegesis. Ratzinger's response to the need for a more "historically conscious" theology, however, has not simply been capitulation to an academic trend. Rather, it has expressed a mode of doing theology that is more spiritually and pastorally rich, given its dialogical and narrative style. The dialogical mode of doing theology is also arguably more capable of plumbing the depths of the essential truth of the Christian vision, which has at its center the mystery of the "tearing of the veil" previously separating heaven and earth and now makes possible intimate communion between God and humanity. Dialogue and encounter

---

57. Joseph Ratzinger, *Pilgrim Fellowship of Faith: The Church as Communion* (San Francisco: Ignatius Press, 2005), 78.

with the *Logos*-made-love in history is at the heart of Ratzinger's theological and pastoral vision.

A consistent concern since Ratzinger's seminary and doctoral studies has been the articulation of how it is that God speaks across the chasm that separates heaven and earth. A theology based on the *Logos*, communicated in dialogue of word and response, is central to his way of dealing with this question. With the *Logos* as the key to his approach, Ratzinger's theology is reasonable, but not abstract. Rather, it is reasonable in a manner that becomes personally attractive when communicated in the context of the biblical narrative as the *Logos* shows itself as visible, incarnate *love* in Jesus Christ. It is for this reason that Ratzinger has from the beginning seen love as the "key to Christianity." When he was asked in an interview about the significance of the common theme from his first publication as an academic to his first encyclical as pope, both of which centered on *love*, he replied:

> Two themes have always accompanied me in my life, then: on the one hand, the theme of Christ, as the living, present God, the one who loves us and heals us through suffering, and, on the other hand, the theme of love . . . because I knew that love is the key to Christianity, that love is the angle from which it has to be approached.[58]

He has made this "angle" his own throughout his theological and pastoral career.

In this chapter I have attempted to establish the centrality of the *Logos* in Joseph Ratzinger's thought. Based on the consistent use of *Logos* in his theology, I have suggested a dialogical principle at work that serves as a kind of unifying principle for all of theology as he undertakes it. I have proposed a few early influences in his philosophical and theological formation that helped to provide a basis for such a dialogical structure in the whole of his thought. I hope that in the next chapters it will become evident how this dialogical principle is at work in particular areas of his theology, beginning with the theology of revelation and then moving on from that basis to his Christology, ecclesiology, and finally his theology of creation and eschatology.

---

58. Benedict XVI, *Light of the World* (San Francisco: Ignatius Press, 2010), 102.

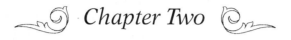

Chapter Two

"Revelation Seen Basically as Dialogue"

> *"In times past, God spoke in partial and various ways to our ancestors through the prophets; in these last days he spoke to us through a son, whom he made heir of all things and through whom he created the universe."*
> *(Heb 1:1-2)*

Because Joseph Ratzinger has never written a comprehensive systematic theology of his own, it is a challenge to know what area of theology to begin with in attempting an exposition of the coherence of his thought. The difficulty of finding a precise starting point is indicative of the nature of Ratzinger's theology. His theological method is always to show the synthetic and holistic nature of the Christian vision and therefore of the whole of the theological enterprise. To speak of sacraments, for example, it is necessary always to have in mind their scriptural basis and the theological as well as philosophical grounding that makes them efficacious. One must never engage in a question of moral theology outside the scope of ecclesiological and trinitarian theologies of communion, etc. Still, it is necessary to start somewhere in the effort to explicate the coherence of his thought, and so I have chosen to begin with his theology of revelation. I do so in order to establish immediately the basis for the thesis that what provides coherence for the whole of Ratzinger's thought is the organizing principle of the communicability of the Word of God.

Ratzinger's theology of revelation is logo-centric, historical in character, and therefore narrative, and in style such that the dynamic it most clearly follows is that of an *unfolding* of the Christian mystery. It can therefore rightly be characterized as dialogical. As he makes consistent use of the appeal to the *Logos* as the principle of coherence for his explanation of how God reveals God's self to humanity he is simultaneously insistent on the *historical* aspect of revelation. As God reveals his Word in human words, he does so always in concrete historical settings and circumstances. Ratzinger learns from Bonaventure that "wisdom is unthinkable and unintelligible without reference to the historical situation in which it has its place."[1] Only from this historical "place" can the *event* of the encounter with the *Logos* unfold. That encounter has the potential to draw humanity "up into the trinitarian dynamic: The Son leads to the Father in the Holy Spirit. It [the Christian mystery] is about God, and only in this do we treat the subject of man correctly."[2] Only by beginning with the divine *actio* of the *Logos* being spoken from above and then seeing how that Logos is spoken "below" in history is it possible to understand the core of the Christian mystery as one of dialogue between God and humanity. In this vision, revelation is not properly understood as a *monologue* from God containing information God chooses to reveal about himself and the world, but rather a *dialogue* between two essential parties, the Eternal "I" speaking to the historical "Thou" of humanity and the historical "I" of humanity responding to the Eternal "Thou." While there is always more to the Eternal Logos than what is expressed in history, the content of this dialogue is the substance of revelation itself.

In the course of this chapter I hope to show first how Ratzinger's study of Bonaventure's theology of history helped to fundamentally shape his thought on the nature of revelation. Second, I will examine

---

1. Joseph Ratzinger, *The Theology of History in St. Bonaventure* (Chicago: Franciscan Herald Press, 1989), 6.

2. Maximilian Heinrich Heim, *Joseph Ratzinger: Life in the Church and Living Theology: Fundamentals of Ecclesiology with Reference to* Lumen Gentium (San Francisco: Ignatius Press, 2007), 2. This passage is taken from Ratzinger's foreword to this study of his own ecclesiology by Heim. He is affirming Heim's sense of the Christocentric and theological structure of the council's teaching about revelation and the life of the church.

his articulation of the nature of the relationship of Scripture and tradition to revelation in an essay published in the course of the council. Next I will highlight the relationship between Ratzinger's approach to the question of revelation and the development of this doctrine from Vatican I's *Dei Filius* to Vatican II's *Dei Verbum*, and then show how the recent apostolic exhortation *Verbum Domini* elaborates on this dialogical structure of revelation. Finally, I will turn to Ratzinger's treatment of the authentic nature of exegesis and theology as *ecclesial* practices. I hope to show how he sees them as ways of participating in the dynamic of revelation insofar as they consist first and foremost of a communal *listening* to the Word in particular historical settings in order that the whole church might be able to better enter into the dialogical event of the unfolding of revelation.

I. Foundations in Bonaventure's Theology of History

After his dissertation on Augustine's ecclesiology, Ratzinger turned to Bonaventure's theology of history for the topic of his *Habilitations-schrift*. He undertook this project in 1953, he says, because the question of salvation history was reshaping the Catholic theology of revelation, "which neoscholasticism had kept too confined to the intellectual realm."[3] He recalls that in the setting of the emerging "historical consciousness" within Catholic theological circles, "Revelation now appeared to no longer be a communication of truths to the intellect but as a historical action of God in which truth becomes gradually unveiled."[4] Though the insistence on historical consciousness being applied to biblical exegesis and dogmatic theology was unsettling to many in Catholic circles, Ratzinger took it as an opportunity to examine the tradition in light of this new question. He did so by reaching back into the resources of that tradition in the thought of St. Bonaventure to "discover whether . . . there was anything corresponding to the concept of salvation history, and whether this motif—if it should exist—had any relationship with the idea of revelation."[5] The fruit of this study was to discover exactly such a

3. Joseph Ratzinger, *Milestones: Memoirs, 1927–1977* (San Francisco: Igna-tius Press, 1998), 104.
4. Ibid.
5. Ibid.

correspondence and to begin to conceive of a contemporary theology of revelation in light of the new "historical consciousness."

Central to this new way of conceiving of revelation was that it is properly understood as essentially a *dialogue that unfolds in history* between God and humanity. It is not merely a monologue from God consisting of truths communicated in the abstract. Indeed, for Ratzinger there is no "revelation" at all without the historically embedded human subject appropriating what is being revealed by God. Whereas it had been common in Catholic theology in the early part of the twentieth century to think of revelation primarily as the objective data given by God to humanity, for Bonaventure revelation is primarily the more foundational *act* by which God reveals what had previously been hidden; it is not the "objectified result of this act."[6] In order for this "unveiling" to properly be said to have happened, the human subject must receive what has been given.[7] Ratzinger explains:

> Here, "revelation" is always a concept denoting an act. The word refers to the act in which God shows himself, not the objectified result of this act. And because this is so, the receiving subject is also always part of the concept of "revelation." Where there is no one to perceive "revelation," no re-*vel*-ation has occurred, because no veil has been removed. By definition, revelation requires a someone who apprehends it.[8]

Ratzinger notes that in modern usage of the term, "revelation" is often simply equated with Sacred Scripture. This would have been entirely foreign to the High Middle Ages, he says. While he starts with Scripture, and sees all of human history through the lens of the narrative of Scripture, Ratzinger argues, Bonaventure conceived of revelation in a much more expansive way, given the association of *revelatio* with *actio*.[9] As he interprets Bonaventure's sometimes convoluted schemas regarding revelation and history, Ratzinger draws out some basic principles more accessible to the contemporary reader. For one, there is always more to revelation than the "letter" that is accessible to the human person. He notes a striking similarity between Scripture

---

6. Ibid., 108.
7. Ratzinger, *Theology of History in St. Bonaventure*, 58.
8. Ratzinger, *Milestones*, 108.
9. Ibid.

and creation in this regard as both sources present a "literal" expression of reality. The challenge for the human subject, however, is always to see behind this immediate presentation of reality to grasp the more transcendent truth of things.[10]

In this regard Bonaventure suggests that if history is properly understood in the light of Scripture, the *future* is "revealed" or accessible on some level to those in the present. By way of Scripture, if understood "in the Spirit," it is possible to apprehend the substance of the future. Also essential to this kind of historical discernment, as one might call it, is constant attentiveness in the present, in light of the scriptural witness.[11] This attentiveness in the present involves a consistent struggle to discover what Bonaventure calls the "mystical meaning" of Scripture that is unveiled from its hidden state in the process of *revelatio*. For the living church, as the Word of God expressed in Scripture is proclaimed and appropriated within the community, it becomes clear to those guided by the Holy Spirit that no immediate interpretation of the texts of Scripture is able to exhaust their meaning. The Spirit who transcends history is the One by whom what is hidden "behind" Scripture is revealed. In this model it is the Spirit who makes the Word intelligible for the faithful living in the church grounded in history.[12] Ultimately, for Bonaventure, what is "unveiled" in the process of *revelatio* is *divine reality* itself.

This divine reality, God's very Self, is encountered in the mystical ascent of humanity, made possible by the grace of God.[13] The content or substance of this *revelatio* of divine essence is not an "exclusive I-Thou relationship, rather it stands in a great cosmic-hierarchical context."[14] As Ratzinger interprets Bonaventure, then, the understanding of God that comes in revelation is not what is apprehended in isolation by one thinker but rather is a discovery that is made in union with the community of the whole church over the course of salvation history. Consequently, what comes to be known by the human person in the process of *revelatio* is not some kind of "clear and distinct" *idea* about God, but rather only the kind of knowledge that comes from personal encounter with God in history. This

10. Ratzinger, *Theology of History in St. Bonaventure*, 84.
11. Ibid., 83–84.
12. Ibid., 85.
13. Ibid., 58–59.
14. Ibid., 72.

encounter does not take place in private between the individual and God but in the context of a whole complex of relations that comprise the church in the present that is always connected to its past.

Controversy: Ratzinger's Dialogical Structure of Revelation

Ratzinger's "dynamic" or "dialogical" interpretation of Bonaventure's theology of history created problems for him in the course of the submission of his *Habilitationsschrift*. The insistence on the role of human reception in the act of revelation from God smacked of a modernist tendency that one of his readers, Michael Schmaus, intended to guard against. Schmaus concluded that Ratzinger was opening the door to what could be understood as the "subjectivization" of revelation and the simultaneous dismissing of revelation's objective and eternal truth.[15] For this reason Schmaus initially rejected Ratzinger's work as unacceptable until Ratzinger deleted this allegedly "subjectivist" aspect of his analysis.[16] This was not a minor edit; it consisted in eliminating over half of his original thesis. He later expanded on the second half of the original thesis in order to make it acceptable to Schmaus. The trauma of this experience, no doubt, left its mark indelibly on the young theologian and would, consequently, sharpen his attentiveness to this aspect of his understanding of the Christian vision as inherently dialogical.[17]

Different Levels of Meaning in Scripture

Because he is convinced of the need always to begin his theology with Scripture, Ratzinger's methodology is never given over to sheer speculation. There is, for him, always the narrative of salvation history to be responded to in doing theology. From this vantage point, revelation itself is understood in these terms. Ratzinger explains that Bonaventure's notion of revelation involves God's communication in the context of historical particulars. Bonaventure is not concerned, as modern theologians are, with the nature of the one revelation, but rather seeks patterns among the many instances of revelation in his-

---

15. Fergus Kerr, *Twentieth-Century Catholic Theologians: From Neoscholasticism to Nuptial Mysticism* (Malden, MA: Blackwell, 2007), 185.

16. Ratzinger, *Milestones*, 108.

17. Benedict XVI, *Gesammelte Schriften*, ed. Gerhard Müller (Freiburg: Herder, 2008).

tory. In this sense then, Ratzinger says, "we could say that Bonaventure does not treat of 'revelation' but of 'revelations.'"[18] These many revelations make up a coherent narrative filled with events that involve a disclosure of meaning. At the heart of this coherent narrative is the principle that God provides revelations as *acts*. Ratzinger interprets Bonaventure's understanding of revelation as being the *act* of revealing by God, not simply the *content* of what is ultimately revealed. Revelation, therefore, is not a static body of data or knowledge but rather always characterized by the dynamic of an *unfolding event*, in turn giving it a narrative texture rather than a propositional one. If this is true, then revelation, strictly speaking, suggests that what is *behind* Scripture is always more than the "letter" of Scripture itself.[19]

Consequently, Ratzinger explains that for Bonaventure the *understanding* of Scripture was itself a "gradual, historical, progressive development . . . which was in no way closed."[20] In terms of this basic grasp of the multivalence of Scripture, Bonaventure proposes three ways of deriving its meaning. The first is the spiritual understanding (*spiritualis intelligentia*), which is identical to the traditional manner of recognizing literal, allegorical, tropological, and anagogical meanings in any given portion of Scripture.[21] In any given text, meaning can be derived that is deeper than the literal sense to allow the reader to understand how certain objects, characters, events, etc., in this or that passage might be representative of other more spiritual realities, how those realities might speak to the importance of moral conversion in the reader, and finally how these realities are instructive about eschatology and divine truth itself. But Bonaventure is not content with this framework for interpreting the texts of Scripture alone. He has in mind the need to understand the *whole* of the Scripture, as one coherent narrative unfolding throughout all of human history.

Consequently, Bonaventure suggests a second manner of interpreting Scripture that calls for analysis of what he terms the *figurae sacramentales* in the whole of Scripture. In this model there are "sacramental figures" that point to the presence of Christ throughout Scripture, especially as conflict with forces of the Antichrist emerge. Failing to cite any specific examples in the Bible, Ratzinger refers to

18. Ratzinger, *Theology of History in St. Bonaventure*, 57.
19. Ibid., 63.
20. Ibid., 75.
21. Ibid., 62–63.

Bonaventure's general dialectic explanation of the whole of the scriptural narrative: "All the mysteries of Scripture treat of Christ with his Body and of the Anti-Christ and the Devil with his cohorts. This is the meaning of St. Augustine in his book on the City of God."[22] Whereas in Augustine's *Civitas Dei*, Ratzinger explains, conflict and duality are what make sense of the whole of history, for Bonaventure the dialectic of conflict between the Christ and the Antichrist is real, but it is relegated to this second of three ways of approaching Scripture.[23]

After the *spiritualis intelligentia* and the *figurae sacramentales*, Bonaventure characterizes the third and most fruitful approach to Scripture as that of the *multiformes theoriae*, through which the reader can apprehend many manifestations of *theoria* or meaning of the one truth, the one Word being spoken throughout the whole of Scripture.[24] Here is Bonaventure's highest level of understanding Scripture. It is not characterized simply by the dialectic struggle between the Christ and the Antichrist but rather by the one unified but "multiform" communication of God for the sake of drawing humanity into relationship. The centrality of the *Logos* is essential for this aspect of Bonaventure's theology of history. The *Logos* through which all things in heaven and on earth are created is the same *Logos* spoken in human history. From Adam and Noah to Abraham, Moses, David, and all the prophets, all the way up to the coming of Christ and in the life of the church founded on Christ, many "*theoriae*" appear in the scope of salvation history, but they are expressive of the one *Logos* or Word of God.

Revelation Unfolding in History: The Many *Semina* of One *Logos*

Bonaventure uses an organic metaphor to concretize this model of the *multiformes theoriae*. Drawing on a philosophical image common since the time of Zeno and the Stoics, who described the *logoi spermatikoi* (seeds of the word) that make creation intelligible,[25] Bona-

---

22. Ibid., 10. Cf. Bonaventure, *Hexameron XIII–XV.*
23. Ibid.
24. Ibid., 7.
25. In a work first published about ten years later Ratzinger spells out the development of this thought from ancient Greek philosophy to its interaction with biblical belief. See Joseph Ratzinger, *Einführung in das Christentum: Vorlesungen über das Apostolische Glaubensbekenntnis* (Munich: Kösel, 1968; new ed. 2000); ET: *Introduction to Christianity*, trans. J. R. Foster (San Francisco: Ignatius Press, 2004), 137–50.

venture suggests that from the one *Logos* of God many *"semina"* or seeds are produced and planted in the soil of human history as well. He writes:

> Who can know the number of seeds which exist? For from one single seed, entire forests grow up; and they in turn bring forth innumerable seeds. So it happens that innumerable theories can arise from Scripture that only God can grasp in His knowledge. As new seeds come from plants, so also new theories and new meaning come from Scripture.[26]

This interpretive image of the seed is key to Bonaventure's whole theology of history because it helps to account for the way the whole of salvation history unfolds: not just within what is recounted in Scripture but including all of human history up to the present moment. The challenge for the present, then, is to understand the meaning of current circumstances in light of the whole narrative until now. True understanding of any present context can only be obtained in light of the earlier *semina* that had sprung forth from the one *Logos* in the past.[27] Though Ratzinger does not indicate this explicitly, it seems evident that there is offered here the underlying principle allowing for development in Christian doctrine as well. The appearance of the church and the way in which the Christian mysteries are articulated in any given age may differ, but there is still coherence to it all in light of the unity and intelligibility of the *Logos*, the original source of the whole story of salvation history from its inception. Indeed, the coherent expression of this principle of the many seeds coming from the one Word is given within Scripture itself. Ratzinger highlights how Bonaventure's theology of revelation in history has to do with the interrelationship of the Old and New Testaments.

For Bonaventure the Old Testament gives way to the New Testament as one seedling begets another.[28] Furthermore, the "seed" of the Word made flesh in the person of Jesus, according to Ratzinger's analysis, characterizes the essence of the identity of the church. In this way, then, both what we call the Old and the New Testaments

---

26. Ratzinger, *Theology of History in St. Bonaventure*, 7, citing *Hexameron* XIII, 2.

27. Ibid., 20.

28. Ibid., 12.

comprise one testament, one expression of the one *Logos* of God who is ultimately revealed in Jesus Christ, who continues to be known within the church.[29] There is, then, a twofold sense of the unfolding of revelation. In one, there is a linear unfolding of revelation in salvation history from the events of the Old Testament leading up to the Christ-event that is the basis of the New Testament. Once the Christ event occurs, however, history is to be conceived, in Bonaventure's view, not in a linear manner but according to the dynamic of concentric circles at the heart of which is the fullness of revelation, the person of Christ, the *Logos* itself made flesh.

Christ as *Center*, not *End*, of History

In this metaphor of the many seeds being planted from the one *Logos*, history begins to be conceived in a progressive manner. This progress, however, is in the mode of a narrative as opposed to the linear character, as is the case in the scholastic tradition based on the teleology of Aristotle.[30] Ratzinger explains: "Bonaventure sees Aristotle's concept of time to be linear; it is an infinite line without ordering. In contrast with this, Bonaventure holds a type of circular movement as the image of Christian understanding of time, the double movement of *egressus* and *regressus*."[31] For Bonaventure the center point of this circular, or perhaps spherical, notion of history is the person of Christ. From the *center* point of history, which is the incarnation of the eternal Word in human history, growth and development flow *outward* until all of history, what lies in the past as well as in the future, is vivified according to the power of what lies at the center.

One of Bonaventure's great contributions, in Ratzinger's view, is the development of this christo*centric* view of human history. Challenged by Joachim of Fiore's vision of salvation history, Bonaventure was forced to deal with the question of history in a new way. He argued against a Joachimism that supposed "new" revelation beyond the age of Christ into the Age of the Spirit. The argument for a deeply Christocentric hermeneutic of Scripture and all of history became central for Bonaventure and is certainly a central principle for Ratzinger. The fruit of his contemplation on the matter left with the church

29. Ibid.
30. Ibid., 143.
31. Ibid., 144.

the early seeds of a kind of "historical consciousness" when it comes to doing theology.[32] This concentric shape of human history is also then complemented in Bonaventure's model by a different sort of circular pattern that is on a vertical plane, connecting eternity and history. In this sense the circular movement of salvation sees history flowing as an *egressus* and *regressus* from God to humanity and back to God through the figure of Christ.[33]

For Bonaventure, Christ is the *center* of history precisely as Word, as the *Logos*. There is communication from God at the center of history, and how and in what way history "progresses" relates to the nature and quality of the human response to that Word. Through the church, the Word continues to be communicated and revealed in history and is the source of coherence in all of history. This *Logos* made flesh is manifested ultimately as love, and is the unifying principle and the source and summit of all of human history. The fulfillment of history comes not when the "end of the line" is reached, but when *love* comes to fruition and prevails in the hearts and lives of the people to whom this love has been offered from the person of Christ. Love itself enters history when the Word becomes flesh in Jesus Christ. Therefore the "end," or better the fulfillment, of history happens when the extension of the Word made flesh in history becomes "all in all" (1 Cor 15:28)—when love is all that remains (1 Cor 13:13).

Historical Consciousness

In Bonaventure's schema history is crucial because of the fact that it is the locus where the Word of love is planted at its heart in order to redeem it from within, from its center. God, who is sovereign over human history, gives new depth to the meaning of history because he enters into it. Ratzinger explains that when the infancy narratives in the gospels proclaim that the incarnation happened in the fullness of time, this itself is a profession of faith in the incarnation, because what makes time "full" is nothing attributable to or discoverable from within the horizon of time itself, but only happens by virtue of the fact that the eternal has entered into the temporal. This *event* that marks the fullness of time becomes the *center* of time

32. Ibid., 106.
33. Ibid., 145–47.

in Bonaventure's theology of history.[34] From this center history itself
begins to be redeemed from the inside because of what has entered
into it from the outside. The orientation toward the future, then,
unfolds based on this *actio divina* from above. In order to understand
the present and anticipate the shape of the future, then, a certain
"historical consciousness" is required that is necessarily eschatological as well.[35]

[margin, handwritten: History redeemed from the inside]

Within Bonaventure's theology of history the virtue of hope becomes
a major reference point for the whole of his vision. Authentic hope in
every age is to be discovered and cultivated from *within history*, not
outside of it. This embodiment of hope from *within* history is what
characterizes the life and mission of the church that gets its life and
purpose from Christ, its center. For Bonaventure, Christ is both the
center and the fulfillment of history. Ratzinger consistently embraces
this same Christocentric view of all of human history that is fundamentally a "movement of *egressus* from God; and *regressus* to him through
Jesus Christ."[36] The inner principle of this movement of history is love
that flows from God and back to God. In this sense a further interpretive mechanism for salvation history comes to the fore, namely, *love* as
what "moves" history toward its gradual fulfillment. The conclusion
of Ratzinger's study of Bonaventure provides a key to understanding
what motivates and informs the whole of his own theology:

> both Augustine and Bonaventure know that the Church which
> hopes for peace in the future is, nonetheless, obliged to love
> in the present; and they both realize that the kingdom of eter-
> nal peace is growing in the hearts of those who fulfill Christ's
> law of love in their own particular age. Both see themselves
> subject to the word of the Apostle: "So faith, hope, love remain,
> these three; but the greatest of these is love." (1 Cor 13:13).[37]

Therefore encountering Christ, encountering love itself in history,
is the foundation for the life of the church, and from this encounter

34. Ibid., 110.
35. Ibid., 106–8. Ratzinger sees this historical consciousness as the great
contribution made by Joachim in theology, even if he arrived at its importance
in an inelegant manner.
36. Aidan Nichols, *The Thought of Pope Benedict XVI: An Introduction to the
Theology of Joseph Ratzinger* (New York: Burns & Oates, 2007), 42.
37. Ratzinger, *Theology of History in St. Bonaventure*, 163.

with love the church's life is to be characterized by that same identity as the locus for the whole world of the dialogical encounter with love. This principle derived from Bonaventure of the centrality of the dialogical encounter with the Word became the basis for the contribution Ratzinger would soon make in the Second Vatican Council.

II. Quaestio Disputata: *"Tradition" in the Deliberations of* Dei Verbum

Ratzinger brought this Bonaventurian understanding of the historical and dialogical nature of revelation to his role as a *peritus* at the Second Vatican Council. The thirty-four-year-old theologian was asked by Cardinal Josef Frings of Cologne to help with the preparatory work before the council began. Ultimately, serving as Frings's *peritus*, Ratzinger would contribute along with several other theologians, including Karl Rahner, to the crafting of the Constitution on Divine Revelation (*Dei Verbum*).[38] Based on this preparatory work, Rahner and Ratzinger wrote independent articles that later were joined together in a book entitled *Revelation and Tradition*, published in German in 1965.[39] The publisher's introduction to the book situates it consciously in the *ad extra* setting of the new ecumenism emerging in the time of the council, as well as *the ad intra* context of the Catholic Church emerging out of the modernist crisis and the problem of historical consciousness posed by it. Their work represents the most proximate efforts by two of the most influential *periti* working on *Dei Verbum* to generate new ways to articulate the essentials of the church's self-understanding in relationship to God's self-communication.

Rahner's introductory chapter for *Revelation and Tradition*, offered first as a lecture at Münster in 1964, begins by acknowledging the *immanentism* of some strands of modernism of the late nineteenth century, in which there can appear to be a certain "inevitable development, immanent in human history, of man's 'religious needs.'"[40] Rahner also notes the reaction to this *immanentism*—the opposite extreme of *extrinsicism* in which revelation comes to be seen as God's

---

38. W. Jared Wicks and Benedict XVI, *Prof. Ratzinger at Vatican II: A Chapter in the Life of Pope Benedict XVI* (New Orleans: Loyola University Press, 2007), 24.

39. Karl Rahner and Joseph Ratzinger, *Revelation and Tradition* (London: Herder, 1966).

40. Ibid., 10.

intervention, "purely from the outside" in humanity's reality, communicating information from God that is extrinsic to God's own identity.[41] The time was now ripe, Rahner argued, for a new understanding of revelation that could bridge the gap between the immanentism and extrinsicism of modern theology. The starting point for his exploration of the nature of revelation is, characteristically, anthropological. Here he explains the necessity to

> assume that every human being is elevated by grace in his transcendental intellectuality in a non-reflex manner; that this "entitative" divinization—which is proffered to freedom, even if it is not accepted freely in faith—involves a transcendental divinization of the fundamental subjective attitude, the ultimate horizons of man's knowledge and freedom, in the perspective of which he accomplishes his life.[42]

While Rahner insists that this "entitative divinization" can occur only in the context of human freedom *in history*, his articulation of the new understanding of revelation is couched primarily in the speculative language of his Thomistic anthropology in dialogue with the existentialism of the day.[43] While he insists on the historical nature of revelation, his description of that historicity remains more conceptual than concrete.

Ratzinger undertook his task in this book from a historical perspective more narrative in style. Beginning with the New Testament proclamation "Jesus is the Christ," he traces in several ways from the Old Testament how it is that the Christ event is the fulfillment of what had been promised over the generations.[44] Underlying the development of these generations is the interaction of the *gramma* and *pneuma*, as St. Paul put it. In the Old Testament the written prophecy had been anticipating its fulfillment. Paul sees Christ as the *pneuma* who makes the rest of Scripture intelligible (2 Cor 3:6-18). Whether it is the prophet Isaiah, Joel, or Jeremiah proclaiming the hope of a

41. Ibid.
42. Ibid., 16.
43. See especially Thomas Sheehan, "Rahner's Transcendental Project," 29–42, and Daniel Donovan, "Revelation and Faith," 83–97, in Declan Marmion and Mary E. Hines, *The Cambridge Companion to Karl Rahner* (New York: Cambridge University Press, 2005).
44. Rahner and Ratzinger, *Revelation and Tradition*, 37–38.

messiah, Ratzinger asserts, "in each case, the time inaugurated by the Christ event now appears as the answer to a line of hope, which expected that in the future age scripture would, in an ultimate sense, be rendered actually superfluous by the immediate proximity of the divine teacher in man himself."[45] Here, then, is the basis for the living tradition that unfolds in the life of the church and follows the basic pattern of the drama of salvation history. The story has primacy over speculation.

Only after dealing with the concrete historical particulars about how the scriptural accounts give way to the life of the church does Ratzinger then offer a reflection on the nature of tradition itself as operating according to the principles of the *analogia fidei*. The Old Testament, he says, is to be understood in light of the Christ event and "also an interpretation of the Christ event itself on the basis of the *pneuma*, which means on the basis of the church's present."[46] The method for understanding tradition, then, does not start with a speculative or philosophical framework, but instead begins with the narrative of Scripture and salvation history and only then attempts to discover patterns of meaning and intelligibility. Many years later Ratzinger would note that it was in the context of writing this book with Rahner that he began to realize they occupied "different theological planets."[47] For Ratzinger the differentiating characteristic of "his planet" was the method of basing his theology of revelation on the experience of the salvation-historical narrative of the Bible that continues in the life of the church as opposed to the more speculative or conceptual mode of Rahner. Though Ratzinger's style is historical, it is not primarily anthropological because the narrative he follows in history is that shaped by the *actions of God* in history. The starting point is not humanity's natural or even supernatural inclinations toward God.

By giving primacy to the *actio divina* in history, to God's revelation of the Word, Ratzinger also found common ecumenical ground on which to stand. Striking a note of concern regarding ecumenism from the beginning, he explains in his first essay that the question of the inner relationship between revelation, Scripture, tradition, and the church has been the source of division among Christians since the

45. Ibid., 38.
46. Ibid., 42.
47. Ratzinger, *Milestones*, 128.

time of Martin Luther.[48] While the Reformers saw the magisterial teachings of the church as accretions of tradition onto the only authentic revelation given by God *sola scriptura*, the basic Catholic understanding has been that the revelation of God, as recounted in Scripture, continues to be deepened in understanding within the living tradition of the church, centered on Christ and enlightened by the Holy Spirit. He notes that even Philip Melancthon conceded that if the church would "allow the Gospel" it would behoove the Reformers to allow for the ecclesiological structures of bishops with the pope primary among them as an important dimension of ministry within the church. This, Melancthon recognized, would allow for the ongoing appropriation precisely of the power of the Gospel in the lives of the faithful.[49] As the Reformers insisted on the primacy of the Word "over" the church, a caricature of the Tridentine position has been the church's insistence on its role as being "over" the Word. Rather, as Ratzinger explains, the true position of Trent was to insist on the fact of the Lord *giving* the Word *to* the church so that the church might always be centered on the Word and be the authentic interpreter of it throughout history.[50] This ongoing appropriation of the Word is what constitutes tradition in the Catholic sense. Therefore, rather than collapsing the Word into an identification with Scripture as is the tendency in the Reformation tradition, the Catholic position has been to see the appropriation of the Word as always beginning with Scripture and then unfolding throughout history in a way that makes possible an ever-developing tradition.

Ratzinger notes the strengths and weaknesses of both the Protestant and Tridentine approaches to the question of the receiving of the Word by the church. In the Protestant tradition, once revelation comes to be identified with Scripture,[51] once the distinction is collapsed and it is asserted that the Word is "over" the church, an interpretive problem emerges. As the Word is given autonomy with respect to the living church, the same Word is "delivered to the caprice of the exegetes."[52] This interpretive problem pointed to in the mid-1960s also characterizes, for Ratzinger, the present-day crisis created by

---

48. Rahner and Ratzinger, *Revelation and Tradition*, 27–28.
49. Ibid., 28.
50. Ibid., 30.
51. Ibid., 34.
52. Ibid., 31.

some of the limitations of the historical critical method. In this situation many modern exegetes have vacated Scripture of the power of the Word of God and consequently Scripture "has become a word of the past" to be dissected by professional experts, as the church all the while sits idly by.[53] On the Catholic side, a certain distortion had emerged in the post-Trent era wherein the insistence on tradition as a "second source" of revelation had too often come to be seen as placing tradition in its own autonomous posture with respect to the Scripture that precedes it. Scandal could be given in this context if it were perceived that the magisterium of the church could teach *apart* from the normative Scriptures.

Ratzinger approached this question of fundamental theology by following the historical developments in the debate about the question of tradition. He does so in his contribution to *Revelation and Tradition* by entering into dialogue with a contemporary and influential work at the time, by the dogmatic theologian from Tübingen, J. R. Geiselmann.[54] Geiselmann's historical analysis of the development of the teaching on revelation in the context of the Council of Trent helped clarify the questions for the deliberations at Vatican II.[55] He demonstrates that in the *Acts of the Council of Trent*, in the early drafts of the document on revelation, the thesis was advanced that what God reveals is to be found *"partim in libris . . . partim in . . . traditionibus,"* partly in Scripture and partly in tradition.[56] This *partial* attribution of revelation to Scripture and *partial* attribution to tradition would have clearly delineated the two-source nature of revelation, indicating that some revelation could be found in tradition that is not explicitly in Scripture. This would also have made reconciliation with Protestantism on this question impossible. In the end, however, the fathers at Trent decided on the simpler formulation, *"in libris scriptis et sine scripto traditionibus,"* indicating that revelation is handed on

---

53. Joseph Ratzinger, *God's Word: Scripture, Tradition, Office*, ed. Peter Hunermann and Thomas Söding (San Francisco: Ignatius Press, 2008), 98.

54. Josef Rupert Geiselmann, *Die Heilige Schrift und die Tradition: zu den neueren Kontroversen über das Verhältnis der Heiligen Schrift zu den nichtgeschriebenen Traditionen* (Freiburg: Herder, 1962).

55. Ratzinger, *Milestones*, 124–27.

56. Herbert Vorgrimler, ed., *Commentary on the Documents of Vatican II*, 5 vols. (New York: Herder and Herder, 1967), 3: 156. Cf. Geiselmann, *Die Heilige Schrift und die Tradition*, 287.

both in written Scripture *and* in unwritten tradition.[57] The fact that
Trent settled on this formulation kept open the door, in Geiselmann's
view, to the possibility of a Catholic rapprochement with Protestant
insistence on seeing revelation as expressed *sola scriptura*. For Geiselmann, by concluding that revelation is found in Scripture *and* in
tradition a Catholic could in good conscience go along with the Reformation doctrine of the "material sufficiency" of Scripture.[58]

Ratzinger, while admiring Geiselmann's scholarship and methodology in examining the historical narrative of developments at Trent,
soon became critical of the interpretive conclusions. In order to avoid
the Protestant mistake of collapsing revelation with Scripture[59] and a
frequent Catholic misinterpretation of the "two-source" theory of
revelation given at Trent that could separate the substance of Scripture
and tradition too drastically, he concluded that the real concern is to
more fundamentally understand the "mode of presence of the Word
of God among the faithful"[60] not in a theoretical way, but as it unfolds
in the contingencies of history. After all, he says, "Revelation always
and only becomes reality where there is faith."[61] We see here the influence of Bonaventure on his thought, keeping historicity always before
him when it comes to the question of revelation. The real task for the
church, he concluded, and ultimately the task the Second Vatican
Council took up so fruitfully in *Dei Verbum*, is to "go behind the positive sources, scripture and tradition, to their inner source, revelation,
the living word of God from which scripture and tradition spring and
without which their significance for faith cannot be understood."[62]
This method he proposed clearly harkens back to his discovery in
Bonaventure of the many *semina* of the one *Logos* in salvation history
as a way of describing the transmission of revelation in history.

57. Vorgrimler, *Commentary on the Documents of Vatican II*, 3: 157.

58. Rahner and Ratzinger, *Revelation and Tradition*, 34.

59. For more on this question see Benedict T. Viviano, "The Normativity of
Scripture and Tradition in Recent Catholic Theology" in *Scripture's Doctrine and
Theology's Bible: How the New Testament Shapes Christian Dogmatics*, ed. Markus
Bockmuehl and Alan J. Torrance (Grand Rapids: Baker Academic, 2008),
125–31.

60. Rahner and Ratzinger, *Revelation and Tradition*, 34.

61. Ibid., 36.

62. Ibid., 34.

Only from the perspective gained once one has "gone behind" the positive sources of Scripture and tradition to revelation itself does it become possible to begin to see the unfolding of the Word in salvation history. Ratzinger explains that this dynamic is at work even in Scripture itself, since the relationship of the Old and New Testaments is rightly understood as one expression of the Word of God *unfolding* in salvation history. In one sense, he notes, only the Old Testament is rightly considered Scripture. For the writers of the New Testament the only Scriptures were those contained in the Old Testament. The New Testament, then, is the Spirit-led interpretation of the Old Testament in light of the Christ-event.[63]

The scriptures (Old Testament) are fulfilled and therefore intelligible only in light of the Christ-event and the beginning of the interpretation of this event is the set of writings contained in what comes to be recognized as the New Testament. Ratzinger notes that in several places in the New Testament, the Old Testament prophecy is seen as the letter (*gramma*) and the New Testament as the spirit (*pneuma*) of the one unfolding revelation of God's Word among his faithful.[64] At work, then, even within the Old and New Testaments is the action of tradition by which what has been received in faith from God in previous generations is handed on, so that faith might take root in the future. At the center of this *traditio* is the Christ-event, the fullness of God's revelation. Here the "letter" of the "old" testament is fulfilled and then only understood according to the guidance of the Spirit, which then makes possible the reception of the "new" testament. The ongoing revelation communicated in the tradition of the church is always founded on Scripture and appropriated authentically only when seen through the lens of the Christ-event. The nature of this principle of the unfolding of tradition is the focus of Ratzinger's concluding remarks in this essay. Jumping ahead a bit, we turn now to his understanding of these questions as he reflected back on the "final product" of the fathers at Vatican II in the promulgation of *Dei Verbum*.

III. Dei Verbum: *Revelation "Seen Basically as Dialogue"*

In his description of the origins and background of the Dogmatic Constitution on Divine Revelation, *Dei Verbum*, Ratzinger recalls

63. Ibid., 37.
64. Ibid., 38.

Archbishop Florit's *relatio* to the council on the first two chapters of the document: "Because of its inner importance as well as the many vicissitudes that it has undergone, the history of the draft on the Constitution on Divine Revelation has fused itself with the history of this council into a kind of unity."[65] The ultimate teaching of the council on revelation would provide an important basis for how to understand the other documents related to liturgy, the relationship of the church to other entities in the modern world, etc. This is so precisely because what was at stake in *Dei Verbum* was the question of how the church conceives of God's most fundamental interaction with the world, reaching from eternity into the contingencies of human history. The council embraced the vision that "the pattern of this revelation unfolds through deeds and words"[66] both in creation and in history. Indeed, in the immediate wake of the council Ratzinger himself described the newly emerging understanding of revelation that is "seen basically as dialogue."[67] This understanding of the unfolding of revelation, expressed in an ongoing dialogue between God and humanity in human history, in turn provided a theological foundation for discussions of other pressing matters, including how the church relates to other Christians, to the Jewish people, to other non-Christian believers, and to the modern world as a whole. While retaining confidence in how God had revealed himself in Scripture and tradition, and most fully through Christ in the Catholic Church, *Dei Verbum* also created space for understanding the ongoing appropriation of this revelation in dialogue with those outside the church.

Again, this category of dialogue is central and always to be understood through the christological hermeneutic that sees the person of Jesus Christ as the fullness of the dialogue between God and humanity. Indeed, the opening words of *Dei Verbum* highlight the role of human receptivity, the "hearing" of the word of God.[68] Only a few years after the young student Joseph Ratzinger struggled to have his *Habilitationsschrift* approved because of his defense of humanity's essential role in it, "this 'novel' understanding of revelation . . . would

---

65. Ibid., 155.

66. Austin Flannery, ed., *Vatican Council II: The Basic Sixteen Documents: Constitutions, Decrees, Declarations* (Northport, NY: Costello Publishing Co., 1996). See *Dei Verbum* 2, 98.

67. Vorgrimler, *Commentary on the Documents of Vatican II*, 3: 171.

68. Flannery, *Basic Sixteen Documents, Dei Verbum* 1, 97.

prove revolutionary at the beginning of the Second Vatican Council and set the tenor for the whole council" in its ultimate insistence on revelation as "historical and contextual" and therefore having everything to do with God's dialogue partner: the human family.[69]

Ratzinger notes the background of the intellectual current that helped to inform the church's ultimate articulation of its teaching on this question.[70] First, the "Romantic movement" had been developing an understanding of tradition, not in material terms but in more organic ways suggestive of the principle of development and growth. Though he does not describe the main figures in this "Romantic movement," he associates it with the need, after the proclamation of the Marian dogma of the Immaculate Conception in 1854, to understand tradition as *developing* and not simply something that is handed down neatly from one generation to the next. He notes Cardinal Newman as one who had been influenced by Romanticism in this regard.[71] The second aspect of the intellectual climate that affected these discussions, in Ratzinger's view, was the challenge posed by historical-critical methods of exegesis that were forcing the church to take more seriously the demands of "historical consciousness" and the role of human factors in the composition of divinely inspired texts. The third important influence was the fact that there had already been in the air, within the life of the church, a new familiarity both at the level of theology and in the piety of "the biblical movement" in which the spiritual resources of the Word of God were being rediscovered by Catholics. In his own analysis in close proximity to the council's conclusion, Ratzinger looked back on the crafting of *Dei Verbum* against the backdrop of these "signs of the times" from which it emerged.

Setting Aside Neoscholasticism for the Language of Shepherds

Ratzinger has described in different places the nature of his dissatisfaction with the original schemata for the council's deliberation on the "Sources of Revelation" that was given to the central preparatory

---

69. Emery de Gaál Gyulai, *The Theology of Pope Benedict XVI: The Christocentric Shift* (New York: Palgrave Macmillan, 2010), 66–67.

70. Vorgrimler, *Commentary on the Documents of Vatican II*, 3: 155–59.

71. Ibid., 155–56.

committee.[72] He was not alone in his dissatisfaction. As the preparatory schemata were introduced to the council by Cardinal Ottaviani in November 1962, several other cardinals immediately gave a *non placet* for various reasons, foremost among them that in their current form they would undermine the basic ecumenical desires of the council.[73] For his own part Ratzinger recalls that while he saw no errors in the initial drafts *per se*, he noticed little evidence of the recent biblical, patristic, and liturgical retrievals (which had the capacity to help ecumenical dialogue). His pastoral concern *within the church* was that "they gave an impression of rigidity and narrowness through their excessive dependency on scholastic theology. In other words, they reflected the thought of scholars more than that of "shepherds.""[74] He notes elsewhere that bishops and theologians alike were discovering that a pastoral body such as this should be "speaking in the language of scripture, of the early church Fathers and of contemporary man" and that technical theological language has its place, but ultimately it "does not belong in the kerygma and in our confession of faith."[75]

In Ratzinger's view the preparatory schemata for *Dei Verbum* initially reflected the notion of revelation as substantial in itself and essentially unrelated to history and therefore not subject to development.[76] Ratzinger notes in his early recollections of the council that the first drafts of the constitution were primarily "anti-modernist" in their scope of concern and consequently rather cold when compared to the warm, hopeful, and innovative tone of the document on the renewal of the liturgy.[77] The initial tendency of the preparatory commission was to continue the magisterial trajectory of the late nineteenth century, beginning with the condemnation of subjectivism with respect to the question of revelation in the *Syllabus of Errors*. Eventually this tendency gave way to a more nuanced understanding

72. Ratzinger, *Milestones*, 156; Vorgrimler, *Commentary on the Documents of Vatican II*, 3; Joseph Ratzinger, *Theological Highlights of Vatican II* (New York: Paulist Press, 1966), 185.

73. Vorgrimler, *Commentary on the Documents of Vatican II*, 3: 160.

74. Ratzinger, *Milestones*, 121.

75. Ratzinger, *Theological Highlights of Vatican II*, 45.

76. Thomas P. Rausch, *Pope Benedict XVI: An Introduction to His Theological Vision* (New York: Paulist Press, 2009), 63.

77. Ratzinger, *Milestones*, 120–23.

of the primacy of the fact of God revealing himself but also took into consideration the dialogical structure of this revelation,[78] in which the receiver of the revelation is essential to the mystery of God's self-revelation.[79]

As the deliberations at the council unfolded, from Ratzinger's perspective it became more and more clear to the fathers that they must treat the question of revelation in terms of its necessarily historical character. Consequently, as they engaged the historical character of revelation they simultaneously shaped the character of theological reflection in the language of the narrative of God's interaction with humanity. As a result, the language of the council and subsequently of much of theological reflection became more accessible pastorally and spiritually to the people of God.

Dei Filius and Revelation as Extrinsic

Ratzinger contrasts the dialogical conception of revelation[80] that was eventually adopted in *Dei Verbum* with an earlier, nineteenth-century view of it crafted in terms of juridical decrees related to a wisdom and goodness ultimately extrinsic to God. The First Vatican Council articulated the mystery of divine revelation in chapter 2 of the constitution *Dei Filius* thus: "it pleased his [God's] wisdom and his bounty to reveal himself and his eternal decrees in another, supernatural way, as the apostle says: in many and various ways God spoke of old to our fathers by the prophets; but in these last days he has spoken to us by a Son' (Heb 1:1-2)."[81] Though the fathers at the First Vatican Council did indicate that God reveals *himself*—se ipsum—Ratzinger sees the emphasis here on the eternal decrees of God's will that are external to God.[82] Consequently revelation is seen as a monologue from God to humanity rather than a dialogue between God and humanity. The theory of the "material tradition" of revelation—the handing down to humanity of something extrinsic to God—

---

78. Vorgrimler, *Commentary on the Documents of Vatican II*, 3: 170.

79. Tracey Rowland, *Ratzinger's Faith: The Theology of Pope Benedict XVI* (New York: Oxford University Press, 2008), 48.

80. Vorgrimler, *Commentary on the Documents of Vatican II*, 3: 171.

81. Jacques Dupuis and Josef Neusner, *The Christian Faith in the Doctrinal Documents of the Catholic Church* (New York: Alba House, 1996), 43.

82. Vorgrimler, *Commentary on the Documents of Vatican II*, 3: 171. Cf. *DS* 3004.

while not erroneous in Ratzinger's eyes, did not seem to do enough to plumb the depths of the fullness of the mystery of salvation.

The reason for this inadequacy, Ratzinger suggests, is in part the neoscholastic philosophical and analytical categories it uses as its first principles. In his commentary on Vatican II he notes that the methodology of Vatican I's *Dei Filius* starts with natural knowledge of God and then briefly touches on the content of revelation before dwelling more on how Scripture and tradition are transmitted. *Dei Verbum*, on the other hand, begins with the narrative, with the *acts* of God in history, and only at the end indicates how it is that, as it turns out, the human person is disposed to receive this revelation from the beginning. Anthropology, then, is seen in light of revelation rather than the other way around. Since, when God speaks and reveals himself, he reveals not just his wisdom and his goodness but his very *self*, revelation penetrates to the very core of humanity that was created by the same Word of God.

Humanity, then, can only be fulfilled or actualized when making a full and conscious response to the Word that is the essence of Scripture and tradition: in *responding* to the act of God's speaking.[83] Because the theological starting point of Ratzinger's thought is God's speaking, humanity is understood in light of the capacity to be in dialogue with God. Such is the nature of the theological personalism of Ratzinger's theology and such is the character of the way divine revelation is presented in the teaching of the Second Vatican Council. What had often previously been matter consigned to the abstract language of propositional statements had, in *Dei Verbum*, been informed by a new theological personalism, thanks in no small part to the contributions of Joseph Ratzinger.[84] Such an analysis rings true when one reads the description of the role of Scripture in the life of the church in the final draft of *Dei Verbum*: "In the sacred books, the Father who is in heaven comes lovingly to meet his children, and talks with them."[85] Given the narrative form of Scripture, it is perhaps easy to see its dialogical nature. But in Ratzinger's theology tradition too follows the same dialogical pattern.

83. Scott Hahn, *Covenant and Communion: The Biblical Theology of Pope Benedict XVI* (Grand Rapids: Brazos Press, 2009), 75.

84. W. Jared Wicks, "Vatican II on Revelation from Behind the Scenes," *Theological Studies* 71 (2010): 637–50.

85. *Dei Verbum* 21.

Tradition as Expressive of Revelation

The Father in heaven meeting and speaking with his children in history is *Dei Verbum*'s personalistic image for how to understand the inner relationship of Scripture and tradition. The pivotal choice by the council fathers to "[go] back to the comprehensive reality of the deeds and words of God" as a starting point made it possible to gain freedom from the problematic *"duplex fons"* theory of revelation that posited two distinct sources of revelation in Scripture and tradition.[86] *Dei Verbum* reflects Ratzinger's plea to "go behind" both Scripture and tradition to see that there is only one unified revelation of God expressed in a twofold manner. This is so because of the nature of God's desire, in which God "graciously arranged that what he had once revealed for the salvation of all peoples [as recounted in Scripture] should last forever in its entirety and be transmitted to all generations."[87] Tradition, then, is the means by which the saving revelation of God is extended to all generations coming after the scriptural era. Though what the church teaches are timeless *truths*, it must never teach them in a way that separates them from the historical context in which its mission to proclaim the living word of God lies. The truth communicated in tradition is to be based on the *Logos* of the Father understood as *Verbum* that unfolds its communication in history and in a relational and communal mode, and not merely as *Ratio* accessible to the individual mind.[88] More will be said on this unfolding understanding of *Logos* in the Christian tradition in the next chapter on Christology. For now, however, suffice it to say that an authentic appropriation of tradition requires attentiveness within the church to both its eternal, universal dimension and its historical, particular expression. This attentiveness demands a "historical consciousness" that is simultaneously informed by the light of faith. This basic framework makes possible Ratzinger's "hermeneutic of reform" within the one subject of the church that both preserves what is constant and also accounts for and is open to genuine development within the living tradition.[89]

86. Vorgrimler, *Commentary on the Documents of Vatican II*, 3: 170.

87. *Dei Verbum* 7.

88. Ratzinger, *Introduction to Christianity*, 189.

89. Benedict XVI, "Address of His Holiness Benedict XVI to the Roman Curia Offering Them His Christmas Greetings," December 22, 2005, accessed at: http://

This hermeneutic has its foundations much earlier in the Christian tradition and in Ratzinger's own formation, namely in his study of St. Bonaventure.

Bonaventurian Echoes in *Dei Verbum*

In *Dei Verbum* we can see the imprint of Ratzinger's dialogical approach to theology, characteristic of the Augustinian tradition to which Bonaventure is a key contributor. What Ratzinger argued for and what ended up being adopted in the vision offered in *Dei Verbum* was a less propositional and more narrative view of revelation that is necessarily and always seen as contingent on how it is received by the church at any given time in history. The condition of the "soil" shapes, in part, how the many "seeds" (*semina*) of the "one Logos" take root, according to the organic metaphor borrowed from Bonaventure.[90] Until God's revelation is received and appropriated, and until that seed of God's Word takes root, there really is no revelation *per se*. In Bonaventurian terms, tradition is what is consistent with the original "seed" of the Word of God's action in salvation history, recorded in Scripture and then proclaimed perpetually at all times and in all places in the life of the church. In this way tradition is unified and coherent and yet always developing.

Revelation in *Verbum Domini*

Nearly a half century after the council, Joseph Ratzinger, now Pope Benedict XVI, promulgated his post-synodal apostolic exhortation *Verbum Domini*, on the topic of the Word of God in the life of the church.[91] Taking up the same topic as *Dei Verbum*, this time synthesizing the deliberations of bishops gathered from around the world, Benedict offered a reflection on these deliberations in light of his own theological vision, which by this point had so significantly helped to shape the universal Catholic teaching on the subject. As the title of

---

www.vatican.va/holy_father/benedict_xvi/speeches/2005/december/documents
/hf_ben_xvi_spe_20051222_roman-curia_en.html.

90. Ratzinger, *Theology of History in St. Bonaventure*, 6–12.

91. Benedict XVI, *Post-synodal apostolic exhortation: Verbum Domini of the Holy Father Pope Benedict XVI to the bishops, clergy, consecrated persons and the lay faithful on the Word of God in the life and mission of the Church* (Vatican City: Libreria Editrice Vaticana, 2010).

the opening section, "God in Dialogue," indicates, priority is given to the divine subject who speaks and who seeks a response from the human listener. Benedict explains: "The novelty of biblical revelation consists in the fact that God becomes known through the dialogue which he desires to have with us."[92] Whether it is God's revelation of himself in creation, accessible through reason, or in salvation history (comprised of both Scripture and tradition), accessible through faith, divine speech is communicated to a human audience capable of entering into dialogue with God. Benedict writes that to speak of the "Word of God" is to enter into a multifaceted reality, to participate in a symphony of words that is reflective of a single Word that, taken as a whole, can be understood as a "polyphonic hymn."[93] This is so because the "Word of God" is unified and coherent first of all as the eternal Word of God, the Second Person of the Trinity. But the "Word of God" is also manifested in many and various ways: (a) in its fullness as the person of Jesus Christ, (b) in creation itself as the *liber naturae*, (c) in the message of the prophets of the Old Testament, (d) in the proclamation of the apostles, (e) in the living tradition as a whole, and finally, (f) in the written texts of Sacred Scripture. For this reason, Benedict argues, Christianity is not rightly considered a "religion of the book" but rather a "religion of the Word of God" that is "living and Incarnate."[94] It behooves us, therefore, to see the various aspects of the study of Christianity as part of a larger whole.

IV. Directions for Exegesis and Theology

In his commentary on *Dei Verbum*, Ratzinger made a direct plea for greater cooperation and interaction between exegetes and theologians, especially dogmatic theologians. He proposed that the two groups of scholars be "independent partners" for each other.[95] The ongoing research of the exegetes would keep the particularities of the Scripture and its historical basis ever before the theologians who reflect on the doctrine that flows from the historical biblical witness. And theologians should be able to support the exegetes with a constant attentiveness to the horizon of faith within the church as a hermeneutical

92. Ibid., 6.
93. Ibid., 17.
94. Ibid. 7.
95. Vorgrimler, *Commentary on the Documents of Vatican II*, 3: 160.

perspective for their own attempt to understand Scripture. Though one group should not dictate the parameters of the method of the other, he argues, they should always be present to one another, so that they might always keep in mind the perspective of the historical on the one hand and the eternal on the other.[96] Some forty years later, in the "Introduction" to the first volume of *Jesus of Nazareth*, Pope Benedict offers a concise yet comprehensive instance of his most mature thought on the nature of authentic biblical exegesis.[97] He challenges exegetes to allow a more theological understanding to inform their work, while remaining true to the directions and innovations taken up in modern historical-critical methods of scriptural study. Fundamental to this theological approach to Scripture is the posture of faith from which one must approach the texts. Operative here is the Second Vatican Council's admonition that Scripture should be read and interpreted in light of the same Spirit by whom it was written.[98] Furthermore, in order to be under the inspiration of the same Spirit it is necessary for the reader to encounter the Scriptures in communion with the whole Spirit-led church, to engage in this dialogue with God from the perspective of the "collective I of the Church," as he had put it forty years earlier.[99] More will be said on these matters from an ecclesiological standpoint in chapter 4. It is enough for now, though, to recognize that Ratzinger's exegetical and theological insistence on a spiritual, theological, and ecclesiological perspective in approaching Scripture is a mark of the holistic approach to theology that always includes both historical-critical biblical exegesis and a hermeneutic of faith by which to interpret the fruit of this exegesis. This is also precisely what provoked the sharpest criticisms of his book on Jesus of Nazareth.[100]

96. Ibid., 45–72. See especially Ratzinger's in-depth exploration of the issue in "The Spiritual Basis and Ecclesial Identity of Theology," 45–72 in idem, *The Nature and Mission of Theology: Approaches to Understanding Its Role in the Light of Present Controversy*, trans. Adrian J. Walker (San Francisco: Ignatius Press, 1995).

97. Benedict XVI, *Jesus of Nazareth: From the Baptism in the Jordan to the Transfiguration*, trans. Adrian J. Walker (New York: Doubleday, 2007).

98. *Dei Verbum* 11–12.

99. Ratzinger, *Introduction to Christianity*, 87–90.

100. For some varying examples of critiques, see Gerd Lüdemann, *Eyes that See Not: The Pope Looks at Jesus* (Santa Rosa, CA: Polebridge Press, 2008); Carlo Maria Martini, "Ardent Testimony on Jesus: On the Book Jesus of Nazareth by

Dogma and Bible

The reluctance on the part of many to allow a robust interaction of dogma and biblical exegesis is one of the great areas of concern for Ratzinger in contemporary theology.[101] In the effort to arrive at "the historical Jesus" he explains, it has been thought necessary by many exegetes to exclude from exegesis the horizon of ecclesial faith and dogma expressive of that faith because it represents an obstruction of the "pure" historical vision. The layers of interpretation of the figure of Jesus and the whole of Scripture seem to cloud the truth of "primitive Christianity." However, by eliminating from the discourse the historical (and faith-shaped) appropriation of the truth of the Scriptures, much of modern scholarship has sterilized Scripture, in Ratzinger's view. Treating Scripture as a mere object for historical analysis, has made it into a genre incompatible with its original form, divorced from communal faith in God's salvific communication in history. Consequently, he explains, "the Bible that has freed itself from dogma has become a document about the past and, thereby, itself belongs to the past."[102]

In order to rectify this distortion he outlines important hermeneutical elements for the renewal of the mission of both Catholic exegesis and theology. What is at stake for Ratzinger is not just a preference within an academic discipline but the question of how well God's revelation will continue to be appropriated in the life of God's people. If exegesis and theology are exercised symbiotically in a spiritual and ecclesial manner they can become an extension of the very revelation of God in history. The Word spoken by God that continues to be authentically received, reflected upon, and communicated is in continuity with the Word originally spoken. The role of the theologian is to translate that Word in new ways in every age and culture according to the logic of revelation itself, which has its roots in eternity and yet is always oriented toward communication in history. In a recent address to theologians from around the world, Benedict explained the role of the theologian, highlighting the "communicative" and dialogical

---

Joseph Ratzinger/Benedict XVI," *Bulletin Dei Verbum* 84/85 (2007): 44–46; Luke Timothy Johnson, "Jesus of Nazareth: From the Baptism in the Jordan to the Transfiguration," *Modern Theology* 24 (2008): 318–20.

101. Ratzinger, *God's Word: Scripture, Tradition, Office*, 91–99.

102. Ibid., 99.

nature of the discipline as it pertains to seeking knowledge of the living God as this is undertaken in the context of ecclesial faith:

> . . . the word "theo-logy" itself reveals this communicative aspect of your work—in theology we seek—through the "logos," to communicate "what we have seen and heard" (1 Jn 1:3). . . . [Furthermore] no theological system can subsist unless it is permeated by the love of its divine "Object," which in theology must necessarily be the "Subject" that speaks to us and with whom we are in a relationship of love. Thus, theology must always be fed by dialogue with the divine *Logos*, Creator and Redeemer. Moreover, theology is not theology unless it is integrated into the life and reflection of the Church through time and space. Yes, it is true that in order to be scientific theology must argue rationally, but it must also be faithful to the nature of ecclesial faith, centered on God, rooted in prayer, in a communion with the other disciples of the Lord guaranteed by communion with the Successor of Peter and with the whole Episcopal College . . . since ecclesial communion is diachronic, so also is theology. The theologian never begins from zero, but considers as teachers the Fathers and theologians of the whole Christian tradition.[103]

Again, Ratzinger's study of Bonaventure is formative. It is worth recalling here the latter's striking insistence on the role of the patristic tradition in understanding Scripture, since the writings of the fathers are in some way part of revelation itself insofar as they appropriated Scripture and communicated the Word of God to the church in the earliest generations. Consequently, our own appropriation of the Word must be done by way of their historical mediation. This inner unity of the fathers and the authentic understanding of Scripture that can only be grasped spiritually is the sole means by which the contemporary church can be transformed by the Word of God. Ratzinger quotes Bonaventure: "By himself, man cannot come to this (spiritual) understanding (of Scripture). He can do this only through those to whom God revealed it, i.e. through the writings of the Saints such as

---

103. "Address of His Holiness Benedict XVI to Members of the International Theological Commission," Vatican City Consistory Hall, December 3, 2010, accessed at: http://www.vatican.va/holy_father/benedict_xvi/speeches/2010/december/documents/hf_ben-xvi_spe_20101203_cti_en.html.

Augustine, Jerome and others."[104] In accordance with this "logic of revelation" that God speaks the Word from eternity through human words in history, Ratzinger also asserts the normativity of accepted translations of Scripture, namely, the Vulgate, as well as traditionally accepted biblical commentary in the patristic tradition as comprising, in some sense, "inspired" tradition. The patristic appropriation of Scripture and the rule of faith are then, in some way, authoritative and as such are part of revelation as they constitute some of the many *semina* of the one *Logos*. Tradition, therefore, is conceived by Ratzinger much more broadly and diversely than simply as the *depositum fidei* of magisterial teachings.[105]

By considering the fathers as part of revelation in some sense, the contemporary theologian is urged to consider in a new light the nature of his or her own task. This reconsidering is central to Ratzinger's theological and pastoral concern. Again, recalling Bonaventure, he rather strikingly asserts that Scripture itself, strictly speaking, is the only real work of theology, for Scripture is simply the direct reflection of Spirit-led writers on the direct action of God in history.[106] Following this pattern, the ongoing work of theology ought to imitate, in some sense, the scriptural authors, to reflect on the experience of God among the faithful in history. Reading Scripture in this new manner, then, becomes what the Second Vatican Council called "a *colloquium inter Deum et hominem* wherein the dialogue with the eternal God is always in the present for the human subject"[107] Consequently, Ratzinger argues, the work of the theologian is always secondary to the experience of the saints, because it is the saint who experiences and enters into profound relationship—dialogue—with the living, speaking God.[108] To put it more precisely, the task of the theologian is not to *say things about* God, but to *treat God as the one who speaks*:

> The beautiful vocation of the theologian . . . means making present the Word, the Word who comes from God, the Word

---

104. Ratzinger, *Theology of History in St. Bonaventure*, 77–78. Cf. Bonaventure, *Collationes in Hexameron XIX*.

105. Vorgrimler, *Commentary on the Documents of Vatican II*, 3: 264–65.

106. Ratzinger, *Theology of History in St. Bonaventure*, 67.

107. Vorgrimler, *Commentary on the Documents of Vatican II*, 3: 171.

108. Benedict XVI, *The Yes of Jesus Christ: Exercises in Faith, Hope and Love* (New York: Crossroad, 2005), 31.

who is God. . . . God, in reality, is not the object but the subject of theology. The one who speaks through theology, the
speaking subject, must be God himself. And our speech and
thoughts must always serve to ensure that what God says, the
Word of God, is listened to and finds room in the world. Thus
once again we find ourselves invited into this process of forfeit-
ing our own words, this process of purification so that our
words may be nothing but the instrument through which God
can speak, and hence, that he may truly be the subject and not
the object of theology.[109]

This posture for doing theology provides an image for the whole
of Joseph Ratzinger's approach to reflecting on the one mystery of
Christian faith. His theology of revelation provides a foundation and
offers shape to the rest of his theology that will be taken up in subsequent chapters. For now, we will take stock of the essential aspects
of his theology of revelation that is, as we shall see, expressed in every
other area of his reflection on the one Christian mystery.

V. Joseph Ratzinger's Dialogical Theology of Revelation

Having outlined the contours of the development of Ratzinger's
own theology of revelation, we turn now to highlight a few of the major
thematic elements of his thought. Lieven Boeve describes Ratzinger's
"concept of dynamic revelation" that is the "turning of God toward
humanity" that "effectively continues to this day—even after the closure
of objective revelation."[110] The "dynamic" process of the unveiling of
the *Logos* in the act of revelation is seen both in the created order and
in the historical, and so the scientist, the philosopher, as well as the
simple person of faith can all be receivers of the one revelation of God's
self.[111] The essential role played by the human subject in the unfolding
of revelation introduces an essential mark of what I call the "dialogical

109. Benedict XVI, "Homily, Eucharistic Concelebration with the Members
of the International Theological Commission," October 6, 2006, accessed at: http://
www.vatican.va/holy_father/benedict_xvi/homilies/2006/documents/hf
_ben-xvi_hom_20061006_commissione-teologica_en.html.

110. Gerard Mannion and Lieven Boeve, *The Ratzinger Reader: Mapping a
Theological Journey* (London: T & T Clark, 2010), 13.

111. Benedict XVI, "Address of His Holiness Benedict XVI to Members of the
International Theological Commission," December 3, 2010, accessed at: http://

structure" of the whole of Ratzinger's theology. The unfolding dialogue between God and humanity culminates in the person of Jesus Christ, who is the definitive instantiation of divine revelation.[112] The church continues to engage in this dialogue with the living God and so appropriates revelation that is "new" in the ongoing development of tradition that reflects on Scripture. Together, then, both Scripture and tradition are the communicated expressions that simultaneously draw on the source of the one revelation, the *Logos* of God.[113] The consequence of this understanding of Ratzinger is that what is unveiled in the positive sources of revelation does not exhaust the substance and content of the whole of revelation. There is always a "surplus" beyond what is revealed. There is always more to the Word than what the eternal Word communicates in historical, human words. This surplus is the basis for the ongoing development of doctrine in the life of the church as expressed in tradition as well as in theological reflection. Though the fullness of the revelation is given in the person of Christ, the way in which the church continues to appropriate and "hear" the Word in history is always characterized as the ongoing dialogue that never ceases to convey new meaning. The ongoing engagement in the dialogue that is revelation is the action by which the Lord "makes all things new" (Rev 21:5) and that also accounts for the possibility of "development of doctrine."

Conclusion:
Revelation as Historically Unfolding Dialogue

In this chapter I have outlined the essential characteristics of Ratzinger's theology of revelation. Beginning with an explanation of the influence his study of Bonaventure's theology of history had on him, I suggest that this understanding of the one eternal *Logos* begetting many *semina* in human history is an organic metaphor for understanding how it is that revelation unfolds in history and is expressed in a twofold

---

www.vatican.va/holy_father/benedict_xvi/speeches/2010/december/documents/hf_ben-xvi_spe_20101203_cti_en.html.

112. Joseph Ratzinger, *On the Way to Jesus Christ* (San Francisco: Ignatius Press, 2005), 82.

113. Mannion and Boeve, *The Ratzinger Reader*, 14. Cf. Ratzinger's essay, "The Question of the Concept of Tradition: A Provisional Response" in *Revelation and Tradition*, 78.

way in both Scripture and tradition. This vision of revelation as unfolding in a dynamic way in history helped to open up a new horizon in the church's own understanding of this mystery at Vatican II. Due in part to Ratzinger's influence, *Dei Verbum* embraced this understanding of revelation "seen basically as dialogue" between God and humanity that unfolds in history. This dialogical structure of Ratzinger's theology of revelation is necessarily historical in character. It is central in the Christian vision, for Ratzinger, that God "doesn't just drop down from heaven and introduce himself." Rather, God makes himself small enough to meet us as a person and "enters fully into an historical context that offers us a way to approach him, one in which he is expected and in which we are able to receive his message."[114] It is precisely because of the historicity of the moments of dialogue in the unfolding of revelation that Ratzinger's theological reflection is always done in a manner attentive to the particulars of history. For it is from history that Scripture and tradition emerge and it is in history that the kerygma is being proclaimed at all times in life of the church. Finally, the most crucial hermeneutical principle at work in Ratzinger's theology of revelation has to do with what has recently been deemed "the Christocentric shift" in some contemporary theology, of which Ratzinger's thought is characteristic.[115] Since Christ, the *Logos* of God made flesh in history, is the fullness of the revelation of God, there is no new public revelation after the New Testament.[116] Consequently Ratzinger sums up his own understanding of the inner unity of the testaments in this way: "The New Testament is nothing other than the interpretation of the Law, the Prophets and the Writings found contained in the story of Jesus."[117] As the person of Christ makes intelligible all that had been anticipated about him in the unfolding of salvation history among the people of Israel, so too does he give shape to and fulfill the identity of those in the church who come after him, seeking to understand the dynamic revelation of God in which they still participate. It is to Ratzinger's understanding of the fullness of this revelation, the person of Jesus Christ, that we now turn.

(margin note: *Divine humility*)

---

114. Joseph Ratzinger and Peter Seewald, *God and the World: Believing and Living in our Time: A Conversation with Peter Seewald* (San Francisco: Ignatius Press, 2002), 206.

115. De Gaál Gyulai, *The Theology of Benedict XVI: The Christocentric Shift*.

116. Ratzinger, *Theology of History in St. Bonaventure*, 69.

117. Ratzinger, *Milestones*, 53.

∽◎ Chapter Three ◎∾

Jesus the Christ:
Eternal Logos-Made-Love in History

There is "a divine plan, which has long been kept hidden and that God himself has revealed in the history of salvation. In the fullness of time, this Wisdom took on a human Face."[1]

On September 30, 2006, the feast of St. Jerome, a year and a half into his pontificate, Pope Benedict XVI signed the foreword to his book *Jesus of Nazareth*.[2] It is striking and indeed unprecedented that a pope approaching an eightieth birthday, while serving as universal pastor for a church of well over a billion members, and in addition to the countless commitments that come with that office, including duties of internal ecclesial governance, international diplomacy, and a steady flow of other occasions calling for written speeches, homilies, and various teachings on every aspect of Christian concern, took the time and made the effort to initiate a three-volume theological treatise independent of these other duties. It is also worthy of note that he made this offering to the world not in a magisterial mode, but

1. Benedict XVI, "Homily, Celebration of First Vespers with University Students," December 17, 2009, accessed at: http://www.vatican.va/holy_father /benedict_xvi/homilies/2009/documents/hf_ben-xvi_hom_20091217_vespri -universitari_en.html. Cf. 1 Cor 2:7.
2. Benedict XVI, *Jesus of Nazareth: From the Baptism in the Jordan to the Transfiguration*, trans. Adrian J. Walker (New York: Doubleday, 2007).

in a very personal way, as the fruit of his lifelong "search for the Face of the Lord."[3] With such an effort Benedict made it unmistakably clear that the figure of Jesus Christ is at the center of his whole project, both theologically and pastorally.

I situate this exploration of Ratzinger's Christology in the immediate wake of an examination of his theology of divine revelation and before an exposition of his ecclesiology because for Ratzinger, Christ is the fulfillment of revelation and yet at the same time able to be truly known only in the context of the believing *ecclesia*. In this chapter I will therefore begin by describing how it is that Ratzinger's Christology flows directly from his understanding of revelation and will conclude with an introduction to the intrinsic link between his Christology and his ecclesiology. The middle of the chapter will be devoted to how his Christology is described as an unfolding dialogical narrative that characterizes the relationship between God and humanity. While the center of this narrative is the incarnation of the eternal Word in Jesus Christ, we encounter the same Word through whom "all things came to be" (John 1:3) in creation and also as the Word toward whom all of salvation history tends. Within the order of creation, then, Christology becomes the lens through which we can discern the ultimate ground of all reality. This metaphysical grounding, when seen in conjunction with salvation history, proves to be one of communicability. The Word (*Logos*) through whom all things were made, when we follow the order of salvation history turns out to be the Word that is ultimately manifested as love itself in Jesus' self-gift on the cross. The systematic framework that makes sense of reality in the order of creation as an expression of divine *Logos* cannot be arrived at outside of tracing the development of salvation history. And so, in Ratzinger's thought, Christology has a logical coherence that is not simply intelligible in the realm of pure speculation but is illuminated by experience in history. The experience of the Word in history illuminates the order of creation that is logically coherent and ends up being most intelligible not as logic alone but as dia-logic—as communication.

I. The Fullness of God's Revelation

In this study of the coherence of Ratzinger's thought we approach his Christology after having examined his theology of revelation.

---

3. Ibid., xxiii, citing Ps 27:8.

There we recognized that his understanding is that revelation is not static and abstract in its essence but rather "dynamic."[4] Characteristic of revelation, as Ratzinger sees it, is that it is unfolding in history and as such *dialogical* and *narrative* in structure. The culmination of this unfolding revelation of God in history is the entrance into the narrative of the figure of Jesus Christ. He *is* the dialogue, the *encounter itself* between God and humanity in one person. As the figure of Jesus Christ is seen as the fullness of the revelation of God, Christology then becomes, for Ratzinger, the hermeneutical key to the whole of theology. Emery de Gaál Gyulai has recently highlighted this Christocentric aspect of Ratzinger's theology. In the epilogue to his book he concludes his remarks on the whole of Ratzinger's thought:

> Life in its varied abundance is far too powerful to be grasped or harnessed by a system. This is the "Christocentric shift." In this sense one would do a great injustice to Ratzinger's theology were one to press it into a self-contained, closed box of timeless truths. He has always avoided such a temptation in his own theology. . . . But amid human frailties, the Word did indeed become incarnate. This is the incontrovertible reality and truth. . . . One cannot doubt it and still be a Christian.[5]

The figure of Christ, then, in de Gaál Gyulai's estimation of Ratzinger's thought, is foundational for the whole of Christian experience and for every aspect of authentic theological reflection in the Christian tradition. He goes on to say:

> As is the case for every Christian, every theology, every theologian, bishop or pope as well, they receive their true greatness by becoming similes or parables for God by participating in the natural, supernatural life of Jesus Christ, who is the *Logos* and thus permitting the Incarnation of God in Jesus to continue to the end of time.[6]

---

4. Jose Granados, Carlos Granados, and Luis Sánchez Navarro, eds., *Opening Up the Scriptures: Joseph Ratzinger and the Foundations of Biblical Interpretation* (Grand Rapids: Eerdmans, 2008), 26.

5. Emery de Gaál Gyulai, *The Theology of Pope Benedict XVI: The Christocentric Shift* (New York: Palgrave Macmillan, 2010), 301.

6. Ibid.

What marks the difference of Ratzinger's theology in this regard is its distancing itself from the "anthropocentric shift" that occurred in many circles in twentieth-century Catholic theology, which ran the risk of trying to make sense of the Christian mystery from within the confines of "a Cartesian egocentric view"[7] that equates meaning with human knowledge. Rather, as de Gaál Gyulai argues, Ratzinger has insisted on the centrality of the "Christian hermeneutics of salvation history."[8] Humanity is rightly understood in light of Christ and not the other way around.

For Ratzinger, the centrality of Christ is evident precisely because of the dialogical nature of the whole of his theology. He explains that Christology is the "new subject and foundation of all theology"[9] because in Christ not only has God spoken to humanity, but humanity is now able to enter into a new subjectivity with respect to God—to speak as a new "I." Ratzinger sees St. Paul's experience as paradigmatic of this new subjectivity, recalling the apostle's declaration of his new identity: "yet I live, no longer I, but Christ lives in me" (Gal 2:20). This was not only Paul's experience; it is the fundamental experience of all Christians and involves a dying of the old "I" that "ceases to be an autonomous subject standing in itself. It is snatched away from itself and is fitted into a new subject. The 'I' is not simply submerged, but it must really release its grip on itself in order to then receive itself anew together with a greater 'I.' "[10] There is, then, at the heart of Christian identity the need to undergo transformational conversion in light of the encounter with the person of Christ. The evangelist John recounts Jesus' own words to his disciples: "Unless a grain of wheat falls to the ground and dies, it remains just a grain of wheat; but if it dies, it produces much fruit" (John 12:24). The disciples will come to see the perfect instance of the one who dies and bears much fruit and so learn how they can do the same in their own lives in union with and in imitation of him. This new fruit that can be produced among the faithful comes as a result of the union with Christ and being drawn into the new subjectivity of Christ. There is a necessary dying of the old human self to become alive again as a

7. Ibid., 300.

8. Ibid.

9. Joseph Ratzinger, *The Nature and Mission of Theology: Essays to Orient Theology in Today's Debates* (San Francisco: Ignatius Press, 1995), 50.

10. Ibid., 51.

new "I" in Christ. This recognition that God has spoken to humanity in Christ as the eternal "I," and that by way of relationship with Christ we can speak in turn to God in a newly acquired subjectivity, is the basis of Ratzinger's understanding of the whole of the Christian mystery, including Christology, ecclesiology, and soteriology.

From the view of the whole of salvation history that culminates in the life, death, and resurrection of Jesus, Ratzinger's method of theological reflection can then look back on the whole of the narrative, going steadily back over salvation history in the presence of the Risen Lord in order to understand it anew in light of the saving experience in Christ. We might characterize this approach to Christology as "dialogical" in that its very shape is following the speech of God and humanity's response throughout history. This dialogue between God and humanity subsequently constitutes a narrative of its own throughout salvation history. Ultimately, the person of Christ himself is the perfection and fullness of this dialogue, both as God speaking to humanity and humanity responding to God.

The Historical Jesus Approached Through a Hermeneutic of Faith

Ratzinger understands clearly that as the figure of Jesus is historical, he is rightly approached by the method of historical analysis. But a historical approach divorced from the perspective of faith is not sufficient for true knowledge of him. In the Foreword to his second volume of *Jesus of Nazareth*, Benedict notes his satisfaction that since the publication of his first volume there seems to be an increasingly robust scholarly discourse on the question of allowing for a theological perspective on exegetical methodology. He says that after two hundred years of historical critical exegesis its "essential fruit" has already been produced. However, if historical-critical exegesis hopes to remain fruitful and not "exhaust" itself it must "take a methodological step forward and see itself once again as a theological discipline, without abandoning its historical character."[11] Developing a familiar theme in his theological vision, building on a focus on biblical exegesis and from there moving to construction of theological perspective, he asserts that scholarly exegesis "must recognize that a properly developed faith-hermeneutic is appropriate to the text and

11. Benedict XVI, *Jesus of Nazareth. Part Two, Holy Week: From the Entrance into Jerusalem to the Resurrection* (San Francisco: Ignatius Press, 2011), xiv.

can be combined with a historical hermeneutic, aware of its limits, so as to form a methodological whole."[12] For Ratzinger, Scripture cannot be understood outside this "methodological whole" that keeps in tension the faith-hermeneutic as well as the historical-hermeneutic. Together they form one authentic perspective on the nature and substance of revelation's two expressions in Scripture and tradition. But what of the "faith-hermeneutic"? What constitutes its shape? For Ratzinger this approach always flows from the ecclesial context in which God speaks and in which he spoke definitively in the person of Jesus Christ.

This "faith-hermeneutic" Ratzinger describes, which is always ecclesial in shape, is outlined in *Dei Verbum* 12:

> since Holy Scripture must be read and interpreted in the sacred spirit in which it was written, no less serious attention must be given to the content and unity of the whole of Scripture if the meaning of the sacred texts is to be correctly worked out. The living tradition of the whole Church must be taken into account along with the harmony which exists between elements of the faith.

This becomes one of the major motifs of Ratzinger's theological and pastoral career. Only in this ecclesial context can Jesus Christ be known: in the context of *encounter* with him, along with others who seek his face, together, in the "collective I" of the church.[13] The vision of the union of God and humanity found in Christ, therefore, is for Ratzinger the "result of a dialogue, the expression of a hearing, receiving and answering that guides man through the exchanges of 'I' and 'You' to the 'We' of those who all believe in the same way."[14] The nature of this inner relationship of ecclesiology and Christology in Ratzinger's theology will be taken up at the end of this chapter as a bridge to the next chapter on the dialogical nature of the church. In the meantime we will more closely examine the particular shape of

---

12. Ibid., xv.

13. For an elaboration of Ratzinger's ecclesial hermeneutic see Maximilian Heinrich Heim, *Joseph Ratzinger: Life in the Church and Living Theology* (San Francisco: Ignatius Press, 2007), 147–53.

14. Joseph Ratzinger, *Introduction to Christianity*, trans. J. R. Foster (San Francisco: Ignatius Press, 2004), 90.

this christological and ecclesiological hermeneutic of faith so central to Ratzinger's methodology.

Christ and the Scandal of Particularity

Ratzinger's exposition of the faith "of those who all believe in the same way" in this ecclesial and christological unity is of course not universally appealing. The vision of apprehending the unity of God and humanity in terms of a dialogue initiated "in the beginning" and fulfilled in the person of Jesus has the capacity to draw the reader in and then immediately stop one short, once the consequences of accepting this narrative become clear. As disarming as the invitation can seem, there is still reason for resistance to it. Though the very structure of dialogue is necessarily "open" to those who seek to enter into it, it is also by its nature *particular* and in that sense manifests a dimension of exclusivity. The believer is invited to take part in *this* dialogue, *this* narrative with its own history, characters, modes of interpretation, etc. It involves entering into a "hermeneutical circle" with its own boundaries. Hence the resistance in contemporary culture to the Christocentrism of someone like Ratzinger becomes evident. The reason for the resistance is that underneath the invitation is a particular proposal, even *promise*, of salvation for all those who are willing to say "yes" to it. The particularity of this promise proves to be a stumbling block in the contemporary context of religious pluralism and the general "dictatorship of relativism" that Ratzinger has so famously diagnosed in contemporary Western culture.[15] Before giving an exposition of the structure of this particular narrative, we pause to acknowledge the nature of the resistance to its consequences as various scholars have responded to Ratzinger's articulation of it.

Pope Benedict's portrayal of the Jesus of the gospels in *Jesus of Nazareth* is attractive, but it also provides a stumbling block for contemporary audiences accustomed to a posture of "objectivity" as the *modus operandi* in a religiously pluralistic context. The christological

---

15. For an in-depth articulation of Ratzinger's understanding of the practical dangers of this relativism, see Joseph Ratzinger, *Truth and Tolerance: Christian Belief and World Religions* (San Francisco: Ignatius Press, 2004). See also his famous homily at the conclave of cardinals gathered to elect John Paul II's successor: "Homily of His Eminence Card. Joseph Ratzinger, Dean of the College of Cardinals," Vatican Basilica April 18, 2005, accessed at: http://www.vatican.va /gpII/documents/homily-pro-eligendo-pontifice_20050418_en.html.

hinge on which this vision turns is given a special clarity in the course of the dialogue he enters into with Rabbi Jacob Neusner.[16] Intrigued by Neusner's attempt to view the figure of Jesus from a thoroughly Jewish perspective,[17] Benedict makes use of the fruit of his friend's contemplation and then lets it shed light on his own long "search for the face of God" in Christ. The rabbi and the pope see a great deal in common regarding the continuity of the figure of Jesus within the tradition of the people of Israel, but it is especially in the place where they part company that Benedict finds confirmation of the unsettling nature of the Christian proclamation of the true identity of Jesus of Nazareth. Benedict relates how Neusner sees claims of divinity by Jesus not only in the more direct statements that he and the Father are "one" (e.g., John 10:30; 17:21), but even within the Sermon on the Mount, which many would regard as the least controversial and most universally appealing of Jesus' teachings. Rabbi Neusner points to this claim to divinity within the Sermon by recalling the Babylonian Talmud in which Rabbi Simelai analyzes the synthesis of the Law from the 613 commandments given to Moses and their steady consolidation from David to Isaiah to Habakkuk and after. Then Neusner, in this dialogue across centuries, "asks" Simelai how Jesus fits into this understanding of the Law. Through the course of this "dialogue" Neusner concludes that Jesus took away nothing from the Law and *added only himself* to it.[18] That is to say, Jesus is consistent with the tradition of Israel up to his inclusion of himself as the fulfillment of the Law and therefore identified with God himself.

Benedict regards this honest exchange with a Jewish friend and partner in dialogue as a model for taking each tradition seriously *from within* and according to its own sources of revelation and subsequently letting the dialogue unfold without fear or manipulation from that point, even if it ends in ultimate disagreement about inter-

---

16. Benedict XVI, *Jesus of Nazareth: From the Baptism in the Jordan to the Transfiguration*, 103–27.

17. Jacob Neusner, *A Rabbi Talks with Jesus: An Intermillennial, Interfaith Exchange* (New York: Doubleday, 1993); Neusner continued the dialogue with Benedict with a simultaneous release of his response to *Jesus of Nazareth*: Jacob Neusner, "Renewing Religious Disputation in Quest of Theological Truth: In Dialogue with Benedict XVI's *Jesus of Nazareth*," *Communio* 34 (2007): 328–34.

18. Benedict XVI, *Jesus of Nazareth: From the Baptism in the Jordan to the Transfiguration*, 105. Cf. Jacob Neusner, *A Rabbi Talks with Jesus*, 107–8.

pretive conclusions. At the center of this dialogue is that "Word" of God, Jesus of Nazareth, who both establishes a bridge to dialogue beyond the church and remains a stumbling block for total agreement with it. This same dynamic is increasingly at work in contemporary culture, the greater the awareness of religious pluralism becomes. For Benedict this ecumenical exchange between two clear-sighted and strong believers honest about their different beliefs regarding the person of Jesus is an especially fruitful moment of dialogue.[19]

Though the ultimate disagreement on the identity of Jesus is obvious in the context of Jewish-Christian dialogue, it becomes problematic within Christian circles as well. John Haught, for example, grapples with the "alleged finality of Christian revelation"[20] consistently held in the Christian tradition. Given the pluralism of today, there emerges a problem with the dialogical theology of someone like Joseph Ratzinger.[21] Precisely because he posits a more personal and even intimate portrayal of God's revelation in Christ, his specificity must be grappled with. If the claims were more general and more philosophical, this difficulty would dissipate. Precisely because Ratzinger takes a narrative approach to theology there is a need to follow the specificity of the one story being told and ultimately to be confronted with the main protagonist of the story, who demands a response and cannot be relegated to the sidelines as one among many characters. The difficulty entailed by the Christocentrism of the church's teaching on revelation against the contemporary backdrop of religious pluralism became abundantly clear in the eruption after the publication by the Congregation for the Doctrine of the Faith of the declaration entitled, *"Dominus Iesus*: On the Unicity and Salvific Universality of Jesus Christ and the Church," on the solemnity of the Transfiguration in the Jubilee Year, 2000.[22]

19. Ibid.

20. John F. Haught, *Mystery and Promise: A Theology of Revelation* (Collegeville, MN: Liturgical Press, 1993).

21. For a survey of some of the responses to *Jesus of Nazareth*, see Roland Deines, "Can the 'Real' Jesus be Identified with the Historical Jesus? A Review of the Pope's Challenge to Biblical Scholarship and the Various Reactions it Provoked," *Didaskalia* 39 (2009): 11–46.

22. *Sic Et Non: Encountering Dominus Iesus*, ed. Stephen J. Pope and Charles Hefling (Maryknoll, NY: Orbis, 2002).

A nerve was certainly touched in the wake of this document from the CDF, headed at the time by Cardinal Ratzinger. The insistence on the unicity of Christ and the church in the divine plan of salvation history struck a chord of dissonance in the contemporary intellectual culture, so conditioned by this time to the landscape of religious pluralism. But Ratzinger's Christology, which centers on the *Logos* as a way of interpreting the Christian mysteries in terms of dialogue and an unfolding narrative of the relationship between God and the world, is vital to keep in mind in reading *Dominus Iesus*. The church itself recognizes the ongoing need to continue to contemplate the mystery of the Word spoken in Christ. The church does not consider itself the possessor of a "monopoly" on truth. At the same time, Christians have very plainly believed from the very beginning that God spoke his Word uniquely and definitively in Jesus Christ. The church itself stands in humility before this mystery along with the rest of humanity, trying to be receptive to listening to what this Word says about who God really is and what humanity is really capable of. This listening is ever unfolding in the authentic Christian vision, and it is characterized by that posture of humble listening and receiving. To *relativize* this Word spoken as equivalent to many other *words* in human history is actually a refusal to stand in humility before the mystery that God has spoken the fullness of God's self once and for all in Jesus Christ. Holding to the truth of this mystery, the church actually maintains the possibility of unity among all peoples precisely because of the particularity of this Word spoken once, in fullness, in history. Indeed, this declaration of the CDF offered thirty-five years after the council draws on conciliar teaching in its conclusion, indicating that only by holding fast to the faith of the church, as *Dignitatis Humanae* urges, can the church be a source for unity in the world among all people.[23] At the center of this faith of the church is the revelation of Christ who is " 'the true lodestar' in history for all humanity," as John Paul II put it in *Fides et Ratio*.[24]

Having taken note of the "scandal" of the particularity of Ratzinger's Christology, we turn now to the difference the unicity of Christ makes in understanding both God and humanity in his theology.

<hr/>

23. *Dominus Iesus* 23. Cf. *Dignitatis Humanae* 1.
24. *Dominus Iesus* 23. Cf. *Fides et Ratio* 15.

Christ Determining Theology and Anthropology

Ratzinger's Christology simultaneously shapes his theology of God and his theological anthropology. Both a new understanding of God and a new understanding of humanity emerge as one follows the narrative that has Jesus Christ as the central character. As the oft-quoted passage from *Gaudium et Spes* puts it, "Christ, the new Adam, in the very revelation of the mystery of the Father and of his love, fully reveals humanity to itself and brings to light its very high calling."[25] Not only is humanity reconceived in light of Christ, but so also is the Godhead. Because of the experience of Christ, God comes to be understood, in Ratzinger's view, "not only as *logos* but also as *dia-logos*, not only idea and meaning but speech and word in the reciprocal exchanges of partners in conversation."[26] He notes that this revelatory and dialogical view of God, who communicates himself, radically challenges the ancient Greek philosophical understanding of reality. As such, God and all being that flows from God's creative will is to be understood anew as perfected not in static unity, simplicity, immutability, and so on. Rather, the perfection attributed to God comes to be reinterpreted in fundamentally dynamic, *relational* terms. God comes to be known as the One who speaks and who, in speaking, shows himself not only to be creative, intelligent, and intelligible but also *essentially* communicative and loving.

A new anthropology is given in Ratzinger's Christocentric vision as well. When he treats the question of God in general in his *Introduction to Christianity*, he notes that the question can be approached by means of speculative philosophy through the themes of being and truth[27] and so on, but also existentially according to the theme of the human *experience of loneliness*. As the "I" of the person experiences longing for the "you" of another, the longing for relationship is fulfilled only partially, he explains, when the "you" is another human person. The longing is fully satisfied only when "a call to the absolute 'You' that really descends into the depths of one's own 'I' "[28] is experienced and responded to. Jesus is the one, in Ratzinger's Christological

---

25. *Gaudium et Spes* 22, in Austin Flannery, ed., *Vatican Council II: The Basic Sixteen Documents* (Northport, NY: Costello Publishing Co., 1996), 185.

26. Ratzinger, *Introduction to Christianity*, 183.

27. Ibid., 106.

28. Ibid.

anthropology, who simultaneously shows humanity what a human response to the longing for the "absolute You" looks like and how the absolute "I" speaks in turn to humanity, which longs to be drawn out of the experience of loneliness into relationship. The human person is fulfilled only when entering into the human–divine, I–Thou dialogue. This encounter makes possible the discovery of the fullness of love that has as its perfect pattern the dialogue that is the love of the Father and the Son, united by the Holy Spirit. The human person is created for participation in this same dialogue. All other human relationships are perfected when flowing from this Trinitarian pattern of dialogue. The figure of Christ, then, opens up new horizons for both the theology of God and that of the human person. In this sense Ratzinger's Christology sets the stage for a profound personalism that can shape our understanding of Christian anthropology. Central to this christological anthropology is the insistence that since eternity has entered into history in Jesus Christ, the human person living in history always has his or her destiny lying ahead in eternity, and this destiny is fulfilled in being drawn into relationship with that same Jesus Christ. The human person, then, seen through a christological hermeneutic, is always both historical and transcendent in nature and in fulfillment.

II. Christ Uniting Faith and History

Throughout the course of Ratzinger's theological explorations, thanks especially to his study of Bonaventure, a constant motif is that of Jesus Christ as the *center* of history.[29] All of salvation history that preceded Christ was leading up to him, and all that comes after him, in the life of the church, is lived out in reference to him as the fullness of the church's identity and as the fulfillment of human history. In beginning the Christology section of his *Introduction to Christianity*, Ratzinger describes Christ as the "central and decisive point of all human history."[30] Jesus Christ is the *locus par excellence* of the encounter of the eternal with the temporal. The redemption of all history is made possible thanks only to the fact of the entry of the divine into human contingency. Furthermore, when it comes to the life of the

---

29. Joseph Ratzinger, *Theology of History in St. Bonaventure* (Chicago: Franciscan Herald Press, 1989), 143–48.

30. Ratzinger, *Introduction to Christianity*, 193.

church and the ongoing struggle to find the path to continual renewal, the shape of that path is always determined by the quality of the encounter of every person, from every age, with the person of Jesus.

As these encounters with Christ happen in the context of the *ecclesia*, so too do the descriptions of Jesus as the Christ emerge from the ecclesial community in the form of various *symbola fidei*. The profession of the symbol of faith (creed) on the part of the ecclesial community is the way in which the community reminds itself at any given moment within history of who it is, from whom it has come, and to whom it is going. At the center of this profession is the acknowledgment of the person of Jesus Christ and the work he accomplishes in redeeming all of humanity. Ratzinger's *Introduction to Christianity* is structured on the Apostles' Creed. While his exposition of the meaning of the different articles of faith is innovative and struck an immediate note of freshness,[31] it is telling that the manner in which this exposition unfolds is not original, but rather traditional and ecclesial in that it proceeds deliberately from *within* the framework of the ancient, established boundaries of the settled dogmatic articulation of the faith in the *symbolum*.[32] From within this framework, however, he articulates the meaning of the articles of faith in dialogue with the questions of his contemporaries. By using the Apostles' Creed, Ratzinger is able to hold in tension the doctrine of Christ that avoids the simplistic extremes of, on the one hand, "the reduction of Christology to history and on the other, abandoning history as irrelevant to faith."[33] Thomas Rausch explains the dynamics here between Ratzinger and his main interlocutors: "The first approach [reducing Christology to history], symbolized by Harnack, purifies the faith of doctrine and creed, making the reconstruction of the historical Jesus determinative for Christology. The other, symbolized by Bultmann, makes faith in the Christ alone important," while the importance of the historicity of the person of Jesus Christ fades.[34] Harnack and Bultmann

31. Emery de Gaál Gyulai calls it a "twentieth century classic" and says that it was received as such with great enthusiasm when it was first published. De Gaál Gyulai, *The Theology of Pope Benedict XVI: The Christocentric Shift*, 129–43.

32. Ratzinger, *Introduction to Christianity*, 82–102.

33. Ibid., 198.

34. Thomas P. Rausch, *Who Is Jesus? An Introduction to Christology* (Collegeville, MN: Liturgical Press, 2003), 4.

are indicated at times in Ratzinger's theology as representative of two trajectories in modern theology that grapple with the question of faith and history, both of which ultimately proceed in ways that truncate the fullness of the Christian mystery. There is a sense in Ratzinger's own self-understanding of the need to stand in the breach created by these two modern approaches to theology in order to achieve a certain synthesis that holds in tension the necessity of the perspective of faith and the importance of history within that same perspective.[35] This is perhaps the most significant mark of division within contemporary Christology, namely, the apparent mutual exclusivity of the "Christ of faith and the Jesus of history." On the one hand, as the challenge of historical criticism became stronger in modern scholarship, historicist exegetes saw the perspective of faith as obscuring the quest for the *historical* and therefore the "real" Jesus. On the other hand, as the figure of Jesus became more and more stripped of vitality under the scalpel of some historical-critical methods, others were compelled to posit Christ as a more strictly spiritual figure that at least would meet some of the needs of the contemporary existential search for God. Yet the more these trajectories developed, the less feasible it seemed ever to reach a point at which they could be reconciled into one person, *Jesus the Christ.*

A Spiritual Christology

Ratzinger consciously walks the line between these two divisions, attempting again and again to respond to the demands of each side and then bringing them into dialogue with one another. On the one hand, in the preface to his book *Behold the Pierced One,* Ratzinger indicates the need for a "spiritual Christology" in contemporary theology. He compares the contemporary need to that seen also by the Third Council of Constantinople, concluded in 681, that sought, after centuries of struggle, to define christological doctrine, to situate the mystery of Christ once more within the spiritual context that makes him accessible to his contemporary followers.[36] The Chalcedonian assertion that Christ is both fully human and fully divine did not adequately account for how it is that the two natures coexist in one

---

35. De Gaál Gyulai, *Theology of Pope Benedict XVI: The Christocentric Shift,* 140.

36. Joseph Ratzinger, *Behold the Pierced One: An Approach to a Spiritual Christology* (San Francisco: Ignatius Press, 1986), 9.

person, Ratzinger explains. Two centuries after Chalcedon, questions about the relationship between the human and divine natures of Christ persisted. In the face of the question of the will of Christ, Ratzinger recalls that the Third Council of Constantinople taught:

> And so we proclaim two natural wills in Him, and two natural operations indivisibly, inconvertibly, inseparably, unfusedly according to the doctrine of the holy Father, and two natural wills not contrary, God forbid, according as impious heretics have asserted, but the human will following and not resisting or hesitating, but rather even submitting to His divine and omnipotent will.[37]

The fully human will of Jesus, then, is fulfilled and perfected as it is lived out in obediential relationship to the divine will. For this reason Ratzinger focuses on the "spiritual" dimension of Christology, which alone has the capacity to indicate the importance of Jesus' own spiritual life that sought only to do the will of his Father.

Ratzinger explains that contemplation of the figure of Jesus leads one to the recognition that at the core of his personality is the fruitful tension between his communion with the Father and his desire to be obedient to him out of love for and trust in him. Focusing on Jesus' prayer allows the contemporary audience to be drawn into the same dynamic of coming to find the fullness of humanity in loving and trusting obedience to the Father. For Ratzinger, while much of the recent history of modern Christology had been devoted to questions of the nature of the hypostatic union, the knowledge and will of Christ, etc., a new awakening has emerged that has led theologians to realize that, as important as these ontological and epistemological questions may be, focusing on them at the expense of the spiritual dimension of Christ's most basic identity can result in a skewed vision of the totality of the Christian mystery, both in Christ's relationship to the Father and the Spirit and in his relationship to the rest of humanity. Ratzinger perceives in his own time the need for a renewed Christology that, while taking seriously the contemporary issues of the day,

---

37. *DS* 291, accessed at http://denzinger.patristica.net/#n1000. See Jacques Dupuis and Josef Neuner, *The Christian Faith: in the Doctrinal Documents of the Catholic Church* (New York: Alba House, 1996), 1006.

never lets the spiritual reality of Christ's identity and work be obscured.

On the other hand, while it is essential to situate authentic Christology in a spiritual context, it must not become merely "spiritualized." For this reason Ratzinger highlights the importance of the historicity of Christ. While it can be easy to get lost in various intricacies of different aspects of the christological controversies over the centuries, it is essential that the most fundamental mystery, which is that God has entered into human history in order to redeem it from *within* history, not be obscured. With the emerging emphasis on historical consciousness in theology, Ratzinger saw that only by taking *human history* seriously is an authentically *spiritual* theology made possible. The question of the relationship between the spiritual and the historical becomes especially poignant in the area of biblical exegesis.

Ratzinger rejects attempts at an exegesis that becomes detached from history and engages the gospels only as a means toward spiritual insight or meaning. In *Jesus of Nazareth* he dismisses, for example, what he calls the theory of the Gospel of John as a "Jesus poem" that is ultimately detached from historical reality. He does so on the grounds of his insistence on the historicity of the salvific kerygma of all the gospels. "A faith that discards history in this manner really turns into 'Gnosticism.' It leaves flesh, incarnation—just what true history is—behind."[38] If Jesus is not the Eternal Word who has descended from above and is really made known in the flesh, in history, there is, for Ratzinger, ultimately no spiritual meaning and efficacy in him. It is precisely the fact that the Eternal *Logos* is expressed in history as *sarx* in Jesus Christ that makes the hope of salvation *within history* real.[39] In Christ, the *Logos* that had been understood as the principle of coherence for all of creation is now seen as a person: the *Logos* made flesh, manifested in love.

What makes possible this union of the perspectives of faith and historical consciousness for Ratzinger is precisely the fact that history is created through the eternal *Logos* and that the same *Logos* continues to be spoken within history. In *Verbum Domini*, Benedict recalls Origen's description of the Word as the *Logos* having been

---

38. Benedict XVI, *Jesus of Nazareth: From the Baptism in the Jordan to the Transfiguration*, 228.

39. Ratzinger, *Introduction to Christianity*, 193–94.

"abbreviated."[40] This abbreviation makes the Eternal Word "shorter," in that it has become historical in order to be apprehended by humanity. As Benedict himself put it in a Christmas homily, "the eternal word became small—small enough to fit into a manger. He became a child, so that the Word could be grasped by us."[41] This is the classic kind of Benedict-ine formulation that is startling in its tenderness and pastoral sensitivity, drawing the suspicious contemporary audience into a highly intimate encounter—the kind of encounter for which the contemporary person longs. This confrontation with the abbreviated word opens up the possibility of a kind of reentry into the drama of salvation history in that, because of this unexpected twist in the narrative, a universal audience can take note and consider participation in this story from a fresh perspective.

The Unfolding of the Meaning of *Logos*

In Ratzinger's thought, not only is the drama of salvation history itself unfolding, but the theological *understanding* of this history is also developing in its own kind of drama within a drama. The whole of his theology is manifested according to the pattern of narrative rather than that of proposition and argumentation. The truth of the eternal *Logos* continues to be appropriated in history in the life of the church. In a crucial way we see Ratzinger following a "narrative" in the history of ideas that traces a development of the understanding of terminology in the Christian tradition. The development of the understanding of the term *Logos* is of special importance here. In a key passage in his *Introduction to Christianity*, Ratzinger produces a brief etymology of the term as it has been appropriated in the course of Christian tradition. He demonstrates that there is nothing static about the term and its meaning. It has, in fact, become multivalent, and it is essential to pay attention to the many layers of meaning the term *Logos* has acquired in the life of the church over time.[42] Following the development of the term and its varying degrees of meaning is a method for tracing the development of the theology of God

---

40. *Verbum Domini* 12.

41. Benedict XVI, "Solemnity of the Nativity of the Lord: Homily of His Holiness Benedict XVI," St. Peter's Basilica, December 24, 2006, accessed at http://www.vatican.va/holy_father/benedict_xvi/homilies/2006/documents /hf_ben-xvi_hom_20061224_christmas_en.html.

42. Ratzinger, *Introduction to Christianity*, 189.

and of Christology. In light of its appropriation in the area of Christology it has implications for the Christian understanding of creation and anthropology as well. In his examination of the historical roots and development of the Judeo-Christian tradition, Ratzinger notes that there was a fundamental choice to be made between *Logos* and myth.[43] Exactly at the time the "gods" of the Greeks were being dismissed thanks to the purifying reason of the philosophers, the oneness and transcendence of God was being more firmly established in the ancient world. The Greek displacement of mythology by philosophy then encountered the biblical worldview of Jews and Christians.[44] The interaction between these two cultures and their mutual challenge and purification produced something new. Myths would no longer do, but neither would philosophical reason alone suffice in the attempt to explain reality. At the heart of this encounter is *Logos*, the meaning of which is expressed ultimately in the concrete personhood of Jesus Christ. The apprehension of the fullness of what this term signifies constitutes a kind of unfolding drama in its own right in the philosophical and theological realm.

In a typically patristic style of theological exposition, in which he likes to emphasize the unity of what seems incompatible, Ratzinger notes the "scandal" of asserting the union of *logos* and *sarx*. In the opening lines of his section on Christ in his *Introduction*, he describes how the second article of the Creed "proclaims the absolutely staggering alliance of *logos* and *sarx*, of meaning and a single historical figure. The meaning that sustains all being has become flesh; that is, it has entered history and become one individual in it; it is no longer simply what encompasses and sustains history but a point in it."[45] Once he has established the tension between the realities that do not seem to "fit together," his audience is open to hearing the central mystery of the Christian vision—the mystery of the person who unites what seems inherently separate—proclaimed in a fresh way. In more

---

43. Ibid., 139–43.

44. Josef Pieper and Romano Guardini, two of the great influences on Ratzinger, focused on this relationship of the development of myth to *Logos* in Western thought. See, for example, Josef Pieper, "The Concept of Tradition," *Review of Politics* 20 (1958): 465–91, and Romano Guardini, *Spirit of the Liturgy* (New York: Herder, 1998).

45. Ratzinger, *Introduction to Christianity*, 193.

recent days and in a more a pastoral setting he proclaims this the only reality that can bridge the chasm between spirit and flesh:

> "The Word became flesh." Before this revelation we once more wonder: how can this be? The Word and the flesh are mutually opposed realities; how can the eternal and almighty Word become a frail and mortal man? There is only one answer: Love. Those who love desire to share with the beloved, they want to be one with the beloved, and Sacred Scripture shows us the great love story of God for his people which culminated in Jesus Christ.[46]

The philosophical question, then, as to how *Logos* and *sarx* can be united is resolved only in following the narrative of salvation history. Tracing this narrative causes us to see the meaning of the eternal *Logos* in new ways—even the *Logos* that provides the basis of metaphysical reality itself—depending on how it is communicated in history. Indeed, as it turns out in the course of human history, the unity of *logos* and *sarx* is communicated dialogically as a word, as a *person* who reveals love itself to all of creation.

From *Ratio* to *Verbum*

Ratzinger notes that the Greeks understood *Logos* to signify something like "meaning." Initially the word was associated in Latin with *ratio*. By the power of this *Logos*, through *ratio*, the Creator creates with intelligence in a way that is accessible to reason. The Creator speaks through creation in such a way that all that comes to be is "Being-thought."[47] Of course, the intelligibility of the created order is not a notion that has its origin in the Christian narrative. The Greek philosophical tradition that for centuries challenged the old "mythology of the gods" was an important transition in intellectual and cultural history toward a rational way of understanding the universe. Philosophy and science had, in this sense, purified religion in the Western tradition. Seeing creation as *being-thought* had become a well-established aspect of Greek philosophy. Still, within this philosophical

46. Benedict XVI, *Urbi et Orbi Christmas Message*, 2010, accessed at: http://www.vatican.va/holy_father/benedict_xvi/messages/urbi/documents/hf_ben-xvi_mes_20101225_urbi_en.html.

47. Ratzinger, *Introduction to Christianity*, 156.

horizon a different limitation was discovered through persistent questioning of the *source* of this being-thought. Is the creation that is "being-thought" generated in freedom, or is it merely a product of a kind of automated determinism?[48] Does the Creator create out of necessity or in freedom? The introduction of the biblical narrative at this moment makes possible an encounter in history between the horizon of philosophy and that of faith that then produces a new kind of synthesis for understanding the relationship between God and the world. With the *Logos* at the center of this union between the worlds of philosophy and biblical faith, both creation and history can be understood as personal expressions of divine communication.

Logos as Person

This new synthesis begins, in a certain way, when John the Evangelist applied the term *Logos* to the figure of Jesus of Nazareth in the prologue of his gospel. Ratzinger notes that the term began to take on new meaning in the history of ideas in this moment. "It no longer denoted simply the permeation of all being and meaning; it characterizes this man: he who is here is 'Word.' . . . He is constantly 'spoken' and hence the pure relation between the speaker and the spoken to. Thus *logos* Christology, as 'word' theology, is once again the opening up of being to the idea of relationship."[49] In this one pivotal moment, then, as salvation history and philosophy meet on a scriptural field, a new reality emerges. By the church's reception of the figure of Christ as the *Logos* itself in the flesh, all of creation and human history begin to be reinterpreted in light of this "*verbum*" who is actually communicated as a *person*.

The *Log*-ic of all reality now begins to be understood not only as "meaning" in the abstract, but meaning as word-spoken that in turn becomes a person. In this sense there is a merging and mutual purification of the realms of mythological religion, philosophy, and human history. The consequence of this pivotal encounter of these ways of thinking also opens up a new horizon for humanity in a world with a person at the center of it and with whom a real relationship is possible. In a homiletic tenor, Benedict explains:

48. Ibid., 157.
49. Ibid., 189.

> At the very moment when the Magi, guided by the star, adored
> Christ the new king, astrology came to an end, because the
> stars were now moving in the orbit determined by Christ. . . .
> It is not the elemental spirits of the universe, the laws of mat-
> ter, which ultimately govern the world and mankind, but a
> personal God governs the stars, that is, the universe; it is not
> the laws of matter and of evolution that have the final say, but
> reason, will, love—a Person. And if we know this Person and
> he knows us, then truly the inexorable power of material ele-
> ments no longer has the last word; we are not slaves of the
> universe and of its laws, we are free.[50]

The freedom of humanity is made possible then by participating in the logi-cal structure of the universe that is not only logical in the sense of its inherent intelligibility but also in the sense of the logic of the communicative structure of reality that is based on the *Logos* who is Word.

The development of the meaning of *logos* from *ratio* to *verbum* is not only a matter of semantic or linguistic preference, in Ratzinger's view. Seeing *logos* not merely as *ratio* but as *verbum* has enormous implications, of course, and it stands at the center of Ratzinger's own "dynamic" understanding of the Christian mysteries, which contrib-uted to his innovative contributions to the church's teaching on reve-lation, as the previous chapter indicated. Jared Wicks, for example, sees Ratzinger's Christology resonating in the compendium on reve-lation he wrote with Rahner, as an early alternative to the neoscho-lastic formulation offered by the preparatory commission at the council. Ratzinger's influence is seen in the description of Christ as the *"vivum Dei verbum quaerens nos."* This living word that has been seeking out humanity throughout all of history is fulfilled in the in-carnation.[51] In light of this historical moment of the incarnation, the *Logos* that had been spoken throughout all of history and indeed from the moment of creation is understood anew.

Moving from *ratio* to *verbum* opened up a necessarily *dialogical structure* to theology that Ratzinger sees as essential to the content of the Christian mystery itself. He explains: "Word never stands on

50. Benedict XVI, encyclical letter *On Christian Hope (Spe Salvi)* (Washing-ton, DC: United States Conference of Catholic Bishops, 2007), 5.

51. W. Jared Wicks and Benedict XVI, *Prof. Ratzinger at Vatican II: A Chapter in the Life of Pope Benedict XVI* (New Orleans: Loyola University Press, 2007), 9.

its own; it comes from someone, is there to be heard, and is therefore meant for others."[52] "Word" by its very nature is communicative and—on being spoken and demanding a response from the one to whom it is spoken—points to dialogue. This central term taken from Scripture is appropriated in a living way that conveys a meaning given to a narrative and dialogical view of the Christian mystery. It moves away from a merely philosophical or theoretical understanding of God and his self-revelation to humanity to an understanding that radically reformulates the approach to these questions. Consequently, as this new dimension of "*logos* theology" comes to be appropriated in the Christian tradition, in Ratzinger's estimation the theology of God, and indeed all of metaphysics, requires a renewed understanding. He writes:

> The experience of a God who conducts a dialogue, of the God who is not only logos but also dia-logos, not only an idea and meaning but speech and word in the reciprocal exchanges of partners in conversation—this experience exploded the ancient division of reality into substance, the real thing, and accidents, the merely circumstantial. It is now quite clear that the dialogue, the *relatio*, stands behind the substance as an equally primordial form of being.[53]

The assertion that God, and indeed all of being, is to be reinterpreted in light of "experience" of the God who engages in dialogue—in revelation—is indeed striking. It also changes the epistemological landscape. Because *relatio* "stands behind" and is therefore constitutive of all being, being can really only begin to be understood not by way of private speculation but in the context of dialogue with God and with the believing community: those who have "experienced" the same God who engages in dialogue.

Ratzinger stresses that the development of the meaning of the term *logos* is not the product of pure human speculation, but rather "it grew in the first place out of the interplay between human thought and the data of Christian faith . . . ."[54] The translation of *logos* as

52. Ratzinger, *Introduction to Christianity*, 210.
53. Ibid., 183.
54. Joseph Ratzinger, "Concerning the Notion of Person in Theology," *Communio* 17 (1990): 439–54, at 439.

verbum in the Vulgate, as well as the ultimate description of the eternal *Logos*-made-flesh as *prosōpon* in the christological and trinitarian debates of the early church, indicate a lively tradition appropriating the "data" of Christian faith as it is handed down from the past. What is "given" in the Christian tradition, as long as the tradition continues to be guided by the original data, continues to be susceptible to mining for deeper and fuller meaning as that tradition extends into new cultures and time periods.

A Person at the Center of Christology and Soteriology

In the introduction of *prosōpon*, for example, the tradition borrows deliberately from the theatrical world precisely because theologians in the Christian tradition viewed Christian faith as the playing out of a literal drama of salvation. Recalling Justin Martyr's analysis of the *Logos* speaking through the prophets of the Old Testament, for example, Ratzinger notes: "The literary artistic device of letting roles appear to enliven the narrative with their dialogue reveals to the theologians *the one* who plays the true role here, the *Logos*, the *prosōpon*, the person of the Word which is no longer merely role, but person."[55] The role of the one who saves has everything to do not just with what he accomplishes but who he *is*. It is evident from the early stages of theological reflection, then, that an inherent unity was perceived between soteriological and christological understanding. How Christ saves is a question inseparable from who he is. Ratzinger's retrieval of this patristic approach to Christology as inherently intertwined with soteriology serves as a corrective of the neoscholastic tradition that tended to separate out questions of the nature of salvation from the philosophical grounding of christological doctrines, including the nature and mode of the hypostatic union, the knowledge and will of Christ, etc. But by highlighting the interplay between philosophy and salvation history as embodied through the mediation of *Logos*, Ratzinger emerges as an important figure in post-conciliar theology that sought to reconnect christological concerns with soteriological ones, reuniting theological reflection on Christ with its biblical context.[56] It is precisely the *person* who reconciles humanity

55. Ibid., 442.
56. Ratzinger, *Behold the Pierced One*, 13–15.

and divinity in his passion and death on the cross who has united humanity and divinity in his own person in the incarnation. His identity and his work are one.

Though the early Christian tradition embraced the understanding of the Word as person, the category of Word itself also kept a certain pride of place, but it did so as understood in light of personhood. The primacy of the category of the Word in Christology did not leave questions in the purely philosophical or speculative realm. The nature of truth itself that *Logos* communicates came to be reinterpreted in light of love in the Christian vision, from a static conception to a more dynamic one. Hence the question of the Word's effect in soteriology remained always prominent. Ratzinger explains this gradual unfolding of the position of the *Logos* as truth as being primary and leading seamlessly to the apprehension of the truth as person:

> Already in Greek philosophy we encounter the idea that man can find eternal life if he clings to what is indestructible—to truth, which is eternal. He needs, as it were, to be full of truth in order to bear within himself the stuff of eternity. But only if truth is a Person, can it lead me through the night of death. We cling to God—to Jesus Christ the Risen One. And thus we are led by the One who is himself Life. In this relationship we too live by passing through death, since we are not forsaken by the One who is himself Life.[57]

Situating the question of truth against the backdrop of the final question of the limit of death moves the whole discussion from the speculative to the existential realm. Ratzinger's argument that "only if truth is a person can it lead me through death" is not, of course, a product of *a priori* speculation. It is rather the fruit of *a posteriori* reflection on the experience of Jesus' life, death, and resurrection given in the scriptural witness. He is the person who is revealed to be truth itself precisely because he leads *through* death—which otherwise would seem to define the limits of the truth of human existence. The experience, then, of the "Jesus of history" who defeats death leads

---

57. Benedict XVI, "Mass of the Lord's Supper: Homily of His Holiness Benedict XVI," St. John Lateran Basilica, April 1, 2010, accessed at: http://www.pcf.va/holy_father/benedict_xvi/homilies/2010/documents/hf_ben-xvi_hom_20100401_coena-domini_en.html.

to the understanding of the same man as the "Christ of faith" precisely because of the fact of the destruction of death and restoration of life that occurs in him in history.

III. The Person of Christ as Key to Scripture and Tradition

In approaching an understanding of the *Logos* ultimately revealed in Scripture as *person*, the question inevitably arises: what kind of person? What are the values of this person? What are the primary relationships? What are the dispositions and aims of this *Logos*-made-person? Careful exegesis is of course central to the task of answering these questions. For Ratzinger the fullness of the identity of the Word of God spoken in the context of ecclesial faith, among the Chosen People of God, is the person of Jesus Christ. Christ both emerges out of the tradition of Scripture and is the summation of the revelation of Scripture, and he is therefore the key to its authentic interpretation.[58] Consequently, he is best approached on his own terms and not according to those who do not have the benefit of the horizon of the communal and ecclesial hermeneutic of faith. He must be approached as he is presented in Scripture and from within tradition. For Ratzinger, Christ is also the *form* of authentic tradition, emerging from the narrative of the past and yet bringing to fulfillment the new development of the revelation of God for all generations. What has been handed on in faith from the time of Abraham to John the Baptist was oriented toward the coming of Christ. And since his coming, the living tradition of the church has had as its *raison d'etre* the ongoing attempt to understand and appropriate the meaning of his identity and how he accomplishes the new and everlasting covenant between God and humanity.

The task of understanding the figure of Jesus of Nazareth has from the very beginning been fraught with difficulty. The gospels themselves offer a kind of paradox when it comes to Jesus' relationship to tradition and the fulfillment of the Hebrew Scriptures. Ratzinger relies on Ernst Käsemann's assessment of the dilemma: the question for

---

58. Again, Wicks attributes to Ratzinger the language of Christ as the "*Clavis Scripturarum, canon interior apriens quod in eis est*" in the compendium on revelation given to the bishops at Vatican II. Wicks et al., *Prof. Ratzinger at Vatican II*, 10.

the modern interpreter of Jesus seems to be the choice between Jesus as a kind of "liberal revolutionary" or a "pious traditionalist." Portions of the gospels give support for each of these conclusions. On the one hand there is the admonition Jesus gives that if anyone departs in the least way from the demands of the Law, that one "will be called least in the kingdom of heaven" (Matt 5:19). At the same time Jesus operates with clear freedom with respect to the Law when he himself reminds the Pharisees that the Sabbath is "made for man, not man for the Sabbath" (Mark 2:27).[59] But the way forward in understanding Jesus is not to choose between these seemingly opposing views, but rather to let the tension between them speak to the whole truth of his identity. Ratzinger explains that Jesus operates in a way that suggests he is obedient to *tradition* and yet free from the constrictions of particular *traditions* that have emerged in the attempt to be faithful to the underlying revelation of the Word of God. To what, then, is Jesus really obedient?

For Ratzinger the fundamental identity of Jesus is not as a follower of tradition or as a revolutionary against it. He is neither fundamentally a liberal revolutionary nor is he simply a traditionalist in his piety with respect to the Law. Rather, his most basic identity is as the Son of the Father.[60] As the Father is the initiator of the covenant, we can see in the Son the fulfillment of the covenant from both the divine and human sides. Jesus both affirms the covenantal relationship of the past and also is critical of the following of it in the present. He is critical in order that the covenant might be fulfilled by the whole People of God in the future. The fulfillment of this covenant is to draw humanity precisely into the Sonship that is at the core of Jesus' identity.[61]

Person as Son

More than a philosophical question, the reality of the divine person entering into human history is a question of entering into a story. At

---

59. Joseph Ratzinger, *Principles of Catholic Theology: Building Stones for a Fundamental Theology* (San Francisco: Ignatius Press, 1987), 95. Cf. Ernst Käsemann, "Was Jesus Liberal?" in idem, *Der Ruf der Freiheit*, 3rd ed. (Tübingen, Mohr [Siebeck], 1968), 19–53.

60. Ibid., 94–99; Benedict XVI, *Jesus of Nazareth: From the Baptism in the Jordan to the Transfiguration*, 24.

61. Benedict XVI, *The God of Jesus Christ: Meditations on the Triune God* (San Francisco: Ignatius Press, 2008), 33–37.

the center of the story are characters with real relationships. There is a sense in which, in Ratzinger's approach, the identity of Jesus as *Son* of the Father unfolds from the identification of him with "the Word." This filial identity of Jesus is another expression of the paradigm of the relationality of Word-spoken-by-speaker and continues to reveal the fullness of the identity of Jesus of Nazareth. This is evident in Benedict's most mature exposition of the figure of Jesus as primarily revealing the character of "Son." Especially in the opening chapter of the first volume of *Jesus of Nazareth*, in his description of the baptism in the Jordan, Jesus is presented as the beloved Son of the Father. This is true at the beginning of his public ministry and then again in the nature of his rejecting the temptations of Satan in the desert by referring back again and again to his relationship with the Father as *the* center of his identity. All the way to his communication with his Father on the cross, it is clear for Benedict what the central characteristic of Jesus' person is, namely, his identity as the Beloved Son of the Father. This identity is then opened up and extended to the followers of Jesus as he teaches them to share in his own relationship with the Father when he teaches them to pray.[62] This filial identity of Jesus, then, also comes to mark the core identity of the whole church as children of the Father.

The centrality of the Sonship of Jesus is made evident, for Ratzinger, not merely from assertions of that identity in Scripture (e.g., "the Father and I are one"). Rather, the import of it is discovered only in following the *whole of the narrative* of the person of Jesus. We see that central to his personhood is the more specific identity of the beloved and therefore obedient Son of the Father. This is an identity that is lived out and is most poignantly recognized in his suffering and death. In *Principles of Catholic Theology*, Ratzinger draws on an observation from one of his most trusted sources of biblical exegesis, Heinrich Schlier. Precisely because of the identity of Jesus as the Son of the Father, there is a way to understand more directly the inner relationship of the incarnation and the cross and what is revealed about God in an unfolding manner through these two central "poles" of the Christian vision. "Word" alone does not adequately communicate the depth of this double revelation from incarnation to cross.

---

62. Benedict XVI, *Jesus of Nazareth: From the Baptism in the Jordan to the Transfiguration*, 9–45; 135–41.

The inherent relationality and the central aspect of sonship-as-love uniquely "carries" the meaning of these two central events in the life of Christ as "Son." Who Jesus is and what he accomplishes, the substance of the "nominal and verbal" confessions of faith, are brought into unity when Jesus is viewed primarily from his *filial* identity. Ratzinger argues that in the letter to the Hebrews, for example, the incarnation is interpreted as an event that is fundamentally a dialogue (lit. word-event, *Wortgeschehen*) in an act of prayer (*Gebetsgeschehen*) between God the Father and God the Son (Heb 10:5) wherein the incarnation is seen as the acceptance by the Savior of the body that will then be offered on the cross.[63] This dialogue of Father and Son, a dialogue that is "in the Spirit," continues all the way to Calvary. For this reason, for Ratzinger, Jesus' sonship from the incarnation to the cross is the basis for the perfect expression of the love of God for humanity and humanity for God.

Double Revelation of the Incarnation and Cross

We come to the point in Ratzinger's Christology that seems pivotal. The understanding of *Logos*, by a process of historical and theological appropriation in the Christian tradition, has gone through various stages of meaning: from *ratio* to *verbum* and then to the appropriation of *verbum* that is communicated as *prosōpon* (person), the primary characterization of which is that of *filius*. Indeed, in Ratzinger's mature reflection on the person of Jesus it seems that, while it does not by any means exclude the importance of the other modes of Christology, "Son of the Father" takes a privileged place among the many titles and modes of understanding Jesus of Nazareth.[64] Ratzinger notes that the real questions about Jesus' identity emerge when crowds wonder at his message in the gospels, when they demand to know where he gets the authority to speak as he does. And if the *identity* is made clear, the *work* Jesus is capable of, the fact that he comes as the one who saves, also comes into focus.

Ratzinger, in attempting to answer these questions, appeals back to the category of Jesus' sonship. What Jesus speaks to the world, he says, flows directly from what is spoken to him by his Father. Coun-

---

63. Ratzinger, *Principles of Catholic Theology*, 20.
64. Benedict XVI, *Jesus of Nazareth: From the Baptism in the Jordan to the Transfiguration*, 1–8.

tering Harnack's famous contention that Jesus spoke only about the
Father and that therefore the dogmatic claims about him developed
in Christology ought to be set aside, Ratzinger responds: "Jesus is
only able to speak about the Father in the way he does because he is
the Son, because of his filial communion with the Father. The Christological dimension—in other words, the mystery of the Son as re-
vealer of the Father—is present in everything Jesus says and does."[65]
The christological definitions of Jesus' identity as divine and human,
then, are not accretions to his sonship but flow directly from this
identity so intimately related to the Father.

But even within the framework of Ratzinger's "Son Christology"[66]
there is no room for complacency. Within the identity of Jesus as Son
of the Father a further tension is ever present, and it is one that has
existed throughout the Christian theological tradition. It is a tension
between theology built primarily from the incarnation and that from
the cross. Ratzinger acknowledges readily that no easy synthesis that
might resolve this tension is possible. Rather, "they must remain
present as polarities that mutually correct each other and only by
complementing each other point to the whole."[67] For Ratzinger,
holding these polarities in tension with one another is the task of the
theologian. He notes the early work done in bringing into dialogue
the "God of the philosophers" and the "God of biblical faith," in jux-
taposing the importance of the categories of "being" and "doing." For
by looking at the figure of Christ as the *Logos*-made-flesh, in a theology of Christ based primarily on the incarnation, as the Greek tradition especially developed it, the Word is seen as that which holds all
being together. At the same time, precisely because of what is encountered on the cross, the Word is communicated not as mere "meaning"
or intelligibility or even simple relationality, but as love itself: that
radical, personal giving away of oneself for another.[68] When looking
upon the figure of Christ, Ratzinger says, we see that if he is held as
the Word through whom all things are made, if he is being itself, he
is being in such a way that being comes to be seen as doing, as "going

---

65. Ibid., 7.

66. Ratzinger, *Introduction to Christianity*, 168. This is the term he uses to
describe the perspective on Jesus given in the Gospel of John, on which he relies
heavily for his own theology.

67. Ibid., 230.

68. Ratzinger, "Concerning the Notion of Person in Theology," 443–47.

out of oneself." *Being* is seen, then, through a christological lens as "exodus," as "transformation." Therefore, he writes, "a properly understood Christology of being and of the Incarnation must pass over into the theology of the Cross and become one with it; conversely, a theology of the Cross that gives full measure must pass over into the Christology of the Son and of being."[69] Such an attempt on Ratzinger's part to keep the polarities of incarnation and cross in tension with one another is illustrative of a key aspect of the renewal of Christian theology that has seen the two poles drift apart from one another at various times.

The tendency in Christian theology to separate too easily the theologies of the incarnation and of the cross was recognized in the deliberations at the Second Vatican Council as well. Jared Wicks notes Ratzinger's warning against this divide in the context of the discussion around *Gaudium et Spes*, which he found at times to be too easily drawn into the optimism of the day, manifesting great trust in the promise of "progress" in modern culture and human development within modernity and using the theology of the incarnation to provide a framework for this naïve, world-affirming vision. Ratzinger warned against the notion of "progress" by our own efforts as theologically justified by the traditional doctrine of the incarnation. Rather, he insists on the necessity of the cross in salvation history, which is an *actio divina* of *amare*, not just *laborare*.[70] He urged the council to keep the tension between incarnation and cross alive, maintaining that a full Christology involves keeping the polarities of the incarnation and the cross in dialogue with one another. The tension, he argued, is essential if the church is to be true to the one Christian narrative given in Scripture. In Ratzinger's eyes, remaining true to this tension also provides the grounding for a more profound anthropological vision, providing a basis for hope that is much deeper than mere optimism about the future based on a superficial ideology of human "progress" in the modern era.

Ratzinger holds that the cross also forces us to reconsider *who God is* who has allowed himself to be drawn into this scandalous humiliation and defeat in the person of Jesus. He explains: "In the face of the crucified Christ we see God, we see true omnipotence, not

---

69. Ratzinger, *Introduction to Christianity*, 230.

70. Wicks, et al., *Prof. Ratzinger at Vatican II*, 12. Cf. *Acta Synodalia III/5*, 562–63; IV/3, 760–1.

the myth of omnipotence. . . . In Him, true omnipotence means loving to the extreme of suffering for us."[71] But this clear vision of who God really is and what love really looks like is not at all clear, precisely because of the cross. In fact, our vision is very much clouded when we look upon the crucified Christ. This seems to be no God at all, but a victim, one who has been defeated. Indeed, there is a sense in which we can have a clearer conception of God, to a limited degree, as Creator, as long as God remains distant and we extrapolate what we think about God by way of what we encounter and know in the created world. Surely it is an intelligent and all-powerful God who can do all this! As God comes close, however, our vision is for a time confused. Our ideas of God can no longer remain so clear and distinct. Ratzinger explains the difficulty that comes into play for a theology of God once God bridges the gap between heaven and earth. "God has come so near to us that we can kill him and that he thereby, so it seems, ceases to be God for us."[72] Only in the contemplation of the *Logos* revealed as the person of Jesus are we confronted with the challenge to see humanity and divinity both in a new light. Specifically, it is through the relationship of Jesus as Son of the Father that we see what is the driving force at work in his life, namely filial love.

The Father Known in Prayer

We have explored before how it is that the Father-Son relation is dialogical. But the Son's experience of the cross demonstrates that there is a particular texture to the dialogical relationship between the Father and him. It is more than just a mutual speaking back and forth. It is a relationship of obedience. The dialogue is one in which the Son hears the Father and then acts out of obedience to him. But what is the source and aim of Jesus' obedience to the Father? Ratzinger notes that this obedience is not mechanical, but rather one that can only be understood in the context of Jesus' twofold relationship (a) to the Father and (b) to humanity. The Chalcedonian framework of his identity that simultaneously asserts the full divinity and humanity

71. Benedict XVI, "Visit to the Pontifical Roman Major Seminary in Honor of the Memorial of Our Lady of Trust," Rome, February 12, 2010, accessed at: http://www.vatican.va/holy_father/benedict_xvi/speeches/2010/february /documents/hf_ben-xvi_spe_20100212_seminario-romano-mag_en.html.

72. Ratzinger, *Introduction to Christianity*, 55.

of Jesus, therefore, is a hermeneutical key to understanding his mission to be obedient in a way that leads to his passion and death. The primacy of his identity as the Son of the eternal Father is precisely the foundation for his mission to take on human nature to save it as God *and* human.[73]

In order to understand this filial, obediential relationship of Son to the Father that leads to his being so radically "for the world," it is necessary, in Ratzinger's view, to enter into the *interior life* of the Son that at its core is a spiritual communion of love with the Father. Only this perspective can shed light for us on the true nature of his identity. One of the central theses in Ratzinger's thought is that since the essence of Jesus is his constant prayerful communion with the Father, we must enter into his prayer in order to get to know who he really is.[74] In this, Christology sets the boundaries for anthropology. Entering into the prayer and relationships of Jesus, opens way for humanity to be fully realized as sons and daughters of the eternal Father. As Ratzinger explains, this is the root of our own true identities, to come to participate in Jesus' sonship, in his prayer to and communion with the Father, by the uniting power of the Holy Spirit: "The question of Jesus' filial relation to the Father gets to the very root of the question of man's freedom and liberation, and unless this is done everything else is futile."[75] The implications for the disciples of Jesus are definitive in light of this filial identity of Jesus. In union with Christ, his followers are able to approach the One who has been invisible until now as Father. Ratzinger explains this unfolding of the double revelation of who God is and who humanity can become by way of union with Christ:

> For one who has grown up in the Christian tradition, the way begins in the "thou" of prayer: such a one knows that he can address the Lord; that this Jesus is not just a historical personage of the past but is the same in all ages. And he knows, too, that in, with and through the Lord, he can address him to whom Jesus says "Father." . . . He sees that this Jesus is truly "Son" in his whole existence, is one who receives his inmost being from another, that his life is a receiving. In him is to be

73. Ratzinger, *Principles of Catholic Theology*, 94–101.

74. De Gaál Gyulai, *Theology of Pope Benedict XVI: The Christocentric Shift*, 5.

75. Ratzinger, *Behold the Pierced One*, 35.

found the hidden foundation; in the actions, words, life, suffering of him who is truly Son it is possible to see, hear, and touch him who is unknown. The unknown ground of being reveals itself as Father.[76]

This revelation of the "unknown ground of being" as Father also becomes the foundation and *raison d'etre* of the life of the church. The nature of the communion that exists in the church gathered around the person of Jesus is the possibility for his followers to find the fullness of life in participation in his filial identity.

The Risen Christ Drawing Humanity to the Father

Only in communion with the Risen Christ, with Jesus who has united himself to humanity in everything, in life, suffering, and even the isolation of death, can the human family be led beyond death into eternal life. It is precisely the Risen Christ who has defeated death, thanks to the radical reception of the Father's love that brings him out of the tomb, the place of the dead. The members of the church who enter into union with the Risen Christ are those who become the members of the Body of which Christ is the head. Particularly in gathering together to listen to the Word of God who is Christ and then in receiving that same Christ in the sacraments, the church is able to participate in Christ's own identity as the Son of the Father.

For Ratzinger, Christ's resurrection makes this union with him and therefore with the Father possible. In providing a unified exegesis of the resurrection narratives from John's gospel he finds the basis for this understanding of the church as grounded in Christ's filial relationship with the Father. First, he notes the puzzling response from Jesus when he appears to Mary Magdalene who, upon recognizing Jesus, attempts to cling to him and return to the former way of relating to him as "My Teacher." Rather, as Jesus rebuffs her and tells her not to cling to him until he has ascended to the Father (John 20:17), he seems to be pointing, in Ratzinger's view, to the need to relate to himself in a familiar yet radically new way in his resurrection.[77] This is confirmed in the appearance to Thomas, insofar as Thomas is indeed invited to come close to touch Jesus only because

---

76. Ratzinger, *Principles of Catholic Theology*, 73.

77. Benedict XVI, *Dogma and Preaching: Applying Christian Doctrine to Daily Life* (San Francisco: Ignatius Press, 2011), 302.

it is clear that he is approaching the one who, bearing the wounds, is indeed the one who died and is now in a glorified state. There is clearly no returning to the former way of relating to Jesus, as the wounds are front and center in this encounter. Ratzinger explains that this presentation of the wounds is meant for Thomas "not to make him forget the Cross, but rather to make it unforgettable."[78] As a result of this presentation of the Crucified and Risen Lord to the church in the person of Thomas, it is now possible for the church to be drawn into communion ultimately with the Father. This is so since "Jesus has now become the one who is exalted at the Father's side and accessible to everyone. Now he can be touched only as the One who is with the Father, as the one who has ascended."[79]

Finally, in the case of the narrative of the disciples on the way to Emmaus, a liturgical element emerges, indicating that this encounter with the Risen Christ is the true basis of the life of the whole church. Following the pattern of the liturgy that is later established, Christ is recognized and truly encountered after a period of listening to the Word, and this recognition is perfected only in the communion of the breaking of the bread. Finally, in Jesus' subsequent disappearing upon their recognition of him there is implicit, for Ratzinger, a sense of the mission of the church: "The worship of the Lord in Word and sacrament is the way in which we can encounter the Risen Lord; the love that shares a meal with him opens our eyes. Then he whom we have recognized disappears, for he calls us to journey farther along the road."[80] The resurrection, then, becomes the essential hinge for Ratzinger upon which turns the subsequent theology of the church. It is to this movement from Christology to ecclesiology that we now turn our attention.

Christological Basis of Ecclesiology

By being drawn into this relationship with Christ, the church is ultimately brought into relationship with the eternal *Logos* who is not only the one revealed gradually in salvation history but the *Logos* through whom all creation came about in the first place (Col 1:15-17). What becomes possible within the church is access to the fullness of

---

78. Ibid., 303.
79. Ibid., 302.
80. Ibid., 303.

truth, as the human person finds the fullness of his or her identity in relationship with the one through whom all things have their being. Ratzinger succinctly articulates this christological vision that links the eternal identity of Christ with his historical identification with the church:

> Only Christ can hold together and unify the whole; when we speak of Christ, we must of course always see the trinitarian mystery in the background; he comes from the Father, and he is present in all of history through the Holy Spirit, who bears witness to Christ and guides believers into all truth (Jn 15:26; 16:13). Universality is God's concern; Christ holds it all together because he is the Son. The Christocentric emphasis is, as such, always a Trinitarian emphasis.[81]

In coming into relationship with Christ, then, one comes into Trinitarian relationship, participating in the filial love of the Son for the Father and being united in the love of the Holy Spirit. What the believer seeks in a personal and genuine dialogue with God—an "I–Thou" dialogue—soon reveals itself to be a dialogue that involves greater multiplicity and dynamism than might have been apparent initially. In a consideration of the Christian roots of the concept of the "person" in Western thought, Ratzinger notes that because of the theological reflection on the questions "Who is the God presented in the Scripture?" and "Who is Christ?" as the Christian tradition slowly comes to understand him, a concept of personhood that sheds new light on our own self-understanding is also given.[82] Seeing the true "person" revealed in Christ makes it clear that relating to God is at the heart of what it is to be a person, not an annihilation of the person. Rather, being in relation to God, "human existence is not canceled, but comes to its highest possibility."[83]

This theological personalism that emerges in the Christian intellectual tradition is perfected, Ratzinger holds, when it is brought into the perspective of the *communio* of the Trinitarian relations. Ratzinger not only asserts a *theological* anthropology in the course of this

---

81. Joseph Ratzinger, *On the Way to Jesus Christ* (San Francisco: Ignatius Press, 2005), 132.
82. Ratzinger, "Concerning the Notion of Person in Theology," 439.
83. Ibid., 452.

consideration of the concept of personhood flowing from christological deliberation. He goes a step further to demonstrate the *Trinitarian*
shape of the relations that provide the foundation for authentic human
relations. He says that Christology that is understood in tandem with
a Trinitarian framework "adds the idea of 'we' to the idea of 'I' and
'you.' "[84] Both the "I" of humanity and the "you" of God, are, as the
Christian narrative unfolds, seen from the perspective of an intimate
personal encounter, but it is not a *private* encounter between two
individuals. Rather, there is multiplicity and community at work on
"both sides" of this encounter that has Christ at its center. In this
regard Christ is not merely an exemplar to be followed, one who
shows the way to union with God. Rather, he is "the integrating space
in which the 'we' of human beings gathers itself toward the 'you' of
God."[85] This notion of Christ as the "integrating space" in which the
whole of humanity can gather makes it clear that this process of being
drawn into his filial relationship with the Father does not annihilate
our personhood but rather fulfills it always in the context of communion with others, with the "collective I" of the church. It also
makes it clear that this filial relationship that involves an obediential
aspect is not a matter of submission to the one God who can easily
be construed as a kind of eternal absolute monarch. Rather, this relationship, this dialogue into which we are drawn through Christ, is
one that not only has "space" on the human side but on the divine
side as well. Ratzinger explains:

> In Christianity there is not simply a dialogical principle in the
> modern sense of a pure "I-thou" relationship, neither on the
> part of the human person that has its place in the historical
> "we" that bears it; nor is there such a mere dialogical principle
> on God's part who is, in turn, no simple "I," but the "we" of
> Father, Son, and Spirit. On both sides there is neither the pure
> "I," nor the pure "you," but on both sides the "I" is integrated
> into the greater "we." Precisely this final point, namely, that
> not even God can be seen as the pure and simple "I" toward
> which the human person tends, is a fundamental aspect of the
> theological concept of the person.[86]

84. Ibid.
85. Ibid., 453.
86. Ibid.

Ratzinger sees continuing to follow the course of the dialogue given in the Scriptural witness and the church's ongoing appropriation of the nature of this dialogue between God and humanity as a great gift given through the church for the whole world. In the offering of this anthropology the church provides a basis for the great dignity of the individual person and then a reason for seeing the individual never as an individual but always as one made for loving relationship with others. Indeed, many of the strikingly contemporary questions about unity and diversity in human relations resonate deeply (and perhaps surprisingly) in this christological and Trinitarian anthropology. Ratzinger writes: "The Christian concept of God has as a matter of principle given the same dignity to multiplicity as to unity."[87] This unity and multiplicity at the heart of the Christian theology of God is also essential to the theology of the church. Since we come to know this harmony of unity and multiplicity most perfectly in the person of Christ, he is also at the center of the church's self-understanding.

Conclusion:
Christ Revealed and Truly Known in the Church

Before moving to an examination of Ratzinger's understanding of the church we pause to recall what has been said about his Christology. The person of Christ, as the fullness of God's revelation of God's self, is the center point of all of human history. Following the narrative of salvation history through the resurrection of Christ makes it possible to look back both on the order of creation and the order of history and reinterpret all of it through a christological lens. The term *Logos* begins to take on different layers of meaning. The *Logos* through whom all things were made is not merely a principle of reason, but rather becomes personalized in the figure of Jesus of Nazareth, shown most perfectly as love itself in giving up his life freely on the cross out of obedient love to his Father and for the sake of the world. Relational, dialogical love then becomes the proper lens for understanding all of history and even being itself. Such is the nature of Ratzinger's Christology and such is the basis of his ecclesiology as well. For Ratzinger, Christ is the center of the church in

---

87. Ibid.

that the very essence of the church is to gather to hear the Word from God spoken and in turn to respond to that Word. The church learns how to do this insofar as it is conformed to the person of Christ who is both the Word spoken from God to humanity and also humanity's perfect response to God. By coming together in worship, then, in hearing the word proclaimed and being given the Word made flesh in the Eucharist, the members of the church are in turn motivated by this christological transformation to begin speaking that same Word of love to the world.[88] It is to this aspect of Ratzinger's theological vision that we turn next.

88. Joseph Ratzinger, *Called to Communion: Understanding the Church Today* (San Francisco: Ignatius Press, 1996), 13–46.

Chapter Four

Church as the Locus
of Divine-Human Dialogue

*Jesus turned around and saw them following him and
said to them, "what are you looking for?" They said to
him, "Rabbi, where are you staying?" He said to them,
"Come and you will see." John 1:38-39a*

Having explored in the previous chapter the contours of the
Christology of Joseph Ratzinger, we now turn to his ecclesiology. The two are intimately linked. Many of the essential
elements of his Christology can be translated into his ecclesiology,
including: (1) the dialogical and narrative understanding of Christ
unfolding in history that always takes place within the body of the
church; (2) how it is that Christ, who reveals God to be *dia-logos*,[1] is
always known in Trinitarian relationality, which then becomes the
essential basis for the structure and identity of the church, and (3)
how Christ's presence and nature are not static but dynamic and are
ultimately made known in the event of the cross, where the fullness
of love is revealed. It is the event of the cross that is experienced ever
anew in the context of the liturgy of the church. For the church, then,

1. Joseph Ratzinger, *Introduction to Christianity* (San Francisco: Ignatius
Press, 2004), 183.

93

this fundamental expression of the love of Christ poured out on the cross and experienced again and again in the eucharistic liturgy becomes *the* criterion by which it can be judged as being true to itself in its mission in the world. Just as the person of Christ must be seen in light of his theology of revelation as the Word of God spoken both in particularity as well as for a universal audience in history, so it is that the life of the church, for Ratzinger, follows the same "once only" as well as "forever" structure of revelation and Christology.[2] In this chapter I will attempt to explicate the christological shape of Ratzinger's ecclesiology. I will describe how his dialogical and narrative way of doing Christology and therefore ecclesiology resonates with the theology of the church offered in *Lumen Gentium*. In light of this conciliar teaching, I will then conclude the chapter with a section on the liturgy as the concrete expression of the theology of the church that then provides the basis for the mission of the church in the world.

I. Church as Place of Dialogue Between God and Humanity

In an essay looking back on and synthesizing the meaning of *Lumen Gentium*, Joseph Ratzinger recalls two important moments from the council.[3] First, Pope John XXIII called the council without proposing any particular themes for it, and yet as the bishops began their deliberations they quickly came to a consensus that it ought to take up primarily the theme of the church.[4] This was due in part to the fact that Vatican I was cut short before it could complete its teaching on the matter. As clear as it became early on that the church ought to be the focus of the council, another voice emerged that resonated with the members as well. In a gathering of the German bishops' conference in anticipation of the council, the elderly bishop of Regensburg urged his brothers that they must, above all, "talk about God. That is what is most important."[5] In Ratzinger's view this is precisely the method adopted by the council fathers. As he interprets the events of the council

2. Joseph Ratzinger, *Called to Communion: Understanding the Church Today* (San Francisco: Ignatius Press, 1996), 123.

3. Joseph Ratzinger, *Pilgrim Fellowship of Faith: The Church as Communion* (San Francisco: Ignatius Press, 2005), 123–52.

4. Ibid., 123.

5. Ibid., 124.

as a whole in hindsight, he explains: "the Second Vatican Council certainly did intend to subordinate what it said about the Church to what it said about God and set it in that context; it intended to propound an ecclesiology that was theo-logical in the proper sense."[6] In this way the church's most authoritative teaching confirms the importance of seeing ecclesiological concerns always in light of the larger theological perspective of the Christian mystery and attempts to ensure that eccle-siological concerns are not swallowed up by a horizon limited to social and political issues. This ecclesiological vision offered in *Lumen Gentium* very much resonates with Ratzinger's own thought on the subject, which is entirely predicated on his understanding of God's self-communication in revelation, as we have already seen.

Logos-basis of *Lumen Gentium*

As has already been discussed in earlier chapters, the primacy of the Word in the theology of Joseph Ratzinger both contributed to and continues to be shaped by the documents of Vatican Council II. His own study of Bonaventure's theology of history, among other things, helped to provide foundation for the writing of *Dei Verbum* and the Christocentrism of the Catholic understanding of revelation. This Christocentrism also finds resonance in the Constitution on the Church, *Lumen Gentium*. Here we are reminded that it is not the church, after all, but Christ, the eternal Word made flesh and center of history, who is the "*lumen gentium*." The church, then, is the means by which the *Verbum* continues to be spoken in human history; it is the locus of the communication between God and man. Implicit in Ratzinger's theology of revelation based on the communicative dynamics of "the Word" is a tension that helped to anchor the teaching of the council in the tradition as well as opening up that same tradition to development in the future. Precisely because the Word is spoken from eternity there is a unity and stability about it. At the same time, because it is spoken from eternity *in history*, the way the Word is heard and appropriated within the life of the church will vary from age to age and culture to culture. This is the basis for an understanding of revelation that is characterized as both developing historically and all the while in continuity with what had been revealed and taught in the past.

6. Ibid., 125.

This tension was highlighted at the council not only with respect to revelation in *Dei Verbum*, but also in the case of the church in *Lumen Gentium*. Ratzinger noted soon after the council's conclusion that previous modern definitions of the church were often formulated as negative arguments against the Protestant notion of the "invisible" church. The response from the Catholic Counter-Reformation into the twentieth century, Ratzinger explains, had often been to stress, alternatively, the institutional and therefore *visible* nature of the church.[7] Consequently, much of the theology of the church had come across as rather static and communicated in propositional terms. The text that was ultimately adopted, Ratzinger notes, embraces the "biblical polarities" of both the sacramental and charismatic notion of the "people of God."[8] By undertaking a more biblical and therefore narrative approach to ecclesiology, *Lumen Gentium* is able to account for the ongoing development of the identity and mission of the people of God—the church—as well as its foundation in the concrete and particular history of the life, death, and resurrection of Christ. Here is another expression of the dialogical and historical nature of Ratzinger's understanding of theology, this time as it pertains to the nature of the church. The church, he says, is always moving toward God who calls. It is not frozen in one structure of the past but rooted in its "changeless center," the person of Christ. And yet the Christ continues to "come," openly and speaking in history.[9] The church, in this christological pattern of identity, is the people of God gathered to be open to this coming, and in responding to this coming and speaking of the Christ it discovers him and in so doing discovers and realizes its true identity.

II. Christological-Pneumatological Tension of the Church

As part of Ratzinger's analysis of the theology of the church at Vatican II, he recalls the essential biblical pillars of the life of the church given in the second chapter of the Acts of the Apostles. This analysis leads him to trace three theological aspects of the church that are present in Acts and are highlighted in a new way in *Lumen Gentium*.

7. Joseph Ratzinger, *Theological Highlights of Vatican II* (Mahwah, NJ: Paulist Press, 2009), 70.
8. Ibid., 74.
9. Ibid., 76.

He sees the church in Acts revealed as *pneumatological, dynamic*, and *liturgical*. He explains that the Lukan vision of the church as given in Acts reveals that "First of all we are faced here with a pneumatological ecclesiology—it is the Spirit who makes the church. We are faced with a dynamic ecclesiology of salvation history, of which the dimension of catholicity is an essential part. Finally, we are faced with a liturgical ecclesiology: the assembly receives the gift of the Holy Spirit in the act of praying."[10] Similar to the rejection of the neoscholastic categories used to try to explain divine revelation in the writing of *Dei Verbum*, when it came to the deliberations on the church there was a similar dissatisfaction with the neoscholastic framework for understanding.[11] Above all, the static notion of the church as defined in scholastic and institutional terms before Vatican II was set aside for a more historical, narrative, and dynamic understanding of the church's nature. Ratzinger notes that Pope Pius XII's encyclical *Mystici Corporis* was an important moment in the development of the church's teaching about its own nature that paved the way for *Lumen Gentium*. In *Mystici Corporis*, he explains, "the Church is seen as determined by pneumatological as well as Christological elements; the Church is charismatic as well as sacramental in nature."[12] Adding the pneumatological tension to the christological understanding of the church[13] made for an ecclesiology that necessarily opened up to the current historical and ecclesial context more fully and was also, therefore, more able to engage the demands of the new spirit of ecumenical relations. Ratzinger describes the church as the christological presence in history,[14] but because of the pneumatological aspect of the church, as the Body of Christ, it is also not simply identical with Christ.[15]

This understanding of Christ's presence in history as the church centered on the person of Christ and yet vivified by the Spirit is, for Ratzinger, the essential aspect of the development of ecclesiology at Vatican II. The basis for such a manner of explaining revelation in history and the church as a carrier of revelation is precisely the inner

10. Ratzinger, *Pilgrim Fellowship of Faith*, 62–63.

11. Ratzinger, *Theological Highlights*, 71–79.

12. Ibid., 74.

13. Ibid., 68.

14. Joseph Ratzinger, *On the Way to Jesus Christ* (San Francisco: Ignatius Press, 2005), 77.

15. Ratzinger, *Theological Highlights*, 74.

Trinitarian tension of christological and pneumatological dynamics in salvation history. While Christ is the absolute center of history and the One through whom all creation came about and toward whom all of salvation history is oriented, the Holy Spirit is the One *in* whom these developments are realized. As the history of the church unfolds, it is always moving from the center of history: the event of the incarnation and paschal mystery of Christ. Yet the church is also vivified and expresses itself in new ways by the ongoing movement of the Spirit. The Spirit's movement, however, is not characterized by a "pneumatic anarchy,"[16] but rather always unfolds in a way that refers the church back to its source of life in Christ. There is, then, both a sense of being anchored in the historical particularity of the Christ event and simultaneously an openness to the future inherent in the character of the church.[17] Acknowledging the tension between the christological and pneumatological characteristics of the church thus opens up a more dynamic understanding of the nature and mission of the church in the modern world. This was the aim of the Second Vatican Council, as Ratzinger sees it.

I would argue that it is important in this regard to recall Ratzinger's appropriation of Bonaventure's theology of history. It seems that his understanding of the pneumatological aspect of the church provides a way of accounting for the fact that the church by its very nature is always unfolding in history. The one *Logos* that begets many *semina* in salvation history is a reality that accounts for both continuity and change in the life of the church. The church is also always either developing or running the risk of corruption and therefore is always in need of reform and renewal. The council's shift away from the language of the church as the *societas perfecta*[18] created a space for greater engagement with those beyond its "borders." The pneumatological nature of the church thus emphasized also opened up an ecumenical horizon that made possible new avenues of dialogue and reconciliation. Earlier conceptions of the church that were more static, he explains, gave the incorrect impression of the absolute identity of the church with the person of Christ. This impression therefore established a kind of stalemate with respect to dialogue with other ecclesial and religious communities such that the only possibility for "develop-

16. Ratzinger, *Called to Communion*, 119.
17. Ratzinger, *Pilgrim Fellowship of Faith*, 178–87.
18. Leo XIII, *Immortale Dei* (1885), 10.

ment" was conversion of others to the fullness of truth in the Catholic Church, or else remaining "in error" and necessarily outside full communion with Christ. This conception of the nature of the church risked what Paul VI called "ecclesio-monism," making the church a kind of idol that could obscure its living vitality. The church is better understood as a pilgrim people sojourning always "on the way" to deeper dialogue and communion with the living God in history.[19] The council set a whole new trajectory for ecclesiology in moving beyond the static understanding of the church defined ontologically as the perfect society identified solely with the figure of Christ. In embracing an ecclesiological vision more biblically based, both christological *and* pneumatological in character, fulfilled and shaped liturgically and therefore expressing an ongoing dynamism in history, *Lumen Gentium* breathed new life into the church's self-understanding that was more dynamic, I argue, precisely because it was more dialogical and relational in nature. Joseph Ratzinger both contributed to this renewed vision and also continues to be shaped by it himself.

Dominus Iesus

A similar tension in understanding the church emerged in more recent years. This time, however, Ratzinger found himself on the opposite side of the debate, one might say. If before the council he was among those arguing, with Paul VI, against the ecclesio-monism that *identified* the church with the Body of Christ, now, at the turn of the new millennium, he was more focused on the need to preserve a direct *association* between Christ and the church. As the debate has unfolded, depending upon his interlocutors and how the balance had shifted in his eyes, it seems that Ratzinger has stressed the pneumatological aspect of the church more in the immediate wake of the council and the christological aspect several decades later. The publication in 2000 of the note *Dominus Iesus*[20] by the Congregation for the Doctrine of the Faith, under the leadership of then-Cardinal Ratzinger, evoked a bitter backlash against the assertion of the unicity of

19. Herbert Vorgrimler, ed., *Commentary on the Documents of Vatican II*, 5 vols. (New York: Herder and Herder, 1967), 3: 162.

20. Congregation for the Doctrine of the Faith, *Declaration* Dominus Iesus: *On the Unicity and Salvific Universality of Jesus Christ and the Church* (Vatican City: Libreria Editrice Vaticana, 2000).

both Christ and the church in the economy of salvation. Perhaps in the forty years since Vatican II theologians and many inside and outside the church had become so accustomed to the pneumatological character of the church (a proposition that had met with such resistance from many at the council) that now there seemed to be a kind of forgetting of its christological character.[21]

In an essay recalling the experience of the "train wreck" of the reception of *Dominus Iesus*, Ratzinger attempted to articulate in more theological terms the canonical and pastoral points made in the document.[22] Underlying this defense is his customary approach to a question based on the twofold dynamic of the *Logos* that both reveals divine reality and in some ways also keeps it hidden. He refers to the basis of the title of the document as that of the confession of faith provided by St. Paul, "Jesus is Lord" (1 Cor 12:3). He calls this early profession of faith "a word that has been given to us by the Holy Spirit and *is* the word of the Holy Spirit."[23] The church is enabled to profess faith in Jesus as the Word made flesh who is Lord of creation and history by the power of the Holy Spirit who in turn points to the Word.

This reliance on the category of the *Logos* is problematic for some contemporary theologians. Thomas Rausch, for example, laments what he sees as Ratzinger's Platonism, which in his view is guilty of "privileging idea over the concrete and the empirical."[24] Rausch sums up the critiques of others based on Ratzinger's placing *logos* over *ethos* when it comes to the church: an approach, they would say, that fails to take history seriously. Rausch cites James Corkery and Walter Kasper in this critique, accusing Ratzinger of an "idealist" ecclesiology.[25] This critique fails, however, to appreciate the nature of Ratz-

---

21. See, for example, José Oscar Beozzo and Giuseppe Ruggieri, *The Ecumenical Constitution of Churches* (London: SCM Press, 2001); Stephen J. Pope and Charles C. Hefling, eds., *Sic Et Non: Encountering Dominus Iesus* (Maryknoll, NY: Orbis Books, 2002); Edmund Chia, *Towards a Theology of Dialogue: Schillebeeckx's Method as Bridge between Vatican's* Dominus Iesus *and Asia's FABC Theology: A Scientific Essay in Theology* (Bangkok, Thailand: Edmund Chia, 2003); Hermann Häring, Janet Martin Soskice, and Felix Wilfred, *Learning from Other Faiths* (London: SCM Press, 2003).

22. Ratzinger, *On the Way to Jesus Christ*, 55–78.

23. Ibid., 55.

24. Thomas P. Rausch, *Pope Benedict XVI: An Introduction to His Theological Vision* (New York: Paulist Press, 2009), 44.

25. Ibid.

inger's theology of history, which, while it has as its source the eternal *Logos* that is *beyond* history, is only really communicated *in* history. It is precisely the primacy of the *Logos*, in fact, that makes it possible to develop a theology of the church that is utterly reliant on history. This is an important ongoing theme in Ratzinger's theology, but again he is able to explain its importance with greatest effect in a pastoral setting, in a homily. In describing the inherently historical nature of the liturgical season of Advent, he says: "there is no period in history for which God would be just the past which already lies behind us and has already been done. On the contrary, for all of us, God is the origin from which we come and yet still also the future toward which we are going."[26] We discover this character of God's lordship over human history only by way of encounter with the Word made flesh who *comes to* us in the incarnation. Only from within what some call his "idealist" theology, then, does dialogue with the living God become possible *within history*, and the whole of history is thereby rendered accessible and intelligible because of it.

Ecclesia Semper Reformanda Est

Because the *Logos* is spoken in history ultimately in Christ and the church that carries the presence of Christ, there is both particularity and universality at the heart of the church's identity. This tension accounts for the simultaneous claims that the church is necessary for salvation in its unique character of holiness and at the same time carries sin within it and is always, therefore, in need of reform. In addressing the problem of the role of Christ and the church in salvation, Ratzinger affirms the unicity and necessity of both in salvation history. He explains:

> For the church to be the means of salvation for all, it does not have to extend itself visibly to all, but has instead its essential role in following Christ, he who is uniquely "the one," and therein the church is the little flock, through which God however intends to save "the many." The church's service is not

26. Benedict XVI, *What it Means to be a Christian: Three Sermons* (San Francisco: Ignatius Press, 2006), 36–37.

carried out *by* all human beings, but is indeed carried out *for* all of them.[27]

It is precisely because of the dialogical and historical nature of the church that it is never complete. It is always in need of being reformed by allowing the person of Christ to be at the center of its life and self-understanding.[28] Because its self-expression is always unfolding in history, the church is always expressing its true identity and at the same time is always being corrupted and drawn away from the dialogue with the Lord that actualizes its true identity. In Ratzinger's view the church is never statically perfect, but rather perfect only in the context of the historical dynamism that is fulfilled in the ongoing dialogue with the living God. Those within the church are often drawn away from this dialogical relationship with the Lord and turn in on themselves in sin. But in every age there are those who heroically and dramatically manifest the fullness of this dialogical relationship with the Lord. Maximilian Heim explains that in Ratzinger's thought these historical figures who carry out such a task are the saints, and they play an indispensable role in Ratzinger's ecclesiology, which is narrative, historically unfolding, and dialogical.[29] The saints are those who stand out as lights in darkness, who specially reflect the light of Christ. They let their relationships with Christ reflect through them and call those around them to greater faith, hope, and love. They are, indeed, at the center of the true identity of the church insofar as they constitute its "real majority."[30]

The Saints as the Normative Majority of the Church

The church, for Ratzinger, is not a group of activists who come together to "set parish life in motion." It is not comprised of those

27. Joseph Ratzinger, "Vicarious Representation," trans. Jared Wicks, SJ, in Scott Hahn, ed., *Letter & Spirit*, vol. 7, *The Bible and the Church Fathers: The Liturgical Context of Patristic Exegesis* (Steubenville, OH: Emmaus Road Publishing, 2011), 218.

28. Ratzinger, *Called to Communion*, 40.

29. Maximilian Heinrich Heim, *Joseph Ratzinger: Life in the Church and Living Theology: Fundamentals of Ecclesiology with Reference to* Lumen Gentium (San Francisco: Ignatius Press, 2007), 396.

30. Ibid. Cf. Benedict XVI and Peter Seewald, *Salt of the Earth: Christianity and the Catholic Church at the End of the Millennium* (San Francisco: Ignatius Press, 1997), 189.

who hold ecclesial offices. All these belong to the church, but the "radius of the 'company' into which we enter by faith reaches farther—beyond the limits of death. . . . The saints are the true normative majority by which we orient ourselves. Let us adhere to them... [for] they translate the divine into the human, eternity into time."[31] This ongoing translation of eternity into time is the echo in history of the Word made flesh. The saints are, to borrow from Bonaventure's theology of history, unique *"semina"* who have been shaped by and sprung from an intimate dialogical union with the one *Logos*. They in turn reflect the light and joy that comes from this union and not only provide encouragement and models for those in the church but serve as a light to those outside the church in the rest of the world.

By way of the saints, then, others are able to imitate and be drawn into the same friendship with Christ they came to enjoy, and thereby are able to be made into saints themselves. In a strikingly tender manner, speaking to a group of children from a school near his summer residence at Castel Gandolfo, Pope Benedict spelled out the possibility of this friendship with God that is fundamental to the identity of the saints. The process begins by listening to God's Word, that fundamental characteristic of the church as a whole:

> Dear children, you go to school and you learn of course, and I was thinking that it has been 77 years since I started to go to school. It was in a tiny village of 300 people . . . yet we learned the essentials. Above all we learned how to read and write and I think it is a great achievement to be able to read and write, for this is how we are able to know what other people think and read newspapers and books . . . . Above all, there is an extraordinary text: God has written a book, that is, he has spoken to us, human beings, and found people who wrote the book that contains the word of God. Thus, in reading it we can also read what God says to us and this is very important: to learn at school everything necessary for life and also learn to know God, to know Jesus and to know how to live well. At school you make many friends and this is beautiful; in this way a large family is formed. Yet, among our best

---

31. Ratzinger, *Called to Communion*, 154.

friends the first one of them, whom we know, must be Jesus,
who is the friend of all and truly set us on the path to life.[32]

This path to holiness that Ratzinger describes, which is accessible
even to the smallest of children (perhaps especially to them!) is characterized by a posture of humility and of receptivity toward God's
word. This must also be the starting point for even the most sophis-
ticated theologian. He describes as the precondition for all of theology,
in fact, the conversion of the theologian into a "new subject," the "I"
of which is no longer an "autonomous subject standing in itself" but
rather the "I" who "has released its grip on itself in order then to
receive itself anew and together with a greater 'I.'"[33] The saint, who
offers a model for this conversion, is important for the theologian but
more important for the whole church. For Ratzinger, to the degree
that the church's members are willing to begin with this posture of
humility and receptivity to the word of the "greater I" and not assert
the church's own agenda, it truly becomes itself.

Obedience to the Word

This understanding of the church as fulfilled in the act of humility
that allows the "I of Christ" to shape the true identity of the church
becomes controversial when it is seen in light of the question of authority, which, of course, causes so much tension in so many corners
of the church today. But the obedience to authority that is called for
in his *"communio"* vision of the church is never an absolutist and
authoritarian quality that is rightly feared. The basis for both authentic authority and truth itself is the same *Logos* expressed as love. This
is a far cry from the modern understanding of authority, separated
from truth and love and manifested only as power. Ratzinger recalls
as a counter-example of this vision Thomas Hobbes, who asserted,

32. "Address of His Holiness Benedict XVI to Students from the 'Paolo VI'
Pontifical Elementary School run by the Religious Teachers Filippini," Courtyard
of the Papal Summer Residence, Castel Gandolfo, Thursday, September 23, 2010,
accessed at: http://www.vatican.va/holy_father/benedict_xvi/speeches/2010
/september/documents/hf_ben-xvi_spe_20100923_maestre-pie-filippini_en.html.
33. Joseph Ratzinger, *The Nature and Mission of Theology: Essays to Orient
Theology in Today's Debates* (San Francisco: Ignatius Press, 1995), 51.

"auctoritas, non veritas fecit legem"—"power, not truth, makes law."[34] Authority looks very different in Ratzinger's ecclesiological vision characterized by obedience out of love. It is always to be seen in light of the very same dialogical relationship of faith and love that is at the core of God's revelation of himself to his beloved children. He explains: "authority in the Church stands on faith. The Church cannot conceive for herself how she wants to be ordered. She can only try ever more clearly to understand the inner call of faith and to live from faith."[35] The church's identity is *given* to it insofar as it allows itself to be shaped by this dialogue with God, which begins with God's initiative and can only be responded to in a spirit of humble obedience that comes from loving trust. The reception of authentic ecclesial identity is ultimately fostered in prayer. This posture of receptivity to the Word is at the heart of what has come to be known as *"communio* ecclesiology," one of whose most prominent advocates has been Joseph Ratzinger. It is to an uncovering of the basic contours of this ecclesiological methodology that we now turn.

III. Ratzinger's "Communio *Ecclesiology"*

Ratzinger describes in his own words the factors involved in the emergence of *"communio* ecclesiology" as a way of trying to interpret what the church taught at Vatican II. He writes, with the aid of hindsight, that "perhaps since the extraordinary synod of 1985, which was supposed to draw up a kind of balance sheet for the twenty years since the Council, there has been a new attempt to sum up the whole of the Council's ecclesiology in one basic concept, which dominates the discussion, under the term *communio*-ecclesiology."[36] He acknowledges that even though the term *"communio"* does not figure prominently in the texts of the council, it is useful nevertheless as a concept that synthesizes its ecclesiological vision. It is also descriptive of his own ecclesiological model, cultivated in his career before the council. Tracey Rowland argues that the whole of Ratzinger's ecclesiology must be seen as a "synthesis of a number of currents. There

---

34. Benedict XVI, *Joseph Ratzinger in Communio* (Grand Rapids: Eerdmans, 2010), 111–12.

35. Joseph Ratzinger, *Images of Hope: Meditations on Major Feasts* (San Francisco: Ignatius Press, 2006), 34.

36. Ratzinger, *Pilgrim Fellowship of Faith*, 129.

are strong resonances of Guardini, de Lubac and von Balthasar."[37] She traces these sources of an emerging "*communio* ecclesiology" in the early part of the twentieth century initially through the thought of Romano Guardini, who stressed the primacy of the experience of the church at worship, especially in the eucharistic liturgy, as the source of the church's life and identity. Henri de Lubac further explored this vision of the church as a *communio* of people "made" from the Eucharist and then identified according to a plurality of charisms within the one body of the church. Rowland also notes that Hans Urs von Balthasar, in his highly literary and narrative approach to theology, also did much in the wake of the council to give flesh to this vision of the church.[38]

The international journal *Communio* came to be a centerpiece and platform for a deepening of this mode of theological reflection with a conception of the church not merely as one more sociological entity with politics and power as its defining characteristics, but rather according to a liturgical and spiritual dynamic of many gifts building up one body (1 Cor 12:4-14). Joseph Ratzinger soon became a part of this theological movement, in part as a way of continuing the new theological developments from the council, and simultaneously realizing almost immediately that serious problems were emerging in the interpretation of those developments in the wider theological community.[39]

Ratzinger situated what he perceived as the problematic dimensions of ecclesiology as it was emerging after the council as a problem of how to interpret a term from *Lumen Gentium* that had become a kind of slogan, seen through the lens of contemporary politics and sociology. He writes:

Marxist view of church

> The crisis concerning the Church as it is reflected in the crisis concerning the concept "People of God" is a "crisis about God": it is the result of leaving out what is most essential. What then remains is merely a dispute about power. There is already

37. Tracey Rowland, *Ratzinger's Faith: The Theology of Pope Benedict XVI* (New York: Oxford University Press, 2008), 103.

38. Ibid., 84–85.

39. Joseph Ratzinger, "Communio: A Program," *Communio: International Catholic Review*, 19 (1992): 436–49.

enough of that elsewhere in the world—we do not need the Church for that."[40]

And so the primary task of ecclesiology is to recover and retain the theological dimension of its study and from within that horizon to see that its transcendent nature is not tantamount to oppression of "the people," but is a quest for the authentic set of relationships that alone can truly liberate the people as they find themselves belonging to and being loved by the God to whom they belong.

Another more recent challenge in ecclesiology is not so much the confusion of a Marxist hermeneutic for understanding the notion of the "people of God," but rather is characterized by the challenge of sensitivity to pluralism. This sense of the church as *communio* relies, in the various appropriations of the term, on the basic fact of the unity of the church. The church in this vision is essentially one, even though there are various manifestations of its essence both among those in communion with Rome and in other Christian communities outside that communion. Contrary to the understanding of the church as fundamentally pluralistic and only secondarily united within that plurality, Ratzinger argues for the "ontological priority" of the one universal church. He explains the biblical basis of this vision of the church's unity:

> The fact that the one Church is a theological entity, and not the subsequent empirical uniting of many churches, certainly emerges convincingly from the New Testament itself. . . . This theological priority is what is meant by the "ontological" priority, which the Fathers then portray—following analogous Jewish traditions—as a kind of pre-existence of the Church. . . . What is essential, however, is not the question of "preexistence" or temporal priority, which is an image, but the question of inner (=theological—"ontological") precedence.[41]

He explains that the evangelist Luke offers the vision that from the twelve apostles various churches emerge, but they come from the one church with theological or ontological priority. Following the narrative of the New Testament, "First the Church as a whole is there; and

40. Ratzinger, *Pilgrim Fellowship of Faith*, 129.
41. Ibid., 249.

then she forms individual Churches; and it is not the individual Churches that gradually come together into one Church."[42] Ratzinger's ecclesiological vision thus allows for diversity in the life of the church while retaining its basis in one of the four traditional marks of the church, namely, unity. Hence yet another of the challenges in current ecclesiology is addressed by this *"communio"* methodology based on the close following of the biblical narrative that establishes the fundamental characteristics of the church today.

As has been noted, in the effort to offer an alternative to the static and propositional definitions of the church Ratzinger consistently favors narrative and descriptive visions of the Christian mystery that unveil the essence of relationality at its center. He consciously uses the term *communio* to capture, though admittedly imperfectly, the various relations and dynamics that make up the church's essence. Recalling three of the four traditional "marks of the church," he notes specifically its historical groundedness in the *apostolic* tradition, the *holiness* of the praying church, and its *unity* throughout it all.[43] These essential marks are seen with special clarity by paying close attention to the dynamics of the liturgy. Ratzinger sees great significance in the fact that the concrete focus and starting point for deliberations at Vatican II was the liturgy (in *Sacrosanctum Concilium*) as the ongoing locus of the "making" of the church. Focus on the primacy of the liturgy as the source and summit of Christian life has also made possible a more dynamic sense of the church being lived out always anew. He explains the perhaps unintended grace given at the council as the fathers took up the renewal of the liturgy as the first order of business: "There were practical reasons for the fact that this was the first. Yet looking back, we have to say that this made good sense in terms of the structure of the Council as a whole: worship, adoration comes first."[44] Situating itself before God as a people made first and foremost for worship then sheds light on other aspects of the church's self-understanding that would be taken up later in *Dei Verbum, Lumen Gentium*, and finally in *Gaudium et Spes*. For Ratzinger this posture of the worshiping church as fundamental to its identity also provides a ground for the essentially relational and therefore unfolding nature

42. Ibid.
43. Ibid., 61.
44. Ibid., 126.

of the church's identity as captured particularly in *Lumen Gentium*'s use of the image of the church as pilgrim. Under this image, Ratzinger noted soon after the council, the church came to be understood as "incomplete and continually journeying with and toward God who constantly called out to it."[45] This multifaceted sense of the church, based always in the absolute center of the Christ event while also being led in ever new ways by the Holy Spirit, is concretized and made new in the celebration of the liturgy. Indeed, Ratzinger argues, following Guardini, it is precisely in the action of the liturgy that the church "subsists" and fulfills its true and deepest identity.[46] In the liturgy, the church realizes its true self.

Biblical Foundation and Liturgical Expression of *Communio*

Ratzinger's decision to settle on the term *communio* to best describe the character of the church is based most importantly on the scriptural witness. He sees both the liturgical and christological links to ecclesiology in the Acts of the Apostles as the foundational biblical source. He calls this book a kind of "first ecclesiology."[47] The character of this ecclesiology is narrative as opposed to conceptual.[48] Specifically, he relies on Acts 2:42, where we are given four essential aspects of the church's own self-understanding: "They devoted themselves to the teaching of the apostles and to the communal life, to the breaking of the bread and to the prayers." As these basic elements are echoed in the *Didachē* as well, it becomes clear for Ratzinger that Christ remains present in the church in the manner that Scripture and the earliest tradition indicate. The consequences for this today are significant in that these four pillars of ecclesial life mark, for Ratzinger, the essential form of the church from the beginning and therefore delimit the essential nature of the church in the present, even though in many ways there has been development and change in its expression of these essential aspects over time.

45. Ratzinger, *Theological Highlights*, 76.
46. Joseph Ratzinger, *God Is Near Us: The Eucharist, the Heart of Life* (San Francisco: Ignatius Press, 2003), 121–29.
47. Ratzinger, *Pilgrim Fellowship of Faith*, 61.
48. Ratzinger, *Called to Communion*, 41.

Relation of Christ and the Church:
Liturgical Confirmation of a Biblical Vision

Ratzinger's insistence on placing the biblical foundations of the church at the fore guarantees a christological basis for ecclesiology, which he believes is sorely needed in the current context. For Ratzinger this is perhaps *the* crucial challenge facing contemporary ecclesiology, namely, the propensity toward a separation from its true basis in Christology. The church can only be its true self insofar as it is the authentic place of encounter with the person of Christ. He writes: "In both her sacramental life and in her proclamation of the Word, the Church constitutes a distinctive subject whose memory preserves the seemingly past word and action of Jesus as a present reality."[49] But this is not easily recognized today. The modern separation of Jesus from the church, he explains, is in part a product of a Protestant exegetical tradition that shaped a biblical understanding of the church based on opposing the themes of *priest* and *prophet* in the Old and New Testaments. The bias behind this exegetical tradition has all too often set up Jesus as the modern liberal prophet rising up and freeing the people of God from the sterile and oppressive institution of cultic, priestly religion.[50] This divide intensified with later Marxist-inspired strands of liberation theology in which Jesus came to be seen as a "revolutionary" standing against the "enslaving power of institutions" of his day, which are in turn associated with the hierarchical nature of the church in modern times.[51]

However, more recent exegetical interpretations have recognized the character of the early church that had Jesus very much as the center of its cultic and liturgical worship. In light of this link between exegesis and the centrality of the liturgy as a source for understanding Christ and the church, Ratzinger acknowledges the important contributions made by Eastern theologians for preserving the focus on the liturgical character of the church in the modern era.[52] In arriving at this perspective on the relationship between Christ and the church within the biblical witness, he acknowledges the great influence of

---

49. Ibid., 19.

50. See his description in Ratzinger, *Introduction to Christianity*, 196–202, of the conception of Jesus coming from the height of liberal Protestantism in Adolf von Harnack.

51. Ratzinger, *Called to Communion*, 112.

52. Ibid., 15–17.

the work of various Orthodox theologians on the eve of the council in helping to shape his own understanding of the spiritual nature of the church that is grounded in the concrete liturgical context. The liturgy as the *locus theologicus* accounts for the various sets of relations that make up the church.[53] He notes the importance of the term *communio* and how it has taken on more significance in light of deficiencies in modern language that make it difficult to fully communicate "the linguistic and conceptual framework of the Bible and of the great tradition."[54] He argues that the term *communio* captures well the relationality of the members of the church among one another in the present as well as the past, the relationality with Christ himself, and the relationality of all those united to Christ both on earth and in heaven. Ratzinger's emphasis on the church's fundamental posture of receptivity of both identity and mission from the prior Word spoken by God in Christ stands in contrast to some other approaches that give priority to the "horizontal *communio*" attempted by the church's own initiative. Tracey Rowland writes: "Rather than analyzing the Church from the vantage point of corporate models he prefers the perspective of the *Communio* ecclesiology which acknowledges the existence of a unified symphonic network of different spiritual missions."[55] This symphonic network is ultimately grounded in the personal and spiritual encounter with God who speaks.

Though the central aspects of this "*communio* ecclesiology" are apparent in the Scriptures, it is really through the lived experience of the church at prayer, especially in the celebration of the Eucharist, in the entering into sacramental communion, that the depth of the meaning of *communio* becomes clear. Ratzinger sees as central to this sacramental reality of the Eucharist as the mutual communion that is a sharing out (*Teilgabe*) and a sharing in (*Teilhabe*) of the communion of the *Pascha* of Christ.[56] Christ offers himself to his people

---

53. Ratzinger, *Pilgrim Fellowship of Faith*, 131 n. 5, with reference to Nicolas Afanasieff, Alexander Schmemann, et al., *La Primauté de Pierre dans l'Église Orthodoxe* (Neuchâtel: Delachaux & Niestlé, 1960); Ludwig Maria von Hertling, "Communio und Primat—Kirche und Papsttum in der christlichen Antike," in idem, *Communio und Primat*, Miscellanea Historiae Pontificiae 7 (Rome: Herder, 1943); repr. *Una Sancta* 17 (1962): 91–125.

54. Ratzinger, *Pilgrim Fellowship of Faith*, 60 n. 1.

55. Rowland, *Ratzinger's Faith*, 89.

56. Ratzinger, *Pilgrim Fellowship of Faith*, 73.

in the liturgy so that they might be drawn into communion with him. And as the people go away from the liturgy, they in turn give themselves away to the world so that the world might be drawn into the same communion with Christ and his Body, the church.

It is this aspect of the *sharing in* and *sharing out* of communion with the Lord in the Eucharist that reshapes the notion of *communio* that existed in the Jewish and Greek ancient worlds before the events testified to in the New Testament. Ratzinger explains that the Greek term *koinōnia*, which becomes *communio* in Latin, is used in one way in the gospels to describe the identities of Peter, James, and John as fishermen.[57] They had a relationship of *koinōnia* restricted to the needs of their livelihood. In the Greek world the term seems to carry a more commercial or professional connotation. In the Jewish world, the Hebrew term associated with the Greek *koinōnia*, *chaburah*, describes a highly intimate relationship. Indeed, *chaburah*, in the Jewish mind, indicates a kind of relationship that is *too intimate* to signify the relationship between God and humanity. For this relationship *berith*, covenant, is used.[58] Only because of the experience of Jesus' disciples at the Last Supper and then their witness to his self-sacrificing love for them on the cross was the stage set for them to enter into the deepest sense of intimacy with him. In their encounter with the risen Jesus it began to become clear that their intimacy with him as friend and teacher was also intimacy with him as Lord, with God himself. Only then, as they began to celebrate the meal that commemorated this act of divine love poured out for them, did they experience an "opening up" of the Lord to them; only because of this experience can *koinōnia*, or *chaburah*, be applied to the human-divine relation. As they looked back on the identity of Christ through the lens of his resurrection it began to become clear to the followers of Jesus that in his person God himself was offering a new *communio*, a new intimacy with them simply by his presence among them, even before the events on Calvary. Ratzinger writes: "In the Incarnation of the eternal Word, there comes about that communion between God and the being of man, his creature, which had hitherto seemed impossible to reconcile with the transcendence of the one God."[59] This *koinōnia* that before could only correspond to human relations does

57. Ibid., 71.
58. Ibid., 74.
59. Ibid., 76.

indeed fortify those human relations now, on the "horizontal" plane, but it does so with much more depth, given the fact that this new *communio* between humans is grounded in the *communio* God has initiated with humanity, on the "vertical" plane, in the incarnation and paschal mystery of Christ.[60] And so for the church to be genuinely open to the source of its identity and self-understanding it must remain in that posture of receptivity to the Word of God. This priority of hearing the Word characterizes the core of Ratzinger's own ecclesiology, which establishes the *communio* itself.

IV. The Priority of Revelation for the Church

In the second chapter I described the course of the conciliar deliberations that produced *Dei Verbum*. Ratzinger recalls that because of the stalemate in the debate on the "material completeness" of divine revelation there, some wanted to give up on a separate document on revelation and simply fold those aspects into the document on the church. Pope Paul VI rejected this possibility, insisting on the Constitution on Divine Revelation and preserving it as a way of emphasizing the priority of revelation for the reality of the church. As Ratzinger puts it, it was necessary to embrace this new understanding of the church as primarily the body that "listens" to the word of God. In this listening, he wrote, the church fulfills its true nature and becomes able to transcend itself by entering into communion with the Word, precisely based upon its prior posture of receptivity to the Word. In this way, Ratzinger asserts, the church fulfills its identity as the *Sponsa Verbi*, and as this spouse of the Word of God it becomes able to bear the Word made flesh in an ongoing way into the world in which it lives.[61] This "new" ecclesiological model grounded in the priority of revelation of God's word, articulated in *Dei Verbum*, would be foundational not only for the church's self-understanding in *Lumen Gentium* but also for how it would conceive of its mission in the world beyond itself, as *Gaudium et Spes* indicates. Having received its identity by listening to the speech of God, the church fulfills its identity by extending that speech from God into the whole world. Fundamentally

[handwritten margin note: Church listens to the Word of God]

[handwritten margin note: Church extends God's speech in the world.]

---

60. Ibid., 72. Cf. Jérôme Hamer, *L'eglise est une communion* (Paris: Cerf, 1962), 176. ET: *The Church Is a Communion*, trans. Ronald Matthews (London: Geoffrey Chapman, 1964), 176.

61. Vorgrimler, *Commentary on the Documents of Vatican II*, vol. 3, 162.

at work in the church's self-understanding here, then, is the dialogical and communicative nature of listening and speaking, standing between God and the world as a dialogue partner for both. For Ratzinger, while the church is to be both a listener and a speaker of God's word, the priority is the mode of listening.

The Listening Church

In the preface to *The Essential Pope Benedict XVI: His Central Writings and Speeches*, the editors note that in the homily preached by Cardinal Ratzinger on the eve of his own election as successor of Peter he struck two main notes: obedience and fruitfulness.[62] Obedience to the truth, to the word of God, begets fruitfulness. Indeed, this is not only an admonition for the faithful but characterizes the very identity of Christ himself, who is the one who is obedient to the Father and thereby the one who bears much fruit. Only because this is the identity of Christ does it follow that this is also who the church is to be: the community of followers, gathered around the Word, trying to live in obedience and thereby becoming the community that bears much fruit in the world. To the degree that the church is able to remain open and obedient it becomes what it is meant to be. For Ratzinger to sound that note in such a historically pivotal moment for the life of the church indeed sheds light on his ecclesiological perspective.

To highlight this characteristic of the listening church, Ratzinger again relies on the narrative in the Acts of the Apostles that describes the earliest days of the church, as the disciples gather to listen to the word of God together and do so in union with those apostles who had been closest to the person of Jesus. The "People of God," as *Lumen Gentium* would come to describe the church, is rightly understood, then, in Ratzinger's view, as "the people" not by their own choosing to come together but rather based on their dialogical relationship with Jesus Christ. In the New Testament this gathering is called the *ekklēsia*. As is customary for Ratzinger's theological method, he pauses to explore the historical and cultural development of the meaning of key terms in this regard. In the Greek world, *ekklēsia* most

---

62. Benedict XVI, *The Essential Pope Benedict XVI: His Central Writings and Speeches*, ed. John F. Thornton and Susan B. Varenne (New York: Harper, 2007), xiii.

often referred to gatherings of men for the sake of civil and political deliberations.[63] The development of its meaning in the Christian community becomes clear only when one looks deeper into the tradition and examines a similar term from their own religious tradition. The Hebrew word *qahal*, with which the earliest Jewish Christians would have been familiar, was a gathering of *all* the people, women and children included, and not just the men who have social and political authority as was the case in the Greek sense of the *ekklēsia*. When the people gather in this way, primarily to listen to God's word, their identity is given to them; they "become a people." The roots of this experience of being formed as a people are in the fundamental experience of the people of Israel who gather at Mount Sinai to listen to and receive the word of God as handed down to them through Moses.[64] It was Moses who had himself spoken with God as one would with a friend (Exod 33:11). By way of this intimate encounter with one man the whole of the people are gradually drawn into this unique and personal relationship with God. This intimate dialogue with God is fulfilled for the Christian community in gathering around the figure of Christ, along with all the others who come to seek the same kind of dialogical encounter with him. In order to demonstrate this authentic ecclesiological pattern, Ratzinger often presents Mary as a kind of icon for this vision of the church, the one subject in history who said "yes" to the Word and in so doing allowed the Word to become flesh within it.

Marian Pattern of Listening to the Word in the Church

In a recent pastoral admonition Pope Benedict challenged his audience to work on establishing an element of quiet in their lives so that they might be able to hear the word of God that is the source of life for them: "[It] is important for us today . . . to know how to make silence within us to listen to God's voice, to seek, as it were, a 'parlour' in which God speaks with us . . . ."[65] The example *par excellence* for this mode of listening in quiet is the figure of Mary, mother of God.

---

63. Ratzinger, *Called to Communion*, 30.

64. Ibid., 31.

65. Benedict XVI, General Audience, Paul VI Audience Hall, September 9, 2009, accessed at: http://www.vatican.va/holy_father/benedict_xvi/audiences/2009/documents/hf_ben-xvi_aud_20090909_en.html.

Ratzinger sets out as a model for the whole church the one who heard and received the Word most radically in her own life and in the flesh. In contemplating the figure of Mary the whole church learns its own deepest identity. He explains:

> . . . Mary was, so to speak, "at home" with God's word, she lived on God's word, she was penetrated by God's word. To the extent that she spoke with God's words, she thought with God's words, her thoughts were God's thoughts, her words, God's words. She was penetrated by divine light and this is why she was so resplendent, so good, so radiant with love and goodness.[66]

This Marian pattern of receptivity of the word that makes possible the Word taking flesh is to be the pattern for the whole church.

For Ratzinger the focus on Mary makes clearer the link between the patterns of Christology and those of ecclesiology. It is for this reason that Mariology is crucial for the whole of theology.[67] The nature of the church cannot be understood apart from the source of the church and what precedes it, namely the figure of Jesus Christ, the Word made flesh. Because of Mary's "yes," the union of God and humanity can take place. In Mary's *fiat* we see a kind of *consummation* of the dialogical relationship between God and humanity that had been unfolding since the beginning of human history. Later in his career, following Hans Urs von Balthasar, Ratzinger explores more explicitly this "nuptial" character not only of Christology but of ecclesiology as well, enriched by the contemplation of Mary as the *Sponsa Verbi*. The nuptial union, which can be understood as the culmination of the dialogical nature of the church, is established again and again in the eucharistic celebration wherein the flesh of the bridegroom is offered to his spouse. Christ goes "beyond himself" to offer himself to the spouse, the church, and the spouse in turn goes beyond self in opening up to receive the Word made flesh in the context of

66. Benedict XVI, Parish Church, Castel Gandolfo, August 15, 2005, accessed at: http://www.vatican.va/holy_father/benedict_xvi/homilies/2005/documents/hf_ben-xvi_hom_20050815_assunzione-maria_en.html.

67. Heim, *Joseph Ratzinger*, 412–13. Cf. Joseph Ratzinger, *Daughter Zion: Meditations on the Church's Marian Belief* (San Francisco: Ignatius Press, 1983), 31–36.

eucharistic communion. This characteristic of "going beyond oneself," for Ratzinger, is what marks the "nuptial" nature of this union.[68] As the church responds in kind to the gift of Christ's whole self, it becomes its true self, and only in this nuptial union with the Lord. We see, then, in this model of intimate dialogue between Christ and the church the intrinsic link between Christology and ecclesiology. Just as there is no authentic way of being the church without a posture of gathering to listen to and encounter the word and the person of Christ, so too it is necessary in coming to genuinely know Christ to do so always in the context of ecclesial communion.

Ecclesial Knowing of Christ

In the third chapter I indicated how the ecclesial manner of coming to know the person of Jesus Christ is central to Ratzinger's Christology. This ecclesial manner is most importantly characterized as communal and historical. God speaks to his people, Ratzinger argues, only through those who have *already* listened.[69] The eternal Word is made known in the flesh in history, precisely in the context of the living tradition of God's chosen people Israel. In the course of the unfolding of the history of the Christian community, Christ can only be truly known not as an object of the past studied scientifically and from a distance but as a living subject knowable in the *present* in the context of the *ekklēsia*. The "I" of the church finds its unity and the possibility of knowing Christ in a coherent way not by the consensus it is able to arrive at by its own analytical efforts but ultimately as a gift given to the church at Pentecost by the power of the Holy Spirit. Only by the gift of the Spirit can Christ be known. As St. Paul reminds the church, only by the power of the Holy Spirit can one confess that Jesus Christ is Lord (1 Cor 12:3).

In the contemporary intellectual landscape, Ratzinger writes, this ecclesial hermeneutic takes on a new viability. He explains that the importance of the concept of the "I" has changed; "it is becoming evident that the 'I' locked securely in itself [as posited by Descartes] does not exist." Rather, "the 'I' is constituted in relation to the 'thou' and

---

68. Fergus Kerr, *Twentieth-Century Catholic Theologians: From Neoscholasticism to Nuptial Mysticism* (Malden, MA: Blackwell, 2007), 181–202.

69. Benedict XVI, *The Yes of Jesus Christ: Exercises in Faith, Hope and Love* (New York: Crossroad, 2005), 27.

. . . the two mutually interpenetrate."[70] There is no "I of the church" without the divine "Thou." Furthermore, the church is, by definition, a collection of subjects who make up the "people of God" and who are given their corporate identity by being in dialogue with the living God. The church becomes a communal "I," a subject, only when there is a common willingness to listen to the word spoken by the divine Thou. This aspect of the gathering of the people *in order to listen* is crucial to the Christian appropriation of the notion of the church. Indeed, "the people" is formed and given its true identity in the unfolding of the dynamic of listening that then leads to response (*Antwort*) to the word (*Wort*) fully spoken in history in the person of Christ.[71]

In following the Word of God in their own communal lives, the people of God become who they truly are. This is so for the people of Israel especially as they gather to receive the Law at the foot of Sinai. In the Christian context, however, a new depth is revealed in the nature of this formation of identity as the *ecclesia* gathers for worship. It is not only a listening and responding to the word that happens in the liturgy. In addition to this listening, the Christian *ecclesia* receives the Word made flesh *sacramentally*. This is the culmination of the gathering of the people. In this verbal *listening* and sacramental *reception*, the dialogue between God and his people is given concrete reality every time the community gathers to participate in the eucharistic sacrifice of the eternal Word made flesh in history. Ratzinger draws on Augustine in asserting that the people of God are given their identity in the liturgy since they are not only established as a communion among themselves but are made into what they eat.[72] As the church deepens its identity as the Body of Christ it becomes who it truly is by being drawn into communion not only with its members on a horizontal plane but into the vertical set of relationships that is rooted in God's very self, the three persons of the Trinity.

V. Church Realized in Trinitarian Communion

The church's participation in Trinitarian communion, for Ratzinger, is a matter not simply of communication between human and divine parties but of the very formation of the identity of the church

---

70. Ratzinger, *Called to Communion*, 35–36.
71. Ratzinger, *The Nature and Mission of Theology*, 26.
72. Ratzinger, *God Is Near Us*, 78. Cf. Augustine, *Confessions* 7, 10.16.

by this experience of communion with Father, Son, and Holy Spirit. As the Old Testament description of the *qahal* of the people of God gathered to listen and be shaped by the encounter with the living God is transposed to the New Testament setting, the nature of the encounter becomes more multifaceted, given that in Christ the God encountered is the one who speaks from an eternal set of relationships that is the triune God. Jesus Christ, as the *Logos* of God, Ratzinger writes, reveals "God who is not only logos but *dia-logos*."[73] This God "who conducts a dialogue" is *essentially* relational, not only *ad extra* toward creation but also *ad intra* in God's eternal Trinitarian relations. That relationality extends to God's own creation and in Jesus we see the culmination and perfection of that dialogue with the apex of creation, the human person. In order for humanity to be drawn into this divine communication, however, a dramatic opening is required. This opening is offered on the cross as the Word spoken in the silence of death, as Love. Jesus finally reveals himself as Love itself, in the form of the beloved and freely obedient Son of the eternal Father offering his life for the salvation of humanity. Ratzinger stresses that we can interpret the *event* of the cross as an act of love primarily based on the *words* of Jesus the night before at the Last Supper. By his freely and consciously speaking of his understanding and willingness to offer himself "for you," the intentionality of what would come about on the cross the next day is made clear. He explains that Jesus' "Eucharistic words" and the free intention behind them are what "transforms death into the spiritual act of affirmation, into the act of self-sharing love."[74] In this sense Jesus fulfills his mission from the Father and for the world on the cross. It is this "word" of silent love spoken from the cross, manifested in his pierced side, that brings to fulfillment the dialogue between God and humanity: the encounter of the "yes" of God's love for humanity and humanity's response of love back to God.[75] For Ratzinger it is only in this final, fullest word of love "spoken" from the cross that the church begins to see who it is in relation to: that this is God who has come from a set of triune relations into the flesh and has spoken to it precisely in this mode. The "people of God," then, starts to become a people with a new identity, born from this

73. Ratzinger, *Introduction to Christianity*, 183.
74. Ratzinger, *God Is Near Us*, 29.
75. Ibid., 27–41.

experience of looking upon "him whom they have pierced" (John 19:37; cf. Zech 12:10) who has accepted this piercing in love.

"Behold Him Whom They Have Pierced"

For Ratzinger the recurring biblical vision given in the passages in which we "behold him whom they have pierced," serves as a key christological source for ecclesiology. This is perhaps the central biblical moment for Ratzinger that provides the link between Christology and ecclesiology. John's exposition of the piercing of the side of Christ on the cross and the subsequent flow of blood and water has long been a sign of the origins of the sacramental life of the church, beginning with baptism and culminating in the Eucharist. Henri de Lubac, for example, in the effort to retrieve the biblical and patristic framework for understanding the church as the Body of Christ, highlights the importance of the image of the pierced side of Christ as the source of the life of the church.[76] Furthermore, for Ratzinger, not only is the church born from the pierced side of Christ but a new creation is begun. From the side of "the new Adam" a new bride is created in the church, which draws its life from the wellspring of his heart, the heart of God that loves in the flesh, all the way to death.[77]

The body-imagery of the biblical narrative of course has spiritual ramifications for Ratzinger. He notes that though the piercing of the heart of Christ on the cross occurs in the realm of the *sōma*, coming to know Christ by way of this piercing is a matter of the *pneuma*. Here the intrinsic link between Christology and pneumatology and how both are the sources of an authentic ecclesiology is made evident. Christ's *sōma* exists in the church as *pneuma*.[78] Those in the church who encounter the *Logos* revealed as love are in turn drawn by the Spirit into that same dynamic of love themselves and so reflect that love in history. Ratzinger writes that the "I" of Jesus is not an independent "I" but one very much dependent on his identity as Son of the Father. This identity of Jesus, he explains, "is identity of *logos* (truth) and love and thus makes love into the *logos*, the truth of human existence. The essence of the faith demanded by a Christology so

---

76. Henri de Lubac, *Catholicism: Christ and the Common Destiny of Man* (San Francisco: Ignatius Press, 1988), 69.

77. Ratzinger, *Behold the Pierced One*, 47–69.

78. Heim, *Joseph Ratzinger*, 241.

understood is consequently entry into the universal openness of un-conditional love. For to believe in a Christ so understood means sim-ply to make love the content of faith. . . ."[79] The church's mission to the world according to this faith, the content of which is love, is the aspect of Ratzinger's ecclesiology to which we now turn.

VI. Mission: Speaking the Word to the World

As I have argued, all of Ratzinger's theology is characterized by a dynamic of unfolding within a framework of dialogue. This is per-haps clearest in his ecclesiology. If the first major characteristic of his *"communio* ecclesiology" is the movement of receptivity of the word of God, the second movement is the outward one to communi-cate the word to the world. Receptivity begets mission. As was noted earlier, Ratzinger sees this Word as ultimately experienced as love itself. The *Logos* of God is ultimately communicated, in the Christian narrative, as *caritas,* most poignantly from the pierced heart of Christ on the cross. This *caritas* is the substance, the content, of the word spoken by God. It is also the force by which the church becomes itself and undertakes its mission in the world. The word it receives is love and the word it speaks in the world is love. Ratzinger recalls a New Testament expression of this link between the love that initiates the church into Trinitarian communion and also directs its identity and mission: "For Christians . . . the words of St Paul are valid: 'The love of Christ impels us' (II Cor. 5: 14). The charity that moved the Father to send his Son into the world, and moved the Son to offer himself for us even to death on the Cross, that same charity has been poured out by the Holy Spirit in the hearts of believers."[80] The Word com-municated through Christ as love has power to "impel" the church into the world, according to Ratzinger's ecclesiological schema.

As those drawn into union with Christ find their most fundamental identity as beloved children of God the Father,[81] a transformation occurs within the heart of the believer that sparks an outward looking

79. Ratzinger, *Introduction to Christianity,* 208.

80. Benedict XVI, Angelus Address, World Mission Day, October 22, 2006, accessed at: http://www.vatican.va/holy_father/benedict_xvi/angelus/2006/documents/hf_ben-xvi_ang_20061022_en.html.

81. Benedict XVI, *Jesus of Nazareth: From the Baptism in the Jordan to the Transfiguration* (San Francisco: Ignatius Press, 2008), 132–33.

to the world in love. The fruit of this transformation leads the Christian to further enact his or her identity in Christ as not only "from the Father" but also "for the world." This twofold identity, at once vertical and horizontal, is the foundation for the characteristic of the church as always essentially missionary.[82] As the foundational identity of Christ is that of the eternal Son of the Father, and as his identity is lived only in dialogue with the Father, his identity as the incarnate Son is worked out not only in dialogue with the Father but also in dialogue with the whole of humanity with whom he has been united in his incarnation.[83] His *identity* as Son, then, seamlessly expresses itself in his *mission* to the world.

The mission of the church, however, is to witness to this love in the world to those beyond the "borders" of the church and to draw all people into the love of Trinitarian communion. Just as Israel was light to the nations, Christ, the *Lumen Gentium* himself, through his body the church, reflects that light so that all might be drawn into Trinitarian participation.[84] The church fails in living up to its true identity, Ratzinger writes, when it spends too much time focused on itself. The church is most fully who it is when communicating the Father's love to the world and, through Christ, communicating the wounded world back to the Father. Being a place where this communication, this dialogue can happen is the real aim of the church and when it fulfills that aim it offers an irreplaceable service to the world. Ratzinger notes that when the church fulfills this identity it offers the ultimate liberation, which is not material but rather an "eternal horizon."[85]

The Church's Offering to the World

Ratzinger believes that only when Christian identity is established by entering into the subjectivity of the person of Christ in the context of the ecclesial community is one ready to look outward to the needs of the world. In his first substantial essay published after his doctoral work he explored the theme of Christian solidarity with the world in

---

82. *Lumen Gentium* 8.
83. Joseph Ratzinger, *The Meaning of Christian Brotherhood* (San Francisco: Ignatius Press, 1993), 75–84.
84. Ratzinger, *Called to Communion*, 126.
85. Ibid., 145.

The Meaning of Christian Brotherhood.[86] He follows here a theological method similar to the one used in other aspects of his theology when he traces the development of the meaning of terms from different languages and cultures of the ancient world and then examines how they come to a new fullness of meaning and depth in the light of the Christ event. In this case he examines the notion of brotherhood as it develops in the Jewish tradition as well as in the context of Greek culture and philosophy.[87] He notes that in the Enlightenment the notion of *fraternité* became a basis for a new rationalist society of *egalité* and *liberté* as well. But in the Christian vision, because of the solidarity with humanity effected by divine initiative of the incarnation of the eternal Word, a new brotherhood among the human community becomes possible. This is based not on human efforts but comes about because we are baptized (plunged) into it by the Father's choice to adopt humanity into the relationship of beloved daughters and sons by way of union with his eternal Son. From this filial relationship established in baptism there emerges a special solidarity of the one baptized not only with Christ but with all of humanity. This is a solidarity based on christological identity. The social consequences of this spiritual and theological reality of Christian incorporation into the family of God are profound, in Ratzinger's view.[88]

Ratzinger's theology of christological solidarity has since become a part of the deposit of the whole church's faith, enshrined in the teaching of Benedict's first explicitly "social encyclical," *Caritas in Veritate.*[89] Here he acknowledges that while it is possible to arrive at a recognition of the equality of all people by reason alone, it is only by way of the revelation of God, by being united in Christ, that the possibility of *fraternity* among people can be established.[90] This deeper bond of love is not something that can be generated by human effort alone, but rather is a gift to be received.[91] The gift is given by God the Father, who sent his eternal Son into our midst to draw us

86. Ratzinger, *The Meaning of Christian Brotherhood*, 93.

87. Ibid., 5–19.

88. Ibid., 21–37.

89. Benedict XVI, encyclical letter *Charity in Truth: Caritas in Veritate* (Washington, DC: United States Conference of Catholic Bishops, 2009), 93.

90. Ibid., 19. Cf. Paul VI, encyclical letter On the Development of Peoples (*Populorum Progressio*), 1967, 21.

91. Ibid., 34.

into intimate union with him and so make possible the raising of our identity and dignity from creatures of God to adopted, beloved daughters and sons of God. This deeper bond of unity is known in the Christian tradition as *caritas*.

From a secular perspective the notion of *charity* in modern times has taken on a negative connotation because, seen solely from within the horizontal social plane, it indicates an inequality and a condescension and demeaning of those who are below by those who are above.[92] The *act* of charity is furthermore undertaken on the terms of those who "have" toward those who "have not" and no real reciprocity or equality of dignity is recognized within that economy of exchange. But for Benedict the Christian dynamic is very different in that all charity begins with God, who is love and who chooses solidarity with all humanity living in poverty of love. Once the faithful have received that love of God in their own lives they necessarily are moved into the world to live according to the same pattern. It is for this reason that Benedict says: "For the Church, charity is not a kind of welfare activity . . . but is a part of her nature, an indispensable expression of her very being."[93] This expression is concretized in direct contact with the materially poor, but it flows from the deeper spiritual reality of the universal spiritual poverty from which God comes to liberate humanity. For Ratzinger, the beginning of that liberation occurs in the experience of meeting the risen Christ in the liturgy.

VII. Word Encountered in Liturgy: Dialogue Made Flesh

Always seeking to personalize and provide a narrative way to explain these mysteries in the Christian life, Pope Benedict recently situated the meaning of the liturgical encounter within the scriptural narrative as well as the story of his own life, with the hope that his audience could make the same connection in their own lives. In his anticipatory address to young people planning on attending the World Youth Day in Madrid in August 2011, after explaining his own path from his youth seeking to live a life full of freedom and meaning and how this path led to the priesthood and ultimately to his service as a bishop and the vicar of Christ, he explains why portraying the sub-

---

92. Christopher Rowland, *The Cambridge Companion to Liberation Theology* (New York: Cambridge University Press, 1999), 260.

93. Benedict XVI, encyclical letter *Deus Caritas Est* 35.

stance of the encounter with Jesus in an ever new way is so essential. Recalling Thomas's disappointment at initially not being able to see the risen Lord in his first appearance to the other disciples, he relates the disciple's experience to those of his audience:

> We too want to be able to see Jesus, to speak with him and to feel his presence even more powerfully. . . . Jesus himself, when he appeared again to his disciples a week later, said to Thomas: "Put your finger here and see my hands. Reach out your hand and put it in my side. Do not doubt but believe" (Jn 20:27). We too can have tangible contact with Jesus and put our hand, so to speak, upon the signs of his Passion, the signs of his love. It is in the sacraments that he draws particularly near to us and gives himself to us.[94]

These few words provide a succinct outline of the essential elements of Ratzinger's method of intertwining Christology, ecclesiology, and the essence of liturgy. The starting point of this Christology, of course, is the scriptural witness to the person of Jesus of Nazareth. From there he links the contemporary "hearers of the word" to the same narrative initiated in Scripture, allowing those in the present to identify with the character seeking Jesus in the past, in this case Thomas. With the aid of the model of Thomas, Benedict acknowledges the obstacles to genuine encounter with Christ in contemporary culture shaped by alternative concerns and perspectives. He then allows his own searching to become a part of this one unfolding narrative, seeking solidarity with his audience around the person of Jesus and pointing the way to the ecclesial, liturgical, and sacramental locus for the fulfillment of this "search." This seeking is not fulfilled until it generates a response in the seeker to then move out into the world in a missionary mode to help others be drawn into the one unfolding narrative that makes possible encounter with the eternal Word spoken in history, in the flesh, in love.

It is in the context of the liturgy that the whole of Joseph Ratzinger's theology comes to life. It is where the whole of theology is consummated and from which it draws its vitality. The liturgical law

---

94. Benedict XVI, Message of his Holiness for the Twenty-Sixth World Youth Day (2011), August 6, 2010, accessed at: http://www.vatican.va/holy_father/benedict_xvi /messages/youth/documents/hf_ben-xvi_mes_20100806_youth_en.html.

of the church acknowledges, too, that the liturgy as a whole is fundamentally marked by a dialogical character: "In a celebration in common or in individual recitation [of the Divine Office] the essential
structure of this liturgy remains the same, that is, it is a conversation
between God and man."[95] When he notes that all Christian revelation
is essentially dialogue,[96] we see how it is in the setting of liturgical
worship that this dialogue takes place most concretely. The word
unfolds to become flesh as the Liturgy of the Word gives way to the
Liturgy of the Eucharist. The liturgy itself follows the framework of
revelation as *logos* is made *sarx*, and in the reception of the *logos*-
made-*sarx* the recipient of this gift is drawn into true worship in spirit
and truth (John 4:23), back into the realm of *logos*. In this dynamic
there is an *exitus-reditus* pattern at work in every particular celebration of the liturgy. As he writes in his book on the liturgy, the title of
which he borrows from Romano Guardini,[97] Ratzinger notes that the
re-velation, the unveiling that takes place in the liturgy is none other
than the one that occurred on the cross, and yet it is recapitulated
daily on altars around the world as Christ comes to his people as he
did in the upper room on Holy Thursday and Calvary on Good Friday.[98]
The definitive unveiling of God's love for humanity marks the turning
point of the human response of love and therefore the return to God.

Ratzinger notes that in every eucharistic celebration the entire
mystery of the life of Christ is reflected. There is a "coming" in the
offertory that is reflective of Advent. At the institution narrative, the
sacrifice of Christ on the cross is recalled and made present again.
Finally, there is an Easter moment of encountering and being united
to the risen Lord in Holy Communion. All the mysteries of the life of
Christ are present and accessible to the faithful in the unfolding of
every eucharistic liturgy.[99] But even before this, what makes it possible for the Christian to enter into this narrative of the life of Christ
is being united to him in baptism. Before looking at the eucharistic

---

95. *General Instruction on the Liturgy of the Hours* (Washington, DC: U.S.
Catholic Conference, 1983), 40.

96. Vorgrimler, *Commentary on the Documents of Vatican II*, 3: 171.

97. Romano Guardini, *The Spirit of the Liturgy* (London: Sheed & Ward,
1930), 148.

98. Joseph Ratzinger, *The Spirit of the Liturgy* (San Francisco: Ignatius Press,
2000), 44–50.

99. Ratzinger, *God Is Near Us*, 69.

liturgy as the source and summit of Christian life, as *Sacrosanctum Concilium* put it, it is essential to consider the role of baptism and its theological significance in order to see the shape of the faith into which one is introduced in this initiatory Christian experience.

In *Principles of Catholic Theology*, Ratzinger outlines the foundational characteristic of baptism and how it provides a pattern for the whole of Christian faith.[100] Acknowledging that in the attempt to emphasize the essential dimensions of the rite of baptism—the need for flowing water and the short formula of Trinitarian faith—what has sometimes occurred unintentionally in the theological expression of this mystery is a kind of abstraction of Christian faith. Since baptism is the entry into faith, he says, the personal and ecclesial nature of baptism and therefore of the Christian faith as a whole must be highlighted in a new way. Above all, the forgiveness of sins makes baptism, and therefore the faith as a whole, a deeply personal encounter with the Lord. Ratzinger notes that Luther perceived this problem of the separation of faith and baptism, and that is why he put so much stress on the personal nature of the forgiveness of sins in baptism. What Luther lacked, however, was the further insight regarding not only the personal but also the ecclesial nature of Christian faith as it is begun in the experience of baptism.[101] The intrinsic link between baptism and Eucharist helps to highlight the ecclesial nature of this unfolding encounter of the faithful with Christ.

Perhaps no other aspect of Ratzinger's theology of the liturgy (broadly conceived, including both baptism and Eucharist) is as important as the insistence on the priority of the *actio divina*. If in the whole of his theology the category of "dialogue" best describes how Ratzinger sees the Christian mystery, it is always a dialogue *initiated* by God. The people of God respond to this initiative. Indeed, not until the people of God respond, provide an *Antwort* to the *Wort Gottes*, do they manifest their true identity.[102] For Ratzinger the divine liberation of humanity begun in baptism is most fully realized in the dynamics of the eucharistic liturgy, wherein Christ, *caritas* itself, comes to the poor of the assembly, speaks to their hearts, and gives them his love, his own heart, sacramentally. What begins with a divine *speaking* to

---

100. Joseph Ratzinger, *Principles of Catholic Theology: Building Stones for a Fundamental Theology* (San Francisco: Ignatius Press, 1987), 27–55.

101. Ibid., 106–8.

102. Ratzinger, *The Nature and Mission of Theology*, 26.

humanity becomes a divine *giving of love*, of self, in the flesh. By way of divine action, then, the church itself becomes who it really is.

The receiving of the Word made flesh is ultimately concretized in the most dramatic way in the context of the liturgy.[103] In this encounter the church is *made*. This is the foundational element of Ratzinger's "*communio* ecclesiology," which he explains is "in its inmost nature a Eucharistic ecclesiology."[104] He describes how, in the encounter of the liturgy, the corporate personality of the church is fulfilled only as it goes beyond itself in the sacramental union with Christ. In this sense the celebration of the Eucharist expresses a nuptial union in which the "I" of the church truly becomes itself only when letting down the barriers of its former "I" and "losing" itself in the "Thou" of Christ, who fulfills his own identity by virtue of his perfect self-donation. Insofar as this losing of self occurs, the church ultimately gains its true self in this sacramental union, because it is in the liturgy that what has separated people from their God is now overcome and they can be reconciled.[105] It is for this reason that the *sacrifice* of Christ, not just the aspect of the *communal meal* of the Eucharist, takes priority for Ratzinger. The communal nature of the liturgy is established only because of the efficacy of the sacrifice that is re-presented on the altar. In the celebration of the Eucharist, Ratzinger writes, Christ "comes to us and begs, as it were, for reconciliation."[106] This is the word spoken by him from the cross: that he *thirsts* for a response from those to whom he is speaking with the word of his self-sacrifice. The same Christ continues to beg for a response, and as the people respond in the affirmative, in acceptance of this word, the Eucharist is given to those who have *let themselves be reconciled* by God.[107] They have let God take the initiative. Christ's passion and the continual celebration of that passion in the eucharistic liturgy, however, do not leave the assembly passive. Rather, in offering an *Antwort* to his *Wort* of suffering love the assembly is reconciled, enlivened, and fulfilled in its identity and given what is necessary to carry out the mission that comes with this identity.[108]

103. Ratzinger, *Called to Communion*, 27.
104. Ratzinger, *Pilgrim Fellowship of Faith*, 131.
105. Ratzinger, *Called to Communion*, 37.
106. Ratzinger, *God Is Near Us*, 40.
107. Ibid., 60.
108. Ibid., 50.

Conclusion: The Actualization of the Dialogue

For Ratzinger, the church's discovery of its true identity and mission in the course of the liturgy is a discovery of the transcendent nature of the human person. This discovery of identity happens in the liturgy because it is a moment of the earthly entry into heaven. Here the temporal is able to enter into the eternal because there has first been an entry into history from the place of eternity. In light of this understanding of the liturgy, it becomes clear that Ratzinger's theology of the liturgy is clearly linked to the concerns of eschatology.[109] What happens once in the once (*semel*) of history on Calvary is recapitulated in such a way that it participates in the always (*semper*) of eternity.[110] This is possible because the one eternal *Logos*, through whom all things are made, the one then encountered in Christ, is the same *Logos* met in the liturgy. This Word of love, then, when received by the assembly, gives confidence to the recipients in the power of love over even death itself. Ratzinger writes: "The event of the Supper consists in Jesus sharing his body and blood, i.e., his earthly existence; he gives and communicates himself. In other words, the event of the Supper is an anticipation of death, the transformation of death into an act of love."[111] It is for this reason that the cross stands at the center of what becomes finally a worship "in spirit and truth" in the liturgy. Ratzinger describes the sacrifice of Christ on the cross as true worship because it flows from a true knowing of who God is and who humanity is. On the cross, Jesus fulfills the authentically human posture of worship toward God the Father. Christians who participate in the sacrifice of praise, then, can themselves take part in true worship that is aimed at eternal life.[112] This true worship also allows the assembly to enter into the eschatological hope that Christ makes possible by his own salvific self-offering on the cross. Ratzinger notes that in the form of speech Christ himself begins to open up this eschatological hope for humanity. In the "eucharistic words" of Jesus at the Last Supper he explains his approach to death. Indeed, historically these words not only disposed him to approach his own death confident in hope, but sacramentally they also effect a bridging

---

109. Ratzinger, *Spirit of the Liturgy*, 60.
110. Ibid., 55–57.
111. Ratzinger, *Behold the Pierced One*, 25.
112. Ratzinger, *Introduction to Christianity*, 287.

of the chasm between life and death for those participating in the liturgy.[113] These eucharistic words of Jesus that both "make" the church and are also the words that confront death in hope play a key role in shaping the Christian eschatological vision as well as the ecclesiological one. And so, from the context of the experience of the liturgy we move our conversation from Ratzinger's understanding of the church to his vision of eschatology: how all of human history is fulfilled in light of the Word spoken across the chasm of the apparent silence of death.

---

113. Ratzinger, *God Is Near Us*, 29.

Chapter Five

Word Spoken from Beginning to End: Creation and Eschatology

"With the Incarnation of the Son of God, eternity entered time and human history was opened to absolute fulfillment in God. Time was, so to speak, 'touched' by Christ, the Son of God and of Mary, and received from him new and surprising significance: it became a time of salvation and grace."[1]

Thus far I have tried to make the case that in the theology of Joseph Ratzinger a dialogical structure is always operative, that is, no matter what the aspect of the one Christian mystery in question, the dynamic is always that of a dialogue between parties, of the eternal *Logos* speaking and being heard. Only from within the tension of this dialogue is the truth of the Christian mystery uncovered. This dialogical narrative has at its center a character named Jesus Christ. All of human history, indeed all of creation, centers on and finds its source and fulfillment in this figure who is the Word made flesh. In the last chapter we explored how it is that in Ratzinger's

---

1. Benedict XVI, Vespers Homily for the Solemnity of Mary Mother of God, Rome, December 31, 2009, accessed at: http://www.vatican.va/holy_father/benedict_xvi /homilies/2009/documents/hf_ben-xvi_hom_20091231_te-deum_en.html.

theology the nature of the church is both established and fulfilled in the communal encounter with the person of Jesus Christ. This is most concretely and poignantly accomplished when the whole of the *ekklēsia* comes together for the liturgy, to hear the word of God spoken in Scripture and given in the Eucharist. The church is made who it is meant to be in this liturgical encounter in which time is opened up into eternity, as every liturgy celebrated on earth shares in the heavenly liturgy.

The nature of this meeting place of history and eternity is the object of focus for this last chapter. We take up here the dialogical nature of Ratzinger's thought as it pertains to his understanding of creation and eschatology. How is it that the creative Word God speaks, by which "the heavens were made" (Ps 33:6) is the same Word that is spoken in the midst of the apparent breakdown of the harmony of creation within human history? How is it that this same Word is being spoken even across the apparently ultimate barrier of silence that is death: the end of creation and history, as it were? And how is it that the Word spoken in death is the basis of resurrection and eternal life? These questions are taken up again and again in Ratzinger's theology and preaching, but in this chapter I will focus especially on two works of his that most explicitly address these issues, namely *Eschatology: Death and Eternal Life*, originally published in German in 1977, and his second encyclical, *Spe Salvi*, on the nature of Christian hope, promulgated three decades later, in 2007. While I will draw on other works of his spanning his theological and pastoral career, these two in particular clearly reveal the dialogical nature of his theology of creation and eschatology.

Given the dialogical structure of creation and history, according to Ratzinger's theology, the human person is able to participate in the intelligibility of creation and enjoy *the* privileged place in the created order as those with whom God desires personal communication and relationship. As he put it in his welcoming address to the hundreds of thousands gathered at World Youth Day in Madrid in 2011, "God is looking for a responsible interlocutor, someone who can dialogue with him and love him."[2] The dialogue that "begins"

2. Benedict XVI, Welcome Ceremony with Young People, Plaza de Cibeles, Madrid, August 18, 2011, accessed at: http://www.vatican.va/holy_father/benedict_xvi/speeches/2011/august/documents/hf_ben-xvi_spe_20110818_32accoglienza-giovani2-madrid_en.html.

with creation, then, is extended throughout the whole of salvation history. Even when this dialogue seems to be silenced, it proceeds. Ratzinger explains that the Word continues to be spoken from God even in the context of human death. Jesus' own resurrection is the pivot upon which a theology of creation, seemingly undermined by the reality of death, continues to unfold into the sphere of eschatology. In order to clarify Ratzinger's contributions in these areas, however, we may first find it useful to surface his most significant interlocutors when it comes to his theology of creation and eschatology. And so we begin with a brief look at the context of the theological discourse from which his theology emerges.

I. Context of Ratzinger's Contributions

Culturally speaking, in the wake of the Second World War and later in the midst of the Cold War that presented the possibility of global nuclear annihilation, a sense of historical stability had been deeply undermined. At the same time, greater global recognition of the plight of the poor initiated a critique of the historical processes that had produced such injustice and inhumanity. For a variety of reasons, then, in the second half of the twentieth century there had emerged a cultural context that Ratzinger characterized as a "historical process in crisis."[3] Theologically speaking, the question of history had become pressing, in part, because of recent exegetical work that explored the nature of Jesus' eschatological preaching, causing these doctrinal matters once again to become the focus of interest among theologians. It is to these cultural and exegetical contexts, from which Ratzinger constructs his new dogmatics based on eschatology, that we now turn.

The Challenge of Political Theology

Ratzinger recognized the contemporary need to clarify the Catholic vision of eschatology against the backdrop of the emergence of the "political theology" pioneered by such theologians as Johann Baptist Metz and Jürgen Moltmann. Later this political theology would develop in the context of Latin American liberation theology

---

3. Joseph Ratzinger, *Eschatology: Death and Eternal Life* (Washington, DC: Catholic University of America Press, 1988), 1.

pioneered by Gustavo Gutiérrez and others. The foundations of "political theology" could be associated with a certain reduction of theology to ethics that emerged in the nineteenth century. In this regard the great figure of Protestant liberalism who looms so large, Adolf von Harnack, set aside the elements of the Christian religion relating to the supernatural realm that are purportedly hard to believe. He instead sought to constitute Christianity as it pertains to the realm of ethics, where all might see Jesus as their brother who lived a heroic life and consequently be motivated to live as one human family comprised of children of one Father in heaven.[4] The political theology of Metz is no doubt influenced by this tradition of identifying theological reality with ethics. At the core of this political theology is the recognition of the need for Catholic theology to speak to the concrete needs of the poor and oppressed in the present, in part by examining and critiquing the history that has systematically produced the conditions for this injustice.[5] Someone like Metz takes history very seriously in the sense that he desires a practical effect in the daily lives of humanity to be shaped by the message of Christ.[6] Ratzinger's critique of this movement in theology, however, points out that this way of taking "history" seriously because of political and social concerns runs the risk of simultaneously *devaluing* history itself in that it can be relegated to the past once the critique against it is leveled. Fergus Kerr recalls Ratzinger's critique of Metz's political theology. Citing a 1982 essay, Kerr recounts the heart of Ratzinger's critique of certain aspects of Metz's thought "in which the enthusiastic option for history represents, at the same time, an equally decisive rejection of the past, a suspension of all reference to tradition in favour of a programme of what is to be done."[7] This potential for antagonism toward history itself as a vehicle for structures of injustice is most potently articulated in the Marxist philosophy of history and concern for revolution for the sake of establishing social justice. Aidan Nichols

---

4. Adolf von Harnack, *What Is Christianity? Lectures Delivered in the University of Berlin during the Winter Term 1899–1900* (New York: G. P. Putnam's Sons, 1903).

5. Ratzinger, *Eschatology: Death and Eternal Life*, 58.

6. Johannes Baptist Metz and James Matthew Ashley, *Faith in History and Society: Toward a Practical Fundamental Theology* (New York: Crossroad, 2007).

7. Fergus Kerr, *Twentieth-Century Catholic Theologians: From Neoscholasticism to Nuptial Mysticism* (Malden, MA: Blackwell, 2007), 188.

argues that Ratzinger sees this "tributary" of Marxism in theological circles of the twentieth century as perhaps the most significant challenge to a proper theological perspective on human history and therefore an authentic vision of eschatology. In the Marxist vision, too, history is taken seriously in the first stages of critique, but history itself is soon relegated to the mere "past" and what becomes important is really only the future that holds the promise of coming revolutions instigated by human effort.[8] The use of history in much of political theology, then, is essential only to diagnose the problem of injustice and suffering and to insist on the improvement of conditions in the future. However, the role of God's ongoing relationship throughout the whole of history seems to recede in importance in comparison to human agency in addressing the problems of human suffering.

Ratzinger acknowledged the fundamental insight that a social and political critique of history was being offered by his twentieth-century peers. He, too, allowed himself to be challenged as a theologian by the reality of those who suffered in the present moment of history. He saw that the matter of Christian hope was perhaps the greatest of the challenges facing the contemporary church and its ability to carry out its mission to evangelize effectively. He wrote:

> The most telling objection against the Christian faith lies in its historical ineffectiveness. It has not changed the world; at least that is how it seems. All theoretical difficulties weigh almost nothing in the face of this oppressive experience. For with it the central word of Christianity, the message of salvation, remains empty. It remains just a word. If through the faith nothing happens, then everything that it might otherwise say is empty theory, lying beyond verification and falsification and—as such—of no consequence.[9]

In echoing the contemporary critique of Christian impotence with respect to history, Ratzinger describes the situation in logocentric terms. It is possible, he observes, that "the central word of Christianity

8. Aidan Nichols, *The Thought of Pope Benedict XVI: An Introduction to the Theology of Joseph Ratzinger* (New York: Burns & Oates, 2007), 111.

9. English in James Corkery, *Joseph Ratzinger's Theological Ideas: Wise Cautions and Legitimate Hopes* (New York: Paulist Press, 2009), 52. Cf. Joseph Ratzinger, "Vorfragen zu einer Theologie der Erlösung," 141–55 in Leo Scheffczyk, ed., *Erlösung und Emanzipation*, QD 61 (Freiburg: Herder, 1973), at 141.

. . . remains just a word." That is to say, it may be that Christianity itself is comprised of nothing but empty theory and ideals. He uses the phrase "just a word," then, to indicate "a word" that remains abstract, trapped in the realm of the speculative. But the nature of his response is to show how this central *word* of Christianity *takes flesh*—becomes concrete in history—and shapes the narrative of the whole of salvation history. Ratzinger's "theology of the Word" that is offered in revelation, fulfilled in Christology, and expressed in ecclesiology and especially liturgy, becomes indispensable now in addressing the contemporary cultural and theological concerns that demand a new eschatology.

De-Mythologized Exegesis

Another major development in twentieth-century theology also contributed, in Ratzinger's estimation, to the undermining of a true sense of the nature of human history in light of divine revelation. The trajectory of exegesis of eschatological texts in the New Testament stressed the importance of history on the one hand and then subsequently dismissed that importance, depending on the particular exegetical lens. This exegetical trajectory produced a school of interpretation not so much political in nature but more privatized and existential in its aim. At the center of this movement had been Rudolf Bultmann, whose "demythologizing" exegesis left the gospels largely devoid of historical foundation.[10] With little of the supernatural left after the demythologizing of the gospel accounts of Jesus' life, ministry, death, and resurrection, what remains is the content of his preaching. For this existentialist school the reader in every era is left with a choice that remains merely private: how to live one's life in imitation of the past historical figure of Jesus of Nazareth. What is therefore demanded is a construction of an existentialist reading of Scripture that would motivate the reader on interior levels, regardless of the truth of the exterior witness given in those same Scriptures. As Ratzinger explains in *Introduction to Christianity*, Bultmann is a key figure in the great question of modern theology: Jesus or Christ? He traces the broad outlines of the debate:

10. Rudolf Bultmann, *New Testament and Mythology and Other Basic Writings* (Philadelphia: Fortress Press, 1989), 168.

> Modern theology begins by turning away from Christ and tak-
> ing refuge in Jesus as a figure who is historically compre-
> hensible, only to make an about-turn at the climax of this
> movement—in Bultmann—and flee in the opposite direction
> back to Christ, a flight, however, that at the present moment
> is already starting to change back into the new flight from
> Christ to Jesus.[11]

In these fluctuations from Christ to Jesus and back again, what strikes Ratzinger as common is the emaciated sense of the nature of history. Either Jesus remains a historicized model who, while personally and existentially inspiring, is nevertheless locked away in the past, or he becomes a figure that floats atop the ocean of history as a kind of spiritualized ideal of faith, but who really has very little relevance to the whole of history itself.[12]

For Ratzinger, then, in every case in which modern eschatology has become problematic there is a problem with biblical exegesis. And the foundational problem with much of contemporary biblical exegesis is an emaciated understanding of the nature of human history. Ratzinger has attempted throughout his theological career to build a more robust understanding of the nature of human history, particularly as he took up questions of eschatology: death and eternal life. He would proceed with this endeavor by relying largely on the nature of the *Logos* that provides for both the transcendent origins and the inner coherence of the scriptural witness and all of human history. The intelligibility of human history as the place where the *Logos* can be heard and appropriated is in turn the basis of creation itself. This logocentric basis of creation deserves closer consideration.

II. Word Spoken in the Orders of Creation and History

Ratzinger begins a collection of reflections on the Catholic understanding of creation and the fall by reflecting on the text of Genesis 1. Taking for granted the beauty and grandeur of the poetry of the text, he immediately acknowledges the question the modern audience brings to it: Yes, this is a beautiful vision of created reality as given

---

11. Joseph Ratzinger, *Introduction to Christianity* (San Francisco: Ignatius Press, 2004), 198.

12. Ibid., 61–63.

by the free, generous, and creative love of God. *But is it true?*[13] After all, there is a common pattern in much of modern thought, even within Catholic theological circles, of quietly setting aside the possibility of the material creation of the universe by a personal God, given the challenges offered by evolutionary theory and a new epistemology fundamentally shaped by strict scientific criteria. This epistemology has also influenced method in theology in such a way that there is a tendency among some modern theologians to consider creation more in existential terms than ontological ones, since the facticity of "creation" as the Judeo-Christian tradition has understood it seems so fragile. Consequently, in Ratzinger's estimation, we run the risk of a "huge (if not total) loss of the reality of faith, whose God no longer has anything to do with matter."[14] He posits the task before him, then, as taking the creation narrative of Scripture, which so clearly has literary elements reflective of the stuff of myth, and reconceiving it in a way that provides a foundation for material realism in the Christian doctrine of creation.

In the Genesis creation narratives, God's Word is the cause of separation of light from darkness, water from land, etc. The same Word is also the efficacious source of the creation of vegetation, land animals, birds of the air, fish of the sea, and ultimately of humanity. God *said* "let there be" these elements of the created order, and they came to be. There is a fundamental reliance in Ratzinger's thinking on the motif of divine speech, which expresses the origins of creation within the scriptural witness. This is a theme that runs consistently through the Old Testament. We think of the book of Wisdom, for example, in which the author proclaims the Wisdom of God that is "mobile beyond all motion." (Wis 7:24). And the Psalmist proclaims in various ways the central vision of creation, namely that "by the Lord's word the heavens were made; by the breath of his mouth all their host" (Ps 33:6). This consistently personal way of conceiving of God's creative action emanating from God's very lips is taken up in the New Testament as well, most foundationally in the Prologue of John's gospel. Here the evangelist re-reads the Old Testament creation and wisdom literature through the lens of the experience of the risen Christ who from "the beginning" is the Word made flesh (John 1:14),

---

13. Joseph Ratzinger, *In the Beginning: A Catholic Understanding of the Story of Creation and the Fall* (Grand Rapids: Eerdmans, 1995), 3.

14. Ibid., xii.

the very same Word who was "with God" "in the beginning" (John 1:1-2). These are the building blocks of Ratzinger's own theology of creation.[15]

In the Christian vision, then, we can know the truth of the world around us because the world was created through the *Logos*. This capacity to know is at the core of the human condition as rational beings. As St. Augustine put it, "Reason has deigned to reveal itself in the things that appear familiar to you."[16] The intelligibility of God and of all that God has created is not only a matter of autonomous intellects apprehending truth about the objects that surround them. Rather, the very possibility of obtaining knowledge is contingent on the free gift of communication given by the personal God who "deigns" to reveal what is true. The possibility of at least some positive intelligibility of God and God's creation and the personalism that underlies this intelligibility are, in Ratzinger's view, essential issues that need to be taken up in modern theology. Given the significant challenges to the doctrine of creation that have emerged in the era of great scientific advances that have so shaped epistemological standards, it becomes that much more necessary to re-present Christianity as able to account for an intelligible creation and an intelligible and loving God who is at the source of that creation.

The Link Between Creation and History

As I indicated in the chapter on Christology, a key component of Ratzinger's "unfolding" theology is the recognition of the *Logos* understood first of all as *ratio*, but ultimately more personally as love itself. The more personal the expression of *Logos* becomes in salvation history, the more possible it becomes to then look back on creation itself as a gift given by a personal and loving God. As he explains in *Introduction to Christianity*, in light of Christ it becomes clear that in the Christian vision all of creation, as "being-thought," is expressed freely and as personal love.[17] He later elaborates on the reasonability

15. Ibid., 15–18.
16. Richard Bosely and Martin Tweedale, eds., *Basic Issues in Medieval Philosophy* (Petersborough, ON: Broadview Press, 1997), 520. Cf. Augustine, *De Ordine* 2.2.30–31 (CCSL 29.124–25).
17. Ratzinger, *Introduction to Christianity*, 59.

of creation and how that reasonability culminates in a personal and relational structure. He explains:

> If Christian belief in God is first of all an option in favor of the primacy of the *logos*, faith in the pre-existing, world-supporting reality of the creative meaning, it is at the same time a belief in the personal nature of that meaning, the belief that the original thought whose being-thought is represented by the world is not an anonymous, neutral consciousness but rather, freedom, creative love, a person.[18]

Ratzinger argues that just as the ancient Greek world influenced by emerging philosophical schools reliant on reason was in the process of dismissing the worldview provided by the ancient myths centered on many capricious gods, the Abrahamic faith of the people of Israel made its way onto the world's stage and offered a kind of union in *one* deity who was personally engaged in human history while at the same time identified with reason, with what the Greeks called *logos*. The nature and depth of this union of *logos* and personal relationship in one God becomes evident in the Christian tradition only by following the narrative of the people of Israel and the Christians who follow them. By tracing the whole of the Judeo-Christian narrative of salvation offered in the Bible, one comes to this conclusion at the end and is able to see that operative throughout has been the *Logos* being spoken by God in every moment. The God of biblical history sheds light on the God of the philosophers and vice versa, such that "this God of the philosophers, whose pure eternity and unchangeability had excluded any relation with the changeable and transitory, now appeared with the eyes of faith as the god of men, who is not only thought of all thoughts, the eternal mathematics of the universe, but also *agape*, the power of creative love."[19] The thread that provides a coherent basis for this theology of God that embraces both the "God of the philosophers" and the "God of men" is the essentially log-ical and, even more accurately, dia-logical character of God.[20] While from one perspective this God of dialogue can be discerned both in creation and in salvation history, the power of God's Word being spoken throughout can also be

18. Ibid., 158.
19. Ibid., 143.
20. Ibid., 183.

called into question. The mystery of death is the ultimate stumbling block for this *Logos*-based vision of both creation and history, and it is important to see how Ratzinger deals with this challenge.

Death as the Silencing of *Logos*?

For Ratzinger it is clear that there are times in the life of the human person when the vision of a beautiful and intelligible creation can be seen, with the eyes of faith, through the lens of the God who has also shown himself as personal and present in history. But there are also plenty of moments when this vision simply does not ring true. Creation appears disordered and history absurd. The *Logos* seems to lose its operative power in moments of suffering and especially death, when creation is apparently defeated and history seems to cease. The consequence of the theology of creation Ratzinger establishes is put to the test when the focus of attention is shifted from the first principles of creation and the nature of being to the "last things" of eschatology.

Aidan Nichols describes Ratzinger's understanding of death as a rupture of communion, of relationship. Rather than being seen as a termination of being or cessation of existence, death is to be understood in dialogical and relational terms.[21] In Ratzinger's theology the problem of death and the possibility of eternal life that death seems to undermine is primarily a problem not simply of how to account for the restoration of *being*, but of how *communication* can be understood to continue even in the face of the radical silence death seems to impose. In an Angelus address at St. Peter's in Lent of 2011, for example, Benedict explains the phenomenon of death in these relational terms: "Indeed, death represents a wall as it were, which prevents us from seeing beyond it; yet our hearts reach out beyond this wall and even though we cannot understand what it conceals, we nevertheless think about it and imagine it . . . ."[22] The longing to "see beyond the wall" is certainly operative in the human heart, and yet that wall cannot be traversed from our side. In the same address he says it is Christ himself who "destroys the wall of death" so that the communion of God and humanity can come to fruition.

---

21. Nichols, *The Thought of Pope Benedict XVI*, 120–21.

22. Benedict XVI, Angelus Address, Rome, April 10, 2011, accessed at: http://www.vatican.va/holy_father/benedict_xvi/angelus/2011/documents/hf_ben-xvi_ang_20110410_en.html.

The Difference Christ Makes

To understand the nature of the communication that can still exist even in death, it is necessary to approach the question in light of what has already been said about the communicative dimension of the origin of human life. Eschatology, in this sense, is necessarily linked to and informed by the theology of creation. Since the Word is the grounding of all creation, precedes creation, and is therefore "beyond" creation, it is also the case that this Word is not silenced at the "end" of created life. The same Word can be spoken even across the chasm of death that appears to be the destruction of creation. The Word speaks into death and draws the dead out of their silence. This would not be the conclusion about the nature of death and eternal life, however, if it were not for the experience of the risen Christ. Ratzinger explains in his work of "spiritual Christology," *Behold the Pierced One*, "Death, which by its very nature is the end, the destruction of every communication, is changed by him into an act of self-communication . . . death, which puts an end to words and meaning, itself becomes a word, becomes the place where meaning communicates itself."[23] The Word spoken in perfect love from the cross is the Word that continues to be spoken even in the silence of death and is indeed the Word that overcomes death itself. For Ratzinger, this is the communication that is the basis of Christian hope. The christological lens is essential as he recalls St. Paul's proclamation that if Jesus is not truly risen, our hope is in vain (1 Cor 15:17).[24] Because of this foundational experience, the nature of who God is as speaker of the eternal Word is reconceived, as is the nature of humanity as hearers of the Word, even in the context of death. God does not remain relegated to the distance, utterly shrouded in incomprehensibility and definitive silence, and humanity is not trapped in the isolation and loneliness of deafness, but rather is able to "hear" even in death. For this reason death becomes the place of the most poignant communication between God and humanity, but only when it is seen through the historical experience of the resurrection of Christ. The experience of being united to Christ's own death and resurrection

---

23. Joseph Ratzinger, *Behold the Pierced One: An Approach to a Spiritual Christology* (San Francisco: Ignatius Press, 1986), 24.

24. Ratzinger, *Eschatology: Death and Eternal Life*, 116.

within the life of the church becomes the basis of each person's hope in the face of death.

In the encounter with death, seeing God simply as the source of *Logos* that gives reason and order to creation is no longer enough, since in death it appears that creation's reason and order comes to a definitive end. The human person has a limited view of the nature of God when God is considered only on the basis of the order of creation. A fuller picture is offered when God is approached under the rubric of the order of salvation history. Ratzinger writes: "God truly enters into human affairs only when, rather than being present merely in our thinking, he himself comes towards us and speaks to us."[25] Only in the fear and isolation that the prospect of death can bring is the fullness of the question of the human condition posed. Only in the face of death does the fullness of the meaning of the *Logos* of God become manifest. The Word spoken from the beginning, which is the basis of all material existence, becomes also the basis for the possibility of hope for the human person in the face of the apparent end of material existence. In the confrontation with the "supreme evil" that is death,[26] the human person is confronted with the ultimate question of the whole of his or her existence. What is the nature of death, and what is called into question about the whole of human existence as a result? For Ratzinger these fundamental human questions are best addressed not in the isolation of private, abstract speculation, but rather in the context of the narrative of salvation history. Such is the first principle of the eschatology he attempted to construct in the wake of the Second Vatican Council, which called for a renewed appropriation of the whole of the Christian mystery in light of both the signs of the times and the salvation history from which those times had emerged.

III. Word Spoken in Death: Basis of a Renewed Eschatology

When Ratzinger moved in 1969 to take up a teaching position at the recently established University of Regensburg he became

---

25. Benedict XVI, encyclical letter *On Christian Hope: Spe Salvi* (Washington, DC: United States Conference of Catholic Bishops, 2007), 23, accessed at: http://www.vatican.va/holy_father/benedict_xvi/encyclicals/documents/hf_ben-xvi_enc_20071130_spe-salvi_en.html.

26. Ratzinger, *Eschatology: Death and Eternal Life*, 9.

reacquainted with Professor Johann Auer, whom he had known earlier while the two were teaching in Bonn. Auer approached Ratzinger to collaborate on a "Short Catholic Dogmatics" he had begun in 1947. Ratzinger agreed, but because he was soon named archbishop of Munich-Freising he was only able to complete one of the two sections assigned to him, namely the volume on eschatology.[27] He later referred to this limited contribution of his as "something I still consider my most thorough work and the one I labored over most strenuously."[28] He elsewhere describes how it is that this work on eschatology served as a chance for him to recalibrate in a comprehensive way his approach to dogmatics as a whole. Having been shaped deeply not only by his own study but by the way the tradition had so recently been renewed in the Second Vatican Council, he sought to let this renewal of the tradition form him in such a way that he would personally approach the major theological questions of his day in light of the return to the sources of Scripture and the Fathers as well as recognizing the need to discern the "signs of the times" when doing theology. He wrote: "After the decisive turning point of the Council, I first tried simply to conceive my whole dogmatics anew, going back again to the sources and keeping abreast of what was being produced. Thus, a vision of the whole gradually grew for me that was nourished by the various experiences and realizations I had encountered along my theological path. I rejoiced to be able to say something of my own, something new and yet completely within the faith of the Church."[29] He realized that much of what must be "new" in the approach to traditional questions of eschatology would be the insights and challenges of recent biblical scholarship, especially those pertaining to the New Testament's treatment of eschatological themes.[30] He noted that for some time eschatology had quietly faded from importance within the broader context of modern theology. What had seemed to be an area concerned with far-off and ethereal speculations about the afterlife had now become a field of theology through which the real nature of history as a whole could be explored.

27. Ibid., xvii.

28. John L. Allen, *Cardinal Ratzinger: The Vatican's Enforcer of the Faith* (New York: Continuum, 2000), 93.

29. Joseph Ratzinger, *Milestones: Memoirs, 1927–1977* (San Francisco: Ignatius Press, 1998), 150.

30. Nichols, *The Thought of Pope Benedict XVI*, 110–33.

In the foreword to their combined work on dogmatic theology, Ratzinger and Auer agree on their methodology. They indicate that they will proceed with the questions before them by focusing on: (1) the biblical foundation of doctrine, (2) the history of individual doctrines, and (3) "the systematic inner coherence of doctrine" taken as a whole.[31] As has been explored in the earlier chapters on Ratzinger's theology of divine revelation and Christology, an essential aspect of his approach to biblical exegesis is to embrace the impetus given by so-called "historical-critical" exegetical models insofar as they lead the reader to take seriously the historical and cultural conditions present at the time of the events recorded in Scripture as well as those of the authors of the texts. At the same time, authentic biblical interpretation cannot remain limited to those questions. The horizon of the contemporary reader who approaches any given text with the eyes of faith must always have a central place in the discourse concerning interpretation, since what is being discussed is always the *living* word of God intended to bring about faith in every age and culture. As helpful and even essential as all the contributions of scientific historical-critical analysis are, it is also the case, for Ratzinger, that "no interpretation from the past is ever completely old hat if in its time it turned to the text in true openness."[32] A true and open turning to the texts of Scripture and to the "text" of the living Christian tradition that appropriated the word of God in history in many different ways would produce today a fresh appropriation of the Christian mystery. It is for this reason that Ratzinger and Auer would quite deliberately take up the questions before them with the multifaceted approach of biblical exegesis as well as the historical development of the relevant doctrines insofar as they had been appropriated in the life of the actual church and not simply taken up in the mode of "objective" theorizing.

This approach to biblical exegesis always considered from theological and pastoral horizons is especially important when it comes to Ratzinger's eschatology. Both disciplines have their "temptations" built into them. He writes: "Dogmatics is always tempted to correct the [exegetical] data for the sake of the results. Exegesis wants to perform the task of transposition into the present, claiming the

---

31. Ratzinger, *Eschatology: Death and Eternal Life*, xxiii–xxiv.
32. Ibid., 24.

competence of an interpreter for work that simply cannot be carried out in that fashion."[33] Appropriating the meaning of an ancient text, allowing it to shed light on circumstances of the present, and orienting an audience to the demands of the future is a multifaceted task that requires great sensitivity to the multiplicity of factors involved in interpretation. Doing the best scientific work to grasp what data the historical critical method can supply gives insight into the text as it was produced and appropriated in history. But then the limits of this method must be recognized, and the interpreter must begin to take into consideration the whole trajectory over the ages of the ways in which the original text has been interpreted. Ratzinger suggests that this variety of viewpoints within the one unfolding history of the tradition ought to lend itself to fostering some humility in the exegete of today, for "[o]nly by listening to the whole history of interpretation can the present be purified by criticism and so brought into a position of genuine encounter with the text concerned."[34]

Ratzinger's insistence on examining the whole of the tradition and how it has tried to articulate various aspects of eschatology becomes that much more intelligible in light of what has already been described of his theology, a primary characteristic of which is its "unfolding" nature. For him, the intelligibility of the whole of the tradition, of the whole of history, is possible precisely because of its transcendent origin. For this reason, in order to make this "listening to the whole history" possible, it is first necessary to establish its metaphysical and transcendent character.

One of the deficiencies of the conception of human history in modern times, for Ratzinger, is that because the strictly "scientific" approach to history has become dominant, an inner principle of the unity of history has been lost. Or to put it another way, the understanding of the metaphysical nature of history has faded. In its place history has come to be seen as lacking any underlying unity because it is detached from the metaphysical reality that transcends history even while it reaches into it. Ratzinger recalls in this context the observation made by Josef Pieper of the growing phenomenon of the "materialistic trivialization of death" whereby, on the one hand, death is to be feared above all realities because it is impossible to see any

33. Ibid., 20.
34. Ibid., 24.

meaning or reality beyond it. On the other hand, there is a sense in which in an age of television "death is presented as a thrilling spectacle tailor-made for alleviating the general boredom of life."[35] Here the shock of the image of death that others undergo is at least an occasion for a temporary awakening from the numbness that comes in living a life devoid of supernatural reality and significance. In both cases, Ratzinger, argues, "[d]eath is to be deprived of its character as a place where the metaphysical breaks through."[36] The prospective in-breaking of the reign of God, of eternity itself, then, is an occasion where the natural realm ends and the supernatural begins. For Ratzinger, keeping in tension the twofold nature of history, having its origins in the eternal *Logos* spoken from an infinite God and "heard" in a finite earthly realm, is essential to understanding the fullness of the Christian mystery as it pertains to death and eternal life. Only in this context does death become the meeting point of history and eternity. Here the theological category of the *Logos* becomes the necessary framework within which it is possible to handle the tensions that arise in the questions posed by an eschatology seeking to respond to the new cultural and philosophical horizons of the modern world.

The Exegetical Problem of an Imminent End

In order to begin to formulate this renewed eschatology, the first task, in Ratzinger's mind, was to address current exegetical challenges. In this case the most pressing question, and the one that had reintroduced the specialization of eschatology to a prominent place in the theological conversation was the need to grapple with the nature of Jesus' preaching and aspects of the New Testament that suggested a vision of the imminent end of the world.[37] He notes that of the 122 times in the New Testament that the phrases "kingdom of God" or "kingdom of heaven" occur, ninety are recounted as coming directly from Jesus' own preaching. Indeed, Ratzinger agrees with the exegetical opinion that this is the "true *Leitmotiv*" of Jesus' preaching.[38] The fact that the mention of the kingdom of God/heaven is almost always in the context of its being "close" or "at hand" or

35. Ibid., 70.
36. Ibid.
37. Ibid., 19.
38. Ibid., 24–25.

"among us" suggests a consistent theme indicating that the reign of God, who is *eternal*, is beginning to take root on earth, in the person of Jesus, in the realm of the *historical*. Ratzinger argues that in preaching the kingdom of God/heaven Jesus is speaking "not of a heavenly reality but of something God is doing and will do in the future here on earth."[39] And yet it remains true that it is God who is acting, and so in this locus of the kingdom of God/heaven history and eternity are meeting, and in that meeting history is facing its "end," i.e., it is being fulfilled in the person of Jesus.

Implicit in this proclamation of Jesus is that the kingdom of eternity is in the process of transforming and somehow overcoming human history. This is to say that Jesus is suggesting that the end of the world as we know it is now upon us. And yet, surely, the "end" did not come. Nothing seems to have happened externally in the world that suggested anything was any different than it had been before Jesus appeared on the scene. If these New Testament sentiments, including the direct preaching of Jesus, did indeed expect the imminent end of the world, what are we to make of the trustworthiness of the scriptural witness when "the end" did not, in fact, come? And since "the end" did not come, can the faithful still find these texts trustworthy in their effort to understand the meaning of history and what to expect in death and beyond?[40] Is New Testament teaching reliable in this area of the questions of death and eternal life?

"Schema and Reality"

Ratzinger's approach to these exegetical problems allows for a diversity of interpretive conclusions. On the one hand, some historians of the texts may be correct in concluding that the New Testament authors and their audiences thought that the end would be near, in their own lifetimes. This did not happen. But the fact that they were proved wrong in one sense of the question does not mean that the writings themselves are in error. In *Eschatology*, Ratzinger describes this interpretive tension inherently built into Scripture as a tension between "literary schema and reality." For the authors of the New Testament, "what interests them is not the question of exact chronological succession or a possible causality of development but the inner

39. Ibid., 26.
40. Ibid., 19.

unity of the whole."[41] The horizon from which these texts were written and within which they are to be properly interpreted is a coherent narrative of salvation history always unfolding. In the moment of the writing of any of the given texts, complete understanding of this inner unity of history is impossible for the particular authors. Yet, in the mind of God, the words spoken in prophecy in Scripture are indeed intimately linked and united to the ultimate reality yet to unfold for those still living in the present. This tension between schema and reality is most clearly uncovered for Ratzinger in the problem of interpreting the person of Jesus in light of the Old Testament. He writes:

> The words of the Old Testament, in which Israel's faith-experience of the word of God is reflected, anticipate the history of Jesus, the living Word of God in this world. It is only in the light of that earlier word that the figure of Jesus becomes theologically intelligible. Jesus is interpreted on its basis, and only thus can his whole existence be acknowledged as itself substantially "Word."[42]

The idea, then, of God's word being spoken throughout history, culminating in the Word itself in Jesus, supplies the fundamental hermeneutical key for understanding all of history. It is precisely the characteristic of the Word as both particular in its expression and yet open with respect to its meaning that makes it so fruitful as a central motif for understanding divine self-communication and the nature and meaning of history.

Hermeneutic of the Word in History

So, for Ratzinger, the foundational interpretive principle that holds together "schema and reality" is one of the Word unfolding in history. What coheres in the mind of God is made apparent to humanity only over time as the whole narrative unfolds. Ratzinger writes:

> The fundamental and all-important hermeneutical insight here is that subsequent history belongs intrinsically to the inner momentum of the text itself. That is: it does not simply provide

41. Ibid., 41.
42. Ibid., 43–44.

retrospective commentary on the text. Rather, through the appearing of the reality which was still to come, the full dimensions of the word carried by the text come to light."[43]

So if reading parts of the text of Scripture in isolation, including the words of Jesus himself, seems to evoke a sense of incoherence or confusion, that need not derail efforts to understand the meaning of the text, since the fullness of the meaning of any given portion of Scripture is ultimately available only in light of the heart of the testimony that pertains to Jesus' resurrection from the dead. Only in light of this *reality* do all the previous *literary schemas* of Scripture become intelligible. Furthermore, only in keeping this tension of "schema and reality" operative in an "authentic appropriation of the word" is the contemporary reader and believer able to avoid the twin pitfalls of "archaism and modernism."[44] For "[i]ssuing as it does from the crucified and risen Christ, the word indicates a given direction which is wide enough to receive all reality into itself, yet clear enough to confront it with a definite measuring-rod of its own."[45] The twin aspects of both the particularity and the openness of "the word" that Ratzinger relies upon become essential for the task of understanding Christ and his message in an ever new way as their meaning continues to be appropriated in history.

Discovering the Kingdom in Person

For Ratzinger, the contemporary person of faith, aided by these historical and exegetical investigations, remains free, and even obliged, to engage the text of revelation in the present, by the light of faith, in order to interpret it as source of faith. This action is what drives the engine of tradition, always anchored in the testimony of the past and always attempting to appropriate the truth of God's words and deeds in history to inform the present and future life of the church. For Jesus to proclaim that the kingdom of heaven is near, then, led many to expect the end of the world in the very near future. But as the narrative unfolds, and in light of Jesus' death and resurrection, it becomes clear that the fullness of the coming of the king-

43. Ibid., 42.
44. Ibid., 43.
45. Ibid.

dom is not an expectation about chronological events in a distant future conceived in a linear fashion but about an openness to an encounter with the kingdom *in person* in the present.[46] Ratzinger recalls the exegesis of Origen from the third century in which he calls Jesus the *autobasileia*, "the Kingdom in person."[47] Only in retrospect, after the resurrection, and guided by the Spirit, does the Christian community begin to realize the full implications of who Jesus had been all the while in their midst. They also came to realize that he remained in their midst *now*, as the Risen One. And so, in light of the new recognition of Jesus' identity as the eternal *Word* in the flesh, they also began to understand the meaning of his *words* in a new way. So it is that Jesus' preaching about the nearness of the kingdom of heaven and the closeness of the end of history must be understood in light of the true identity of Jesus himself. The Christian community discovers that, as the very presence of God in the flesh in history, Jesus himself is the presence of the reign of God of which he spoke. He is the fullness and in that sense the "end" of human history in his very self. Consequently, Ratzinger argues, "Eschatology's meaning and driving force depend upon the power of this waiting on Christ, not on temporal expectations of the world's end or transformation, no matter of what kind."[48] In this christological hermeneutic, then, the only proper way to understand any of the *ideas* associated with eschatology and the nature of history must be in light of the *person* of Christ.

Maranatha vs. Dies Irae

As a sort of case study of an application of this historically sensitive methodology in eschatology, Ratzinger takes up the contrast drawn by many theologians within the Christian tradition between the ancient biblical cry of *"maranatha"* ("our Lord, come!") and the thirteenth-century Latin hymn, *Dies Irae* ("day of wrath").[49] If it is true that the *lex credendi* is formed by the *lex orandi*, what are we to conclude about the Christian belief regarding the final judgment when looking at these two apparently diverging prayer texts? The note of

46. Ibid., 34.
47. Ibid.
48. Ibid., 11.
49. Ibid., 4–15.

confidence in God's mercy struck in the utterance *maranatha*, asking him to come close, stands in sharp contrast with the spirit of fear of that same God's wrath that characterizes the *Dies Irae*. What to do with this tension? Ratzinger first focuses on an examination of the prayers themselves. Beginning with *maranatha*, he notes that current exegetical scholarship is somewhat divided between the possibility that *maranatha* was a plea *asking* that the Lord *might* come close and others who say the prayer is a proclamation of what has already occurred: "the Lord has come."[50] In either case, however, the prayer strikes a note of confidence in the coming of the *Savior* who is at the same time the *judge* of humanity. The eschatological sense of this proclamation intimates a mingling of both judge and savior within the one identity of Christ in the ancient church that seems to allow the faithful to approach the end-times, whenever they might come, with confidence, hope, and even joy.

In a different historical and cultural setting, however, in the case of the emergence of the *Dies Irae* in the medieval church, the prospect of judgment seems to have been separated from the mercy of the Savior. While this certainly appears to be the case, Ratzinger points out that there were also other strands of liturgical life even in the medieval church that kept alive the reality of the mercy of the Savior and the hope with which the faithful could approach death. He points here to the development of the Litany of the Saints, which became such a crucial communal prayer in the medieval church. In the litany and in the communion of saints it calls upon, he argues, the faithful find their true identity and home as Christians who can face earthly death with confidence. In the litany, he explains, the Christian "gathers the redeemed of all ages around him and finds safety under their mantle. This signifies that the walls separating heaven and earth, and past, present and future, are now as glass. The Christian lives in the presence of the saints as his own proper ambience, and so lives 'eschatologically.' "[51] Thus, in Ratzinger's schema, with Christ at the center of history, final judgment becomes not necessarily the stuff of fear and dread, but of hope and joy based on the personal encounter with the center of history himself, Jesus Christ.[52] When Ratzinger

50. Ibid., 6.

51. Ibid., 9.

52. Joseph Ratzinger, *The Theology of History in St. Bonaventure* (Chicago: Franciscan Herald Press, 1989), 108.

considers the whole of the Christian tradition of the *lex orandi*, then, the underlying confidence in the *maranatha* sheds more light on eschatology than the fear elicited by the *Dies Irae* when it is separated from the true identity of Christ, whose mercy fulfills his justice. The person of Christ who faces death and defeats it in love becomes essential for a theology based on hope even when confronting death. More precisely, the figure of Christ, as he is met in the life of the church, especially in the liturgy, is crucial in filling out the context of genuine eschatological hope in the Christian vision, and it is to this liturgical aspect of Ratzinger's renewed eschatology that we now turn.

Saved by Hope

Benedict acknowledges in his second encyclical, *Spe Salvi*, on the nature of Christian hope, that when discussion moves from the origins and nature of created reality to the final questions posed at the end of life, we can and must ask, "what may we hope?"[53] The fulfillment of this hope even in the face of death is offered and given a foretaste in myriad ways in the liturgical life of the church. Indeed, in the church's life perhaps the best explanations of these mysteries come precisely in the context of the liturgical setting, for it is in these settings that the people of God, the church, are most opened up and receptive to truly "hearing" the word spoken to them. In anticipation of the celebration of the paschal mystery, the universal church proclaims the word of God that calls the faithful listener to be open to the Word that is spoken and can be heard even across the boundaries of death. For Christians, being "united" to Christ in baptism is an experience of having been "engrafted onto the death of Christ."[54] The foundational experience of baptism as a participation in the death of Christ in order to share in his victory over death in his resurrection is a further hermeneutical key to the problem of death that Benedict offers in *Spe Salvi*.[55]

53. Benedict XVI, *Spe Salvi* 22, 24.
54. Ratzinger, *Eschatology: Death and Eternal Life*, 115.
55. See also the chapter entitled "On the Theology of Death" in Benedict XVI, *Dogma and Preaching: Applying Christian Doctrine to Daily Life* (San Francisco: Ignatius Press, 2011), 243–54.

Death, as we have said, presents itself to the human person as the apparent silencing of the word of life. But for the Christian, hope consists in continuing to have faith that the Word is being spoken from God even in the context of death. This is at the core of the vision of the paschal mystery. But there is a muting of this word of hope in contemporary Western culture especially. This muting is part of the landscape Benedict addresses in his introductory observations in the encyclical. Precisely in cultures that have been historically Christian, the word of hope, perhaps because it has become too familiar, has been drowned out. He writes: "We who have always lived with the Christian concept of God, and have grown accustomed to it, have almost ceased to notice that we possess the hope that ensues from a real encounter with this God."[56] The single thing the human person longs for is confidence that there is hope for the fullness of life, even eternal life. Yet there is also something in the human heart that makes us balk at this prospect. Among other reasons, there is a fear that eternal life might turn into a kind of relentless drudgery. After all, he writes, " 'Eternal,' in fact, suggests to us the idea of something interminable, and this frightens us."[57] As long as eternal life and the hope that makes this life possible remain offered in the realm of abstraction and proposition, that fear is justified. But as Benedict consistently emphasizes, Christian hope does not flow from an *idea* offered to the mind but rather from a concrete *encounter* that is available to the whole person. Moving from concept to encounter, then, makes all the difference in opening a contemporary culture back up to authentic hope.

Hope is possible, Benedict's argument goes, only in the context of this encounter. This dialogical and relational model of hope is in contrast to the secular virtue of mere optimism, which, for Ratzinger, is a product of an ideology of progress. It is embraced and cultivated in the isolation of individualism. This individualism refuses the need for dependence on another that is necessary for relationship within the human community and ultimately with God. Hope is not an intellectual conclusion drawn from an ideology thought about in isolation but rather the product of a dynamic relationship, an encounter. He explains something of the effectiveness of this dynamism as he describes the power of the Gospel itself in his introduction to *Spe Salvi*:

56. Benedict XVI, *Spe Salvi* 3.
57. Ibid., 12.

So now we can say: Christianity was not only "good news"—
the communication of a hitherto unknown content. In our
language we would say: the Christian message was not only
"informative" but "performative." That means: the Gospel is
not merely a communication of things that can be known—it
is one that makes things happen and is life-changing. The dark
door of time, of the future, has been thrown open. The one
who has hope lives differently; the one who hopes has been
granted the gift of a new life.[58]

If hope is not informative but performative, what is achieved in it?
What "things happen"? His answer: "redemption."[59] Pope Benedict
draws immediately upon the example of a recently canonized saint,
Josephine Bakhita, to illustrate this hope that "is redemption."[60] By
way of Bakhita's life he is able to provide an icon of the liberation that
is found in coming to know the person of Christ and how through this
encounter, through entering into dialogue with Christ and therefore
cultivating a real relationship with him, one's present circumstances
of suffering can be approached with new confidence. Josephine Bakhita, the nineteenth-century Sudanese slave-turned-religious-sister,
had been sold numerous times and endured several brutal beatings
at the hands of various masters. She was ultimately sold into servitude
to a master who took up residence in Venice. Benedict describes how
she there came to know a very different kind of master, (*paron* in
Venetian dialect). He recounts her experience:

> Up to that time she had known only masters who despised and
> maltreated her, or at best considered her a useful slave. Now,
> however, she heard that there is a *"paron"* above all masters,
> the Lord of all lords, and that this Lord is good, goodness in
> person. She came to know that this Lord even knew her, that
> he had created her—that he actually loved her. She too was
> loved, and by none other than the supreme *"Paron,"* before
> whom all other masters are themselves no more than lowly
> servants. She was known and loved and she was awaited. What
> is more, this master had himself accepted the destiny of being
> flogged and now he was waiting for her "at the Father's right

58. Ibid., 2.
59. Ibid., 3.
60. Ibid., 3–4.

hand." Now she had "hope"—no longer simply the modest hope of finding masters who would be less cruel, but the great hope: "I am definitively loved and whatever happens to me—I am awaited by this Love. And so my life is good."[61]

Benedict goes on to explain the further transformation that came in St. Josephine's life thanks to the word that she had heard regarding this new kind of relationship with a new kind of *paron*. Upon recognizing that she is loved, the next step for her was to let others come to know this freedom she had only recently discovered. That next step in the unfolding of her new identity in Christ was missionary in character. Upon being baptized, confirmed, and receiving First Communion from the Patriarch of Venice in 1890, she was received into the Canossian Sisters, with whom she became a kind of missionary within Italy, telling the story of her experience of "the liberation that she had received through her encounter with the God of Jesus Christ." Benedict goes on to explain that "she felt she had to extend [this message], it had to be handed on to others, to the greatest possible number of people. The hope born in her which had "redeemed" her she could not keep to herself; this hope had to reach many, to reach everybody."[62]

Here, encapsulated in this one story of one saint, is really the pattern for the life of the whole church in Ratzinger's theology. One who is trapped in slavery, darkness, and suffering comes to hear the word of God in his or her life. As the seed of that word is planted, it begins to take root. The more clearly the word of God is heard in that person's life, the greater the transformation that begins to unfold. This is a transformation undergone not in isolation, but always in the context of the ecclesial community comprised of many who seek to hear the word together. The hearing of this word culminates in the sacramental life of the church, where the Word is given in the flesh, in love. Upon reception of this Word in the flesh, the one who has been transformed by this love seeks to respond in love, in the flesh. Bakhita, as Benedict tells her story, first heard about the possibility of a new kind of *paron*, but that level of hearing involved only words that could easily fade away. Not until she "heard" that word of promise in deeds as well as words, did it begin to take flesh. She encountered that word in the action taken by her owner in giving her freedom,

61. Ibid., 3.
62. Ibid.

and she continued to experience that freedom she discovered in Christ in the context of prayer, especially in the sacramental encounter with Christ. In using St. Josephine Bakhita as an image of Christian hope, Benedict points to the theological reality that hope is not a mere idea of progress that one assents to in the intellectual realm, but an experience of the whole person as one comes into contact with the God who has come close in Jesus Christ. It is to this christological shape of hope as Benedict sees it that we turn now.

Hope in Entering the "I" of Christ

In *The Yes of Jesus Christ*,[63] Ratzinger describes the "situation today" in which people are torn between the desire for God and the impulse to be "free" from God to seek the more immediate needs and desires of our hearts. In this situation "[w]e cannot break away from God, but neither do we have the strength to break through to God: with our own resources we cannot build the bridges that would lead to a definite relationship with this God."[64] In light of this dilemma on the human side of that chasm, Ratzinger explores the Christian proposal that uncovers the power of the love God has for humanity in the creative "assent," one might call it, that God makes to humanity. Since "human beings cannot completely dispel the strange twilight that hangs over the question of the eternal," he explains, "God must cross over to them and talk to them if real relations are to be established with him."[65] God definitively says "yes" to humanity in the incarnation and on the cross. Drawing on Josef Pieper's definition of love in the affirmation, "it is good that you exist,"[66] he explains the power of this utterance when God directs it to humanity. When that word that is "yes" from God, that Word that is the origin of creation itself is uttered in the context of human isolation from God, this utterance becomes another creative act, and from those words a new creation emerges. Human beings need this affirmation in order to live. "Biological birth is not enough," Ratzinger writes, "man can only accept his personality, his 'I,' in the power of the approval of his being

63. Benedict XVI, *The Yes of Jesus Christ: Exercises in Faith, Hope and Love* (New York: Crossroad, 2005).

64. Ibid., 26.

65. Ibid., 26–27.

66. Ibid., 89.

that comes from another, from 'you.' "[67] For Ratzinger, the human person is first able to fully accept this personality in the person of Christ, who fully receives approval from the Father. In the person of Christ, then, it becomes possible for the I–Thou affirmation of God for humanity, begun in creation and continuing to unfold in salvation history, to reach its fulfillment in the eschaton.[68] What allows this affirmation ultimately to take place and come to fulfillment is the dialogical structure of the relationship between God and humanity.

The eschatological dimension of this dynamic of entering into the "I" of Christ becomes clearer as Ratzinger explains the link that exists within Jesus' own teaching about himself in John's gospel. The bread of life discourse of the sixth chapter and the narrative of the raising of Lazarus in the eleventh mutually inform each other in this regard.[69] For Ratzinger, to enter into communion with Jesus is to enter into communion with God who both transcends history and has taken flesh within it as well. This communion serves as a kind of bridge, then, between history and eternity, death and eternal life. Ratzinger notes that in the narrative of Lazarus's death and resuscitation in John 11, even before Jesus' own resurrection, there is a promise of the bridge across death. His *word* to Martha, "I am the resurrection," is spoken in conjunction with his *deed* of raising his friend from the dead. The consistency of his word and deed signifies an underlying presence that spans earthly and transcendent reality and is echoed also in eucharistic terms. Ratzinger conjoins these realities when he writes:

> The bond with Jesus is, even now, resurrection. Where there is communion with him, the boundary of death is overshot here and now. It is in this perspective that we must understand the Discourse on the Eucharist in John 6. Feeding on Jesus' word and on his flesh, that is, receiving him by both faith and sacrament, is described as being nourished by the bread of immortality. The resurrection does not appear as a distant apocalyptic event but as an occurrence which takes place in the immediate present. Whenever someone enters into the "I" of Christ, he has entered straight away into the space of unconditional life.[70]

67. Ibid., 90.
68. Ibid., 91.
69. Ratzinger, *Eschatology: Death and Eternal Life*, 117.
70. Ibid.

This "space of unconditional life" that is hoped for beyond this life is simultaneously entered into in this life in the sacramental encounter of the church with the Lord, in the eucharistic liturgy. This encounter is possible only because of what is accomplished in history in the death and resurrection of Jesus. To see more closely how Ratzinger conceives that the entrance into the "I of Christ" is contingent on the resurrection of Christ, we turn now to the key to this link, in my estimation: the fact that the resurrection of Christ is the moment in history in which the dialogue between God and humanity is fulfilled.

IV. Dialogical Fulfillment of Resurrection

To help formulate an overview of Ratzinger's thought on the eschatological import for humanity of Jesus' resurrection, it makes sense to start with his own recent attempt at such an overview. In his present-day foreword for that thirty-year-old work on eschatology, his starting place is the scriptural witness itself, where he recalls the challenge posed to Jesus by the Sadducees on the possibility of resurrection from the dead. Jesus calls them "greatly misled" in denying the resurrection, since God had already revealed himself in the Scriptures of the Jewish people as the God of Abraham, Isaac, and Jacob and is therefore "not God of the dead but of the living" (Mark 12:27). Ratzinger sees in Jesus' answer to the Sadducees a key to a proper understanding of the whole of the Christian mystery that includes both the foundations of creation and the vision of life after death in the *eschaton*. "This theo-logical interpretation" that Jesus offers, he argues, "is just as much a dia-logical interpretation of the human being and of human immortality."[71] He then explains the distinction in a footnote: " 'Theo-logy' discloses a discourse about *theos*, God. A 'dia-logical' interpretation is a sharing of the *logos* in the form of a conversation (*dialogos*)."[72] What seems to have passed away in death, from the perspective of the Sadducees, has indeed *not* passed away from the perspective of Scripture as Jesus interprets it. The whole of human history, in fact, is present within the context of the dialogue eternally taking place within God. Since there would be no creation or human history if these had not emanated from within God, who is a communion of relations and therefore characterized by dialogical

71. Ibid., xx.
72. Ibid. n. 5.

dynamics, all of creation and history find their principle of coherence precisely within this dynamic of dialogue. It is for this reason, then, that the Christian understanding of the possibility of human immortality is grounded in the fact that we exist from the very beginning in the mind of God. Ratzinger says that we exist at all only because "we are inscribed into God's memory. In God's memory we are not a shadow, a mere 'recollection.' Remaining in God's memory means we are alive, in a full sense of life. We are fully a 'we.'"[73]

Thus in this one description of human existence being sustained from within the mind, the memory of God, Benedict gives the grounding for both the origins and the "end" of human existence. Even before his own death and resurrection, Jesus is interpreting the history of Israel as foundational for the promise of eternal life for us. The grounding for this hope for eternal life is a structure of creation and history that is, at its base, dialogical and conversational. The "we" of humanity that possesses the potential for eternal life does so based on the fact that our very existence is within God and in relation to God. This potential for humanity that Jesus points to in his own teaching ministry is not fulfilled and opened up to all, however, until his own death and resurrection.

For Ratzinger, the Christian is drawn into a foretaste of eschatological fulfillment and the inner dynamic of new creation insofar as he or she participates in the paschal mystery of Christ. Participation in the liturgy is the entrance *par excellence* of the members of the church into the "'I' of Christ." For Ratzinger, to "enter into the 'I' of Christ" is fundamentally to step into the dialogical relationship between divinity and humanity. It is to enter into the story of that unfolding relationship as it has occurred throughout the narrative of salvation history fulfilled in the death and resurrection of Jesus. When he discusses the New Testament understanding of the link between the resurrection of Christ and the possibility of eternal life for all of humanity, he emphasizes this dialogical dynamic that unfolds through salvation history. In one such explanation of the resurrection in his second volume of *Jesus of Nazareth*, Benedict takes as a starting point Paul's formula of the confession of faith given in 1 Corinthians, where he asserts: "Christ died for our sins in accordance with the scriptures" (1 Cor 15:3). He takes those two elements of interpretation—that the

---

73. Ibid., xx.

death was "for us" and that it was "in accordance with the scriptures"—to be essential to the Christian meaning of Jesus' death and resurrection.[74]

In examining Benedict's analysis of these two parts of Paul's confession of faith we can detect the dialogical principle at work again in both instances. For Benedict, I would argue, Paul's proclamation is fundamentally a dialogical reality. First, behind the resurrection is a divine action *for* humanity. Jesus' death on the cross is God's most perfect word of love to humanity, and the power of that love is not recognized by humanity until the resurrection that follows the death. Second, the resurrection is the fulfillment of the saga of salvation history, marred early on by the disobedience of humanity in the fall of Adam. There is an attempt to correct this rupture of the relationship between God and humanity through the giving of the Law and the prophets until finally, in Jesus, a new Adam emerges who is a human being able once again to be obedient to and live in union with God, as humanity is created to be. The resurrection is the fruit of this obedience and thereby represents *the* moment of a new creation that is also the eschatological fulfillment of all of salvation history. Benedict writes: "It [the resurrection of Jesus] belongs in the context of God's ongoing relationship with his people, from which it receives its inner logic and its meaning. It is an event in which the words of Scripture are fulfilled; it bears within itself Logos, or logic; it proceeds from the word and returns to the word; it surrounds the word and fulfills it."[75] At the very heart of the meaning of Christ's free gift of self-sacrificing love on the cross, then, is *Logos*: an event of communication. And if it is communication, then it is a communication between two parties, God and humanity. It is for this reason that the two aspects of Paul's confession—both that the death and resurrection that mark the pinnacle of the relationship between God and man that is salvation history were "in accordance with the scriptures" and that they were "for our sins"—indicate the dialogical nature of the paschal mystery. Jesus' death and resurrection form an event of communication at the center of which is a word *from God* and *for humanity*. Benedict writes: "Because his death has to do with the word of

74. Benedict XVI, *Jesus of Nazareth. Part Two, Holy Week: From the Entrance into Jerusalem to the Resurrection* (San Francisco: Ignatius Press, 2011), 251.

75. Ibid., 252.

God, it has to do with us, it is a dying 'for.' "[76] If the original sin of refusing to listen to God's word ended in the isolation of death for humanity, it is in the "yes" of God to humanity and humanity back to God, in Jesus' death, that eternal life is made possible for humanity. Only this event of the perfect dialogue between God and humanity overcomes the disruption of that dialogue that death signifies.

Resurrection as Re-creation in History

For Ratzinger it is essential to emphasize that the resurrection of Jesus—the perfection of the human/divine dialogue—happens in *history* and is not merely an abstract idea proposed to the intellect. Furthermore, in describing how essential it is that it was not merely one isolated event, one person's dying and return to life, Benedict emphasizes the radical uniqueness of this event and its meaning for the whole of human history. He writes: "Even if man by his nature is created for immortality, it is only now that the place exists in which his immortal soul can find its 'space,' its 'bodiliness,' in which immortality takes on its meaning as communion with God and with the whole of reconciled mankind."[77] It is here in the context of the death and resurrection of Jesus that the Christian understandings of both creation and eschatology begin to converge. What was begun in the moment of creation that came about through the effectiveness of the Word of God being uttered now comes to fulfillment. The resurrection of Jesus, Benedict writes, is not merely a noteworthy moment in history; it marks an "evolutionary leap" in the very heart of being, an "ontological leap . . . opening up a dimension that affects us all, creating for all of us a new space of life, a new space of being in union with God."[78]

Resurrection of the dead in the Christian vision, then, is not simply about individuals living after death on a spiritual plane. It is also bodily. As such, it points to the eschatological fulfillment of what the human person was created for "in the beginning." For Ratzinger, resurrection is about communion both with God and with the rest of created humanity. It is has both human and divine consequences. It is individual and communal. It is eternal as well as historical. The

---

76. Ibid.
77. Ibid., 274.
78. Ibid.

resurrected self enters into eternity only because eternity has entered into temporality. Ratzinger's reliance on the *Logos* both in his theology of creation and his eschatology makes it possible to hold these dimensions together, since the *Logos* is both spoken from eternity and always remains in eternity, while also spoken in and communicated in creation, in history. Since the *Logos* is spoken in history, it enters into a realm of the contingent, because it depends on the receptivity of free humanity to what is spoken. The direction taken by the response on the part of humanity remains an open question. When it comes to the eschatological question of the final judgment, then, the fragility of the nature of this dialogue between God and humanity becomes clear. Having established the "fact" of the resurrection, then, Ratzinger also takes up the question of how humanity, which remains free to enter into the dialogue or refuse it, chooses to respond. This must be our next focus.

V. Human Freedom and Divine Love in the Final Judgment

If resurrection and eternal life for the human person are about the fulfillment of the dialogue with God offered in Christ Jesus, and if it is true that God never ceases speaking his eternal Word to us out of love, is it really possible for the human person to definitively and once and for all refuse this dialogue? Could final judgment result in damnation, in hell? Or is there always a chance of reopening the dialogue? The traditional doctrines of hell and damnation are of course very much called into question in the modern era, and Ratzinger notes the challenge implicit in keeping the traditional doctrine while finding a way to articulate it in more contemporary and personalist terms. He recalls the famous theological proposal of Origen in the third century: that in the end, all would be saved. Ratzinger writes that this assumption arises out of Origen's Platonic theory that evil has no real substance and God's being would ultimately overcome all distortions of reality.[79] Coming partially to Origen's defense, he reminds the reader that Origen proposed this as a *hypothesis*, but his ultimate conclusion was determined primarily by the metaphysical *system* he had worked out, which provided a framework for understanding aspects of the

---

79. Ratzinger, *Eschatology: Death and Eternal Life*, 215.

Christian faith. In this sense Origen neglected the scriptural witness pertaining to the reality of hell. And so Ratzinger uses that scriptural witness as his starting point.

There is no doubt that the Bible testifies to the reality of hell. But what is its nature? Proceeding from an essentially biblical basis, he argues that human freedom has a privileged place in this schema and that this freedom is always operative. And so, while divine love is always offered to free human beings, it is not thrust upon them. While this freedom is respected, "what can be given to the creature . . . is love . . . . And yet the freedom to resist the creation of that assent [to divine love], the freedom not to accept it as one's own, this freedom remains."[80] The human person always remains free to receive this love, to hear this word of love spoken from God and allow it to transform her or him, or else to reject it. Hell, then, in Ratzinger's schema reveals a great deal about the fragile dynamic that characterizes relationship: the offer of love, a word of invitation to love, and the uncertainty of the response. Whether it is rejected or embraced depends on the second party. The Word of love spoken from the divine "I" can be received or rejected by the human "thou." It is a fragile process because it is dialogical in nature. The prospect of hell, or heaven for that matter, in Ratzinger's view, is not a matter of the unilateral action taken by the all-powerful juridical authority of God, who either dispenses salvation or damnation as he sees fit, but rather Judgment takes on the tenuous character of a relationship, the outcome of which remains to be seen. For this reason hell remains very much a reality for a free humanity. And yet, the reality of hell can be faced in hope. This hope, he writes, "does not emerge from the neutral logic of a system . . . instead, it derives from the surrender of all claims to innocence and to reality's perduringness, a surrender which takes place by the Cross of the Redeemer. Such hope, however, cannot be a self-willed assertion. It must place its petition into the hands of its Lord and leave it there."[81] This is the hope that can "take on" hell not as an endeavor of the isolated individual but only as the act of one who is fundamentally in dialogue with the Word himself who is spoken as love, in the face of death, on the cross.

---

80. Ibid., 216.
81. Ibid., 218.

Hell and Heaven

For Ratzinger, in the absence of the ultimate hope that is based in dialogue with the Lord, hell becomes a very real possibility; indeed it is a likely outcome. Benedict explains near the end of *Spe Salvi*:

> There can be people who have totally destroyed their desire for truth and readiness to love, people for whom everything has become a lie, people who have lived for hatred and have suppressed all love within themselves. This is a terrifying thought, but alarming profiles of this type can be seen in certain figures of our own history. In such people all would be beyond remedy and the destruction of good would be irrevocable: this is what we mean by the word *Hell*.[82]

On the other hand, he says, there are people who are so radically open to God and to their neighbors that upon their death they move directly into that fullness of communion with God and all the angels and saints in heaven. While that radical openness to relationship with God and others is possible, just as is a radically closed disposition to that relationship, realistically, he says, neither of these situations is very common in the human condition. Most who reach the point of historical death have at least a degree of openness to the eternal fullness of that relationship with God and the rest of sanctified humanity, but there is also a need for a purification of heart before that communion can take place. It is for this reason that *purgation* is required.

Benedict notes the opinion of "some recent theologians"[83] when he explains the notion that

> . . . the fire which both burns and saves is Christ himself, the Judge and Saviour. The encounter with him is the decisive act of judgement. Before his gaze all falsehood melts away. This encounter with him, as it burns us, transforms and frees us, allowing us to become truly ourselves. All that we build during our lives can prove to be mere straw, pure bluster, and it collapses. Yet in the pain of this encounter, when the impurity and sickness of our lives become evident to us, there lies

82. Benedict XVI, *Spe Salvi* 45.
83. Ibid., 47.

salvation. His gaze, the touch of his heart heals us through an undeniably painful transformation "as through fire."[84]

It is in this encounter with Christ, whose identity is both Savior and Judge, that the work of God's justice as well as God's mercy is expressed. This work of both justice and mercy unfolds as a "painful transformation" that occurs in the course of the encounter with Christ. Benedict situates this transformation in the context of the true nature of hope that relies on both justice and mercy, or "grace," as he calls it: "The judgement of God is hope, both because it is justice and because it is grace. If it were merely grace, making all earthly things cease to matter, God would still owe us an answer to the question about justice—the crucial question that we ask of history and of God. If it were merely justice, in the end it could bring only fear to us all."[85] It is worth noting here that the twofold nature of divine judgment that reveals itself first as justice and then as mercy is consistent with the entire mode of Ratzinger's theological reflection, which is narrative and unfolding in character. Because the final judgment is based on the unfolding of the relationship between God and humanity as it plays out in the context of salvation history, justice is accomplished but also gives way to the fulfillment of justice that is God's mercy. Neither justice nor mercy is a mere concept to be grasped. One cannot be understood without the other, and neither can be understood if both are not attended to throughout the course of the unfolding narrative of salvation history. The flexibility of this mode of doing theology to which Joseph Ratzinger has become accustomed in the course of his career enables him to handle the apparent contradictions that would arise if this theological reflection were being done in more propositional terms that required precise and self-contained definitions of divine justice and divine mercy as mere ideas that could be analyzed a-historically. Rather, his salvation-historical approach to these questions allows for the dynamic of understanding a particular theological problem always in the context of the relationship between God and humanity that is continually unfolding.

Another dimension of this unfolding relationship between God and humanity as it culminates in final judgment is that the relationship is always a communal one of the whole of humanity relating to

84. Ibid.
85. Ibid.

God and one another. It is for this reason, Benedict explains, that even after death the bonds of love among the faithful still exist and remain an essential dimension of how a given person undergoing divine judgment enters into that encounter with the Lord. This is never done in isolation, but always in the context of the web of human relationships the person enjoyed while alive on earth. While each individual person does undergo a particular judgment, she or he does so potentially with the support of other aspects of love in her or his life. Benedict writes:

> The souls of the departed can, however, receive "solace and refreshment" through the Eucharist, prayer and almsgiving. The belief that love can reach into the afterlife, that reciprocal giving and receiving is possible, in which our affection for one another continues beyond the limits of death—this has been a fundamental conviction of Christianity throughout the ages and it remains a source of comfort today. Who would not feel the need to convey to their departed loved ones a sign of kindness, a gesture of gratitude or even a request for pardon?[86]

Certainly, on a phenomenological level, that need among the bereaved to want to speak a word of love to and on behalf of their beloved departed exists, but theologically a question remains: how can this "word" spoken by other people become a word that is effective in the unfolding of the beloved's reception of divine justice and mercy? Benedict takes up this problem when he asks:

> Now a further question arises: if "Purgatory" is simply purification through fire in the encounter with the Lord, Judge and Saviour, how can a third person intervene, even if he or she is particularly close to the other? When we ask such a question, we should recall that no man is an island, entire of itself. Our lives are involved with one another, through innumerable interactions they are linked together. No one lives alone. No one sins alone. No one is saved alone. The lives of others continually spill over into mine: in what I think, say, do and achieve. And conversely, my life spills over into that of others: for better and for worse. So my prayer for another is not something extraneous to that person, something external, not even after

86. Ibid., 48.

death. In the interconnectedness of Being, my gratitude to the other—my prayer for him—can play a small part in his puri-fication. And for that there is no need to convert earthly time into God's time: in the communion of souls simple terrestrial time is superseded. It is never too late to touch the heart of another, nor is it ever in vain.[87]

This touching of the heart of another, even across the chasm of death that is marked by the gap between history and eternity, can be done in love, most perfectly when that love is grounded in the heart of Christ and in the context of ecclesial prayer, in which the church prays from within "the 'I' of Christ."

Conclusion: Eternal Dialogue

In this meditation on the last things in *Spe Salvi*, then, we see something of the profound interconnectedness of the various aspects of Ratzinger's theology. He offers a theological anthropology that insists on a true identity for humanity, one that is constituted of soli-darity among people and established at a spiritual level, one that is fulfilled in prayer and love for one another. This prayer is made pos-sible and fulfilled in the person of Christ. And the solidarity into which we are able to enter, through Christ, is one that stretches across the orders of creation and history into eternity. For Ratzinger there is no proper understanding of eschatological realities without seeing them through the lens of the identity and work accomplished by Christ, whom he sees as the perfection of the dialogue between God and humanity. We recall here from the second chapter of this book that Ratzinger sees revelation "basically as dialogue." And if Christ is the fullness of the revelation of God then, as I argued in the third chapter, Christ is the dialogue itself: both the speaking of God to humanity and humanity's response back to God. Ratzinger's Christology, draw-ing from his study of Bonaventure, has Christ at the center of history and as the fulfillment of the plan of God for humanity's salvation, precisely as Word. Christ, the Word made flesh in history, is also the Word who continues to speak from eternity, calling the whole of his-tory into the life and love of the Father. This Logo-centric under-standing of Christology—one that is only understood within the " 'I'

87. Ibid.

of Christ" actualized for humanity in the life of the church—further elucidates the matter of eschatology. It is precisely because of the framework of the *Logos*, because of the communicative and dialogical way of understanding Christ and salvation history, that certain tensions implicit in eschatology can remain creative and enlightening even though they always escape the precise grasp of human understanding. The communicative, dialogical framework of Ratzinger's theology allows for this tension. For Ratzinger, the *eschaton* is nothing other than the fulfillment in eternity of the narrative of salvation history shaped by the dialogue between God and humanity.

Epilogue

We come, then, to the end of this exploration of the thought of Joseph Ratzinger. We have concluded with an examination of the last things, but in this examination we see the first things still at work. There has been a constant dynamic throughout his thought and it is this dynamic that, in my estimation, makes the whole cohere. The dynamic has been one of dialogue both within God, in all eternity, and also between God and humanity in history. The dialogue that is at the very heart of reality is one that has bridged the chasm between eternity and history. There is simplicity at the core of Ratzinger's articulation of the Christian mystery. God speaks. Humanity listens . . . or not. To the degree that humanity does listen to the Word spoken by God, it opens up to the possibility of responding to the Word, thereby fulfilling what it means to be truly human. In this speaking and listening a relationship is established, a transformation occurs, a story is told. But this simplicity can be deceiving. It is not the simplicity of a one-dimensional exposition of Christianity. Quite the contrary. For Ratzinger, as I have attempted to demonstrate, there is always a tension at work in this reality of the Christian vision. Precisely because God is not only logical but dialogical, so too is all of reality not only logical, but dialogical.

There is fragility in dialogue. The whole of the mystery emerges as the dialogue unfolds. It cannot simply be grasped and then set aside. It must be lived from within and, if it is to remain in touch with reality, it is necessary to remain _within_ this dialogue—with our fellow human beings, with the tradition that has preceded us, with those in heaven who have gone before us, with the story of Scripture that has been told to us, with the experience of the liturgy that is the perfection of that dialogue in daily life. Throughout it all, in all the ways that we remain "within" the dialogue of human existence, we get our bearings as to how this dialogue really works by looking to the figure of Jesus Christ, the one who is the dialogue itself, in one person, the one who is both the eternal Word of God spoken to humanity and humanity's perfect response back to God.

Not long ago I had a brief conversation with a student at a Jesuit university. We had just concluded celebrating a 10 p.m. Mass on a Tuesday night. I had not seen him at that Mass before. He was in his senior year and was a theology major. He asked if we could speak for a moment and I agreed. He asked what he ought to do, since he had recently noticed that the more he immersed himself in his theological studies the less he was drawn to prayer. His spiritual life was drying up as he was nearing the completion of his theology degree. When he was a freshman, he said, he prayed often, went on retreats, even seriously considered becoming a Jesuit one day. It was because of this devotion that he had decided to study theology in the first place. And now that devotion seemed to be fading. There was sadness and longing in his voice. As he described his predicament, an immediate rush came over me of all that I had been studying and writing about in the last year and a half based on the preaching and theology of Joseph Ratzinger. "This is why Benedict has done what he has done," it struck me. This is why he has undertaken theology in such a manner: for people like this young man before me. For Benedict, theology is an attempt to give words to what the Word has spoken in history and to what ordinary people have experienced of that Word in their lives. Theology is meant to describe and deepen the sense of what, exactly, is the nature of this encounter. And when theology is done well, it ought to lead one directly back into that encounter and not away from it so that Christianity can be examined from a safe, "objective" distance. To my mind Joseph Ratzinger, now Pope Benedict XVI, does theology well. It is my hope that, having reflected on his thought, I might do a little better at it myself.

 *Bibliography*

Allen, John L. *Cardinal Ratzinger: The Vatican's Enforcer of the Faith*. New York: Continuum, 2000.

Balthasar, Hans Urs von. *The Word made Flesh*. San Francisco: Ignatius Press, 1989.

Benedict XVI, Pope. *The Essential Pope Benedict XVI: His Central Writings and Speeches*. Edited by John F. Thornton and Susan B. Varenne. New York: Harper, 2007.

———. *Gesammelte Schriften*. Edited by Gerhard Ludwig Müller. Freiburg: Herder, 2008.

———. *The God of Jesus Christ: Meditations on the Triune God*. San Francisco: Ignatius Press, 2008.

———. *Images of Hope: Meditations on Major Feasts*. San Francisco: Ignatius Press, 2006.

———. *Jesus of Nazareth: From the Baptism in the Jordan to the Transfiguration*. New York: Doubleday, 2007.

———. *Jesus of Nazareth. Part Two, Holy Week: From the Entrance into Jerusalem to the Resurrection*. San Francisco: Ignatius Press, 2011.

———. *Light of the World: The Pope, the Church, and the Signs of the Times: A Conversation with Peter Seewald*. Translated by Michael J. Miller and Adrian J. Walker. San Francisco: Ignatius Press, 2010.

———. *The Yes of Jesus Christ: Exercises in Faith, Hope and Love*. New York: Crossroad, 2005.

Bockmuehl, Markus, and Alan J. Torrance, eds. *Scripture's Doctrine and Theology's Bible: How the New Testament Shapes Christian Dogmatics*. Grand Rapids: Baker Academic, 2008.

Bonaventure. *Collationes in Hexaëmeron, et Bonaventuriana quaedam selecta adfidem*. Edited by Ferdinandus Delorme. Florence: Collegii S. Bonaventurae, 1934.

Buber, Martin. *I and Thou*. Translated by Walter Arnold Kaufmann. New York: Scribner, 1970.

Bultmann, Rudolf. *New Testament and Mythology and Other Basic Writings*. Edited by Schubert Miles Ogden. Philadelphia: Fortress Press, 1989.

Casel, Odo. *The Mystery of Christian Worship, and Other Writings*. Translated by Burkhard Neunheuser. Westminster, MD: Newman Press, 1962.

Chia, Edmund. *Towards a Theology of Dialogue: Schillebeeckx's Method as Bridge between Vatican's Dominus Iesus and Asia's FABC Theology: A Scientific Essay in Theology*. Bangkok, Thailand: Edmund Chia, 2003.

Congregation for the Doctrine of the Faith. *Proclaiming the Truth of Jesus Christ: Papers from the Vallombrosa Meeting*. Washington, DC: United States Catholic Conference, 2000.

Corkery, James. *Joseph Ratzinger's Theological Ideas: Wise Cautions and Legitimate Hopes*. New York: Paulist Press, 2009.

Deines, Roland. "Can the 'Real' Jesus be Identified with the Historical Jesus? A Review of the Pope's Challenge to Biblical Scholarship and the Various Reactions it Provoked." *Didaskalia* 39 (2009): 11–46.

Denzinger, Heinrich, and Clemens Bannwart. *Enchiridion Symbolorum: Definitionum Et Declarationum De Rebus Fidei Et Morum*. Freiburg: Herder, 1908.

Dulles, Avery Cardinal. "From Ratzinger to Benedict." *First Things* 160 (Fall 2006): 24–29.

_____ . *Models of Revelation*. Maryknoll, NY: Orbis Books, 1992.

Dupuis, Jacques, and Josef Neusner, eds. *The Christian Faith in the Doctrinal Documents of the Catholic Church*. New York: Alba House, 1996.

Flannery, Austin, ed. *Vatican Council II: The Basic Sixteen Documents: Constitutions, Decrees, Declarations*. Northport, NY: Dominican Publications, 1996.

Gaál Gyulai, Emery de. *The Theology of Pope Benedict XVI: The Christocentric Shift*. New York: Palgrave Macmillan, 2010.

Geiselmann, Josef Rupert. *Die Heilige Schrift und die Tradition: zu den neueren Kontroversen über das Verhältnis der Heiligen Schrift zu den Nichtgeschriebenen Traditionen*. Freiburg: Herder, 1962.

Gordo, Jesús Martinez. *The Christology of J. Ratzinger–Benedict XVI in Light of his Theological Biography*. Barcelona: Cristianisme i Justicia Booklets. 132 (February 2009).

Granados, Jose, Carlos Granados, and Luis Sánchez Navarro. *Opening Up the Scriptures: Joseph Ratzinger and the Foundations of Biblical Interpretation*. Grand Rapids: Eerdmans, 2008.

Guardini, Romano. *The Spirit of the Liturgy*. London: Sheed & Ward, 1930.

Hahn, Scott. *Covenant and Communion: The Biblical Theology of Pope Benedict XVI*. Grand Rapids: Brazos Press, 2009.

Hamer, Jérôme. *L'eglise est une communion.* Paris: Cerf, 1962.

Harnack, Adolf von. *History of Dogma.* Boston: Roberts Brothers, 1895.

Haught, John F. *Mystery and Promise: A Theology of Revelation.* Collegeville, MN: Liturgical Press, 1993.

Heim, Maximilian Heinrich. *Joseph Ratzinger: Life in the Church and Living Theology: Fundamentals of Ecclesiology with Reference to Lumen Gentium.* San Francisco: Ignatius Press, 2007.

Johnson, Luke Timothy. "Jesus of Nazareth: From the Baptism in the Jordan to the Transfiguration." *Modern Theology* 24 (2008): 318–20.

Käsemann, Ernst. "Was Jesus Liberal?" 19–53 in idem, *Der Ruf der Freiheit.* Tübingen: Mohr, 1968.

Kerr, Fergus. *Twentieth-Century Catholic Theologians: From Neoscholasticism to Nuptial Mysticism.* Malden, MA: Blackwell, 2007.

Lamb, Matthew L., and Matthew Levering. *Vatican II: Renewal within Tradition.* New York: Oxford University Press, 2008.

Lubac, Henri de. *Glauben aus der Liebe: Catholicisme.* Translated by Hans Urs von Balthasar. Einsiedeln: Johannes Verlag, 1970.

Lüdemann, Gerd. *Eyes that See Not: The Pope Looks at Jesus.* Santa Rosa, CA: Polebridge Press, 2008.

Mannion, Gerard, and Lieven Boeve, eds. *The Ratzinger Reader: Mapping a Theological Journey.* London: T & T Clark, 2010.

Martini, Carlo Maria. "Ardent Testimony on Jesus: On the Book Jesus of Nazareth by Joseph Ratzinger/Benedict XVI." *Bulletin Dei Verbum* 84/85 (2007): 44–46.

Miles, Jack. "Between Theology & Exegesis." *Commonweal* (July 13, 2007): 134.

Mills, Clifford W. *Pope Benedict XVI.* New York: Chelsea House, 2007.

Neusner, Jacob. *A Rabbi Talks with Jesus: An Intermillennial, Interfaith Exchange.* New York: Doubleday, 1993.

Nichols, Aidan. *The Thought of Pope Benedict XVI: An Introduction to the Theology of Joseph Ratzinger.* New York: Burns & Oates, 2007.

O'Malley, John W. *What Happened at Vatican II.* Cambridge, MA: Harvard University Press, 2008.

Peukert, Helmut. *Science, Action, and Fundamental Theology: Toward a Theology of Communicative Action.* Translated by James Bohman. Cambridge, MA: MIT Press, 1984.

Pope, Stephen, and Charles Hefling, eds. *Sic Et Non: Encountering Dominus Iesus.* Maryknoll, NY: Orbis Books, 2002.

Rahner, Karl. *Hearers of the Word.* New York: Herder and Herder, 1969.

———— and Joseph Ratzinger. *Revelation and Tradition.* London: Herder, 1966.

Ratzinger, Joseph. *Behold the Pierced One: An Approach to a Spiritual Christology.* San Francisco: Ignatius Press, 1986.

──────. *Called to Communion: Understanding the Church Today*. San Francisco: Ignatius Press, 1996.

──────. "Communio: A Program." *Communio: International Catholic Review* 19 (1992): 436–49.

──────. "Concerning the Notion of Person in Theology." *Communio: International Catholic Review* 17 (1990): 439–54.

──────. *Der Gott des Glaubens und der Gott der Philosophen*. Munich: Schnell & Steiner, 1960.

──────. *Dogma and Preaching: Applying Christian Doctrine to Daily Life*. San Francisco: Ignatius Press, 2011.

──────. *Eschatology: Death and Eternal Life*. Washington, DC: Catholic University of America Press, 1988.

──────. *God Is Near Us: The Eucharist, the Heart of Life*. San Francisco: Ignatius Press, 2003.

──────. *God's Word: Scripture, Tradition, Office*. Edited by Peter Hünermann and Thomas Söding. San Francisco: Ignatius Press, 2008.

──────. *In the Beginning: A Catholic Understanding of the Story of Creation and the Fall*. Grand Rapids: Eerdmans, 1995.

──────. *Joseph Ratzinger in Communio*. Edited by David Schindler. Grand Rapids: Eerdmans, 2010.

──────. *Introduction to Christianity*. San Francisco: Ignatius Press, 2004.

──────. *The Meaning of Christian Brotherhood*. San Francisco: Ignatius Press, 1993.

──────. *Milestones: Memoirs, 1927–1977*. San Francisco: Ignatius Press, 1998.

──────. *The Nature and Mission of Theology: Essays to Orient Theology in Today's Debates*. San Francisco: Ignatius Press, 1995.

──────. *On the Way to Jesus Christ*. San Francisco: Ignatius Press, 2005.

──────. *Pilgrim Fellowship of Faith: The Church as Communion*. Edited by Stephan Otto Horn, Vinzenz Pfnür, and Henry Taylor. San Francisco: Ignatius Press, 2005.

──────. *Principles of Catholic Theology: Building Stones for a Fundamental Theology*. San Francisco: Ignatius Press, 1987.

──────. *The Spirit of the Liturgy*. San Francisco: Ignatius Press, 2000.

──────. *Theological Highlights of Vatican II*. New York: Paulist Press, 1966.

──────. *The Theology of History in St. Bonaventure*. Chicago: Franciscan Herald Press, 1989.

──────. *Truth and Tolerance: Christian Belief and World Religions*. Translated by Henry Taylor. San Francisco: Ignatius Press, 2004.

──────. "Vicarious Representation." Translated by Jared Wicks, SJ, in Scott Hahn, ed., *Letter & Spirit*, vol. 7, *The Bible and the Church Fathers: The Liturgical Context of Patristic Exegesis*. Steubenville, OH: Emmaus Road Publishing, 2011.

————. *Volk und Haus Gottes in Augustins Lehre von der Kirche.* Munich: Zink, 1954.

Rausch, Thomas P. *Pope Benedict XVI: An Introduction to His Theological Vision.* New York: Paulist Press, 2009.

Rush, Ormond. *Still Interpreting Vatican II: Some Hermeneutical Principles.* Mahwah, NJ: Paulist Press, 2004.

Rowland, Tracey. *Ratzinger's Faith: The Theology of Pope Benedict XVI.* New York: Oxford University Press, 2008.

Rutsche, Markus. *Die Relationalität Gottes bei Martin Buber und Joseph Ratzinger.* Norderstedt: GRIN Verlag, 2007.

Schall, James V., and Benedict XVI. *The Regensburg Lecture.* South Bend, IN: St. Augustine's Press, 2007.

Schlier, Heinrich. *On the Resurrection of Jesus Christ.* Translated by Michael Sullivan. Rome: 30Giorni, 2008.

————. *Der Geist Und Die Kirche: Exegetische Aufsätze Und Vorträge 4.* Edited by Veronika Kubina and Karl Lehmann. Freiburg: Herder, 1980.

————. *Gotteswort im Menschenmund: Zur Besinnung.* Edited by Veronika Kubina and Karl Lehmann. Freiburg: Herder, 1982.

————. *The Relevance of the New Testament.* New York: Herder and Herder, 1968.

Söhngen, Gottlieb. *Die Einheit in der Theologie: Gesammelte Abhandlungen.* Munich: Zink, 1952.

Valente, Gianni, and Pierluca Azzardo. "That new beginning that bloomed among the ruins: Interview with Alfred Läpple." *30 Days* 1 (2006): 60.

Vorgrimler, Herbert, ed. *Commentary on the Documents of Vatican II.* 5 vols. New York: Herder and Herder, 1967.

Wicks, W. Jared. "Vatican II on Revelation from Behind the Scenes." *Theological Studies* 71 (2010): 637–50.

————, and Benedict XVI. *Prof. Ratzinger at Vatican II: A Chapter in the Life of Pope Benedict XVI.* New Orleans: Loyola University, 2007.

For encyclicals, speeches, and homilies of Pope Benedict XVI and other documents of the Holy See, see www.vatican.va.

Index

Abraham, 12, 28, 79, 159
Acts of the Apostles, 96–97, 109, 114
Adam, 28, 65, 120, 161
Analogia fidei, 35
Aristotle (Aristotelianism), 8, 30
Auer, Johann, 144–45
Augustine, St., 2, 11–13, 23, 28, 32, 51, 118, 139

Bakhita, Josephine, St., 155–57
Balthasar, Hans Urs von, viii, 11, 16, 106, 116, 152, 168
Bonaventure, St., viii, 2, 22–33, 38, 46, 50–51, 53, 66, 95, 98, 103, 168
Buber, Martin, 13–16, 103
Bultmann, Rudolf, 67, 136–37

Canossian Sisters, 156
Caritas in Veritate, 123
Cartesian, 58
Casel, Odo, 7–9, 14
Chalcedon, Council of, 69
Chalcedonian structure of theology, 68, 85
Civitas Dei, 28
Communio, 6, 18, 89, 104–13, 115, 121, 128

Confessions of St. Augustine, 13
Constantinople III, Council of, 68–69
Corkery, James, SJ, 100

Dei Filius, 23, 43–44
Dei Verbum, 15, 23, 33, 38–49, 54, 60, 95–97, 108, 113, 115
Dies Irae, 151–53
Dignitatis Humanae, 64
Dominus Iesus, 63–64, 99–100
Dulles, Avery Cardinal, SJ, 1–2

Ecclesia semper reformanda, 101

Fides et Ratio, 64
Florit, Archbishop Ermenegildo, 40
Frings, Joseph Cardinal, 3, 33

Gaál Gyulai, Emery de, 15, 57
Gaudium et Spes, viii, 65, 84, 108, 113
Geiselmann, Josef Rupert, 37–38
Gramma, 34–39
Guardini, Romano, 7, 9, 106, 109
Gutiérrez, Gustavo, 134

Harnack, Adolf von, 67, 83, 134
Haught, John, 63

Heim, Maximilian Heinrich, 102
Hobbes, Thomas, 104

Isaiah, 34, 62

Jacob, 159
Jeremiah, 34
Jerome, St., 51, 55
Joachim of Fiore, 30
John XXIII, Pope, 94
John Paul II, Pope 3, 64
John the Baptist, 79
John the Evangelist, 58, 70, 74,
    112, 120, 138, 158
Justin Martyr, 17, 77

Käsemann, Ernst, 79
Kasper, Walter, 100
Kerr, Fergus, 134

Läpple, Alfred, 11
Lex orandi lex credeni, 10, 151, 153
Logos, xiii, 6, 9, 78–79, 82, 83, 85,
    88, 91, 93, 95, 98, 100–101,
    103–14, 119–21, 126, 129, 131,
    137, 139–41, 143, 147, 159,
    161, 163, 169
Lubac, Henri de, viii, 11, 106, 120
Lumen Gentium, 94–97, 99, 106,
    108–9, 113–14, 122
Luther, Martin, 36, 127

Magdalene, Mary, 87
Maier, Friedrich, 5
Maranatha, 151–53
Marxism, 107, 110, 134–35, 153
Mary, Mother of God, 115–16, 131
Melanchthon, Philip, 36
Metz, Johann Baptist, 133–34
Moltmann, Jürgen, 133
Mörsdorf, Klaus, 7
Moses, 8, 10, 12, 28, 62, 115
Mystici Corporis, 97

Neoscholasticism, 4, 7–8, 23, 41
Neusner, Jacob, Rabbi, 62
Newman, Blessed John Henry, 41
Nichols, Aidan, OP, 134, 141

Origen, 10, 70, 151, 163–64
Ottaviani, Alfredo Cardinal, 42

Pascher, Josef, 7
Paul, St., 34, 58, 100, 117, 121,
    142, 160–61
Paul VI, Pope, 3, 99, 113
Pieper, Josef, 146, 157
Pius XII, Pope, 97
Plato (Platonism), 8, 100, 163
Pneuma (Pneumatology), 34–35,
    39, 96–100, 120

Rahner, Karl, SJ, 33–35, 75
Rausch, Thomas, SJ, 67, 100
Rowland, Tracey, 16, 105–6, 111

Sacrosanctum Concilium, 108,
    127
Schlier, Heinrich, 81
Schmaus, Michael, 7, 26
Simelai, Rabbi, 62
Söhngen, Gottlieb, 2, 7, 10–11
Spe Salvi, 132, 153–54, 165, 168
Stoics, 28
Stummer, Friedrich, 6
Syllabus of Errors, 42

Taylor, Charles, 16
Thomas, Apostle, 87–88, 125
Trent, Council of, 36–38

Vatican Council I, 23, 43–44, 91
Vatican Council II, 1, 3, 15–16,
    23, 33, 37–39, 41, 44, 48, 51,
    54, 84, 95–98, 100, 105, 108,
    143, 144

Verbum Domini, 23, 46, 70

Vulgate, 51, 77

Wisdom, book of, 138

World Youth Day, Madrid, 124, 132

Wright, Tamra, 14

Zeno, 28